State Formation and Democracy

in Latin America, 1810–1900

STATE

FORMATION

and DEMOCRACY

in LATIN AMERICA,

1810~1900

Fernando López-Alves

DUKE UNIVERSITY PRESS   Durham & London   2000

© 2000 Duke University Press

All rights reserved

Printed in the United States of America on acid-free paper ∞

Designed by C. H. Westmoreland

Typeset in Plantin with Pabst display by Keystone Typesetting, Inc.

Library of Congress Cataloging-in-Publication Data

appear on the last printed page of this book.

We are grateful to the Institute for Latin American Studies in London for

permission to reprint the chapter on Uruguay; part of chapter 2 in this volume

originally appeared in *Between the Economy and the Polity in the River Plate:*

Uruguay, 1811-1890 (London: ILAS, *1993*).

TO AURORA ALVES, TANIA LOPEZ, AND

HELENA PASQUARELLA

Contents

Illustrations

Tables

Acknowledgments

Data gathering and writing were facilitated by the generosity of two Fulbright grants, support from the University of California at Santa Barbara, and a grant from the Center for Chicano and Latino Studies at UCSB. For four years, I have been privileged to share a National Endowment for the Humanities grant for another project with my colleague David Rock, which allowed me access to priceless data on nineteenth-century Uruguay and Argentina. Some of those data have been used to enrich the construction of the cases in this book.

I owe a debt of gratitude to many people. The first must go to Diane Johnson, who with unabashed enthusiasm labored so many long hours in carefully editing and providing critical comments on earlier drafts. The second must go to the perceptive and thoughtful comments of the two anonymous reviewers from Duke University Press, which reshaped the book into a more readable and much improved manuscript.

Kate Bruhn contributed insightful comments that have been incorporated into the first two chapters. José Pedro Barrán made available precious and almost unattainable data on nineteenth-century Uruguay. Charles Bergquist enthusiastically supported this project at its early stages and unselfishly shared data on nineteenth-century Colombia. Miguel Centeno contributed data on war making in the region, as well as insightful comments. Adan Griego, one of the finest librarians one could imagine, donated precious hours to revealing many sources that I would not otherwise have been able to obtain. Over many lunches, Alan P. Liu's wise advice and sagacious remarks greatly helped the organization of the argument and definitely convinced me that sound work demands more patience and time than I had ever expected. I hope the final result does not disappoint him. Cynthia Kaplan's resourceful suggestions on an early draft helped the organization of the argument and improved its comparative scope. Helena Pasquarella patiently spent many hours editing and improving figures and tables. Jonathan Rosenberg, whom I must thank for believing in this book from the very beginning, has consistently contributed support, excitement, and crucial criticism. Thomas Schrock generously spent many hours over breakfasts giving suggestions and advice that greatly improved the presentation of the argument and the organization of the manuscript; whether or not this book lives up to the standards of his comments, I am certain that his words have, in one way or another, been naturally absorbed throughout. I am extremely grateful to David Rock for his valuable comments and generosity in sharing unpublished work on two crucial and previously poorly researched decades of state making in Argentina, the 1860s and 1870s. My deepest intellectual debt goes to Charles Tilly, whose work has in many ways inspired my own and whose enthusiasm and steady support for this book have remained a comforting foundation through many drafts.

Many of my graduate students were patient enough to comment on earlier versions. The critical enthusiasm of Erik Ching and lengthy conversations with Fernando Rocchi helped to convince me that perhaps I was on the right track. Michelle Lipka, Alistair Hattingh, Robert Porter, and Lia Roberts improved tables and text. Finally, I must add that none of the aforementioned persons are in any way responsible for any omissions, errors, or misinterpretations that might remain.

Introduction

As the proverb says, "getting started is half the battle," and a good
beginning we all applaud. But in my view a good start is more than
"half," and no one has yet given it the praise it deserves.
—PLATO, *The Laws*

Riddles and Cases

During the eighteenth century, concepts such as "nation" and "nationalism" became part of Europeans' everyday political jargon. Whether
nationalism stemmed from deep structural changes, self-conscious political ideologies, or—as Benedict R. Anderson (1983:7) has suggested—
a cultural (and imagined) "deep horizontal notion of comradeship,"
sovereign nations started to become the norm while dynastic empires
and monarchical institutions became the exception. In nineteenth-
century Latin America, state makers were frantically at work. They designed republican institutions, elaborated on the concurrent notions of
common citizenship and popular sovereignty, tried to centralize power,
and created, along the way, a different ladder of social stratification
responding to new notions of civil society and societal discipline. Their
degree of success varied. The final product differed, in some cases
radically, from the ideas and the political practices of the first generations of state makers. In other cases, the final outcome bore some
resemblance to the original design. But in no case did the political
institutions of the nations emerging in the early twentieth century remain similar to either the colonial period or the republicanism that
triggered independence.

If we were to conceive of the process of nation building studied in this book as "postcolonial," then the emphasis should be placed on "post." The agrarian societies that emerged from the convulsive nineteenth century definitely represented, in Barrington Moore's (1966) terms, different "paths" of institution building and regime formation. They differed in natural endowments, levels of development, and the use of labor. But the most striking difference was political. In countries such as Chile, Uruguay, and Colombia, political parties prevailed. In others such as Argentina and Brazil, weaker parties—similar to loose cliques or movements—confronted serious obstacles to becoming party machines. Even where they succeeded, as in Argentina, some still faced constraints in forming party systems. In terms of state institutions, Chile, Argentina, and Mexico grew stronger and were able to monopolize coercion, but others such as Uruguay, Colombia, and Venezuela remained weak and maintained only a feeble presence in the countryside.[1] State makers also differed from one another across countries. A political elite, alongside the traditional coalition of landed and mercantile interests, crafted the state in Colombia, Chile, Uruguay, Argentina, and Peru; in Venezuela and Paraguay, however, the military and associated militias virtually created the state.

This book seeks to solve two riddles that are essential to explaining these differences. The first riddle deals with the complexities of state formation. It involves problems of power centralization, state building, and the design of government institutions. A central question is how and to what degree the organization called the "state" gains control of the principal means of coercion within a defined territory.[2] To survive, this entity must maintain a relatively centralized, differentiated, and autonomous structure. Charles Tilly (1990:131) writes that this is accomplished "by creating an organization that is at least partially distinct from those that govern production and reproduction in the territory, by seizing, coopting or liquidating other concentrations of coercion within the same territory, by defining boundaries, and by exercising jurisdiction within those boundaries." We will seek to explain two parallel but not always directly correlated processes of state formation: the building of state capacity and autonomy.[3] Because the evolution of the state bureaucracy and the armed forces were not necessarily identical, the case studies in this book treat them separately.

In adopting this conventional definition, I have purposely left in the *"state" cultural construct.*

IMPACT of Culture on State making

background the notion of "a state" as a cultural construct. We shall see how cultural components of state making can comfortably dialogue with structural and collective action theories. In comparing Uruguay and Argentina (countries that have very similar cultural backgrounds) with Colombia, Paraguay, and Venezuela (countries that have very different cultural makeups), the chapters tangentially explore the impact of culture on state making, although a fuller exploration will be left for another time in order to sharpen the book's focus. By the same token, this analysis does not give center stage to the personality, ethnicity, and cultural background of state makers, important components in the nation-building process. The choices that state makers made, and the strategies that they followed, apparently affected institution building, but the book does not exclusively concentrate on the process of individual decision making to explain outcomes.[4] A strong emphasis on the cognitive processes of state makers based on a broad sense of "rationality" proved limiting, and defining "irrationality" poses a theoretical problem. Considering the broad sense in which rationality is often described, one could come to the surprising conclusion that during more than 230 years of history (when one combines the three main cases of this book), actors made no "irrational" choices.

The second riddle involves problems of coalition formation and seeks to discover the conditions under which more open and democratic regimes may emerge. State building is directly related to coalitions and regime type. Since Aristotle, people have disagreed over precisely what to include in the definition of "regime" (e.g., institutions, values, and rules). They also disagree as to how regimes rise and evolve, and how to classify them.[5] My interest here is in types of coalitions and their impact on regime formation. The book adopts the definition of regime given by Ruth Berins Collier and David Collier (1991:789), which includes the method used to select the government and representative assemblies (such as coups or elections), formal and informal mechanisms of representation, and adopted patterns of repression. This definition rejects the identification of a regime with its incumbents or the public policies they choose, unless these policies change the regime itself. A central query of this book is whether these agrarian societies carved distinctive "paths to democracy"; thus this second riddle relates to democratic theory and the conditions under which democracy can emerge in nonindustrial settings. The definition of democracy used here refers to political democracy, as opposed to social democracy or economic democracy, and echoes the "procedural" version of democracy that Robert Dahl (1956, 1971) has called "polyarchy."[6]

Comparisons, the Argument, and the Cases

To answer these riddles, this book studies two scenarios: first, societies that shared a number of economic, cultural, and social features but did not breed similar institutions or regimes; and second, societies that did not have much in common structurally, culturally, and socially but bred similar states and regimes. These scenarios allow us to explore any correlation between the timing of power centralization and regime formation. For instance, did the rise of stronger states in the early stages of nation building contribute to a tendency toward more corporatist and state-centered policy making? Did slower processes of power centralization encourage pluralism, stronger party politics, and robust local governments? Or is there even a correlation between the type of ruling coalition and different processes of power centralization?

The book finds that when either political parties or armies took the more active role in institution building during the process of state formation, the resulting regimes were more or less democratic. As a consequence, states also differed in their degree of power centralization, the strength of their bureaucracies, and the scope of their capacity and autonomy. Civil-military relations lay at the core of state building. I suggest that the balance within this equation depended on the characteristics of civil and external conflict, combined with the pace, type, and range of rural mobilization. Therefore, war and the collective action of the rural poor provided central engines of institution building. They contributed to the construction of the central army, the rise of new social classes, and the emergence of civilian organizations. They determined the pace of state making and the growth of a shared notion of nationality among populations that varied geographically and culturally. And finally, they marked the geographic boundaries of the state.

Rather than focusing on the causes of war, the book emphasizes the impact of war on classes, institutions, and coalitions. In nineteenth-century Latin America, conflict resulted from the conventional causes identified by most of the literature: invasions, territorial expansion, competition for resources, control over domestic or international trade, participation in decision making, class interests, military pressures, and disagreements over institutional design.[7] This study, however, is not about war alone or the often too general notion of "conflict." Rather, it offers an empirically grounded argument about types of war in combination with types of rural mobilization, and the resulting states and regimes. It was the type of war, rather than the frequency of war, that shaped a country's "path" of state making. And it was the type of rural mobilization, rather than the type of rural economy, that shaped political parties, modified systems of labor relations, and often set the limits on state capacity. My argument neither neglects the enormous impact of capitalist development and the world economy on nation building nor dismisses structural theories of state formation that focus on types of economies, the exploitation of natural resources, and the characteristics of financial, agrarian, or industrial capital. Nonetheless, it does reveal the limitations of these popular premises.

My argument is grounded in an in-depth comparison of three cases—Uruguay, Colombia, and Argentina—during their most intense phase of state and regime formation, from approximately 1810 to 1900. To broaden the book's comparative scope and make theory testing more reliable, Paraguay and Venezuela serve as "control" cases. These last two cases pose the question of whether authoritarian-militaristic outcomes in Latin America resemble other types of authoritarian rule in Eastern Europe or Asia and help to sharpen the book's focus on civil-military relations. Indeed, unlike in the three main cases, the army became the major state maker in Venezuela and Paraguay.[8] These two can also be considered "negative cases," since the argument emerging from the comparison of the three main cases does not seem fully to account for the outcomes we see in Venezuela and Paraguay. Thus, their addition allows for falsification, adjustment, and reconsideration of my major claim. Brief references to state formation in the United States further sharpen the book's argument, which is fully spelled out in chapter 1.

The existing literature on the political evolution of the three main cases frequently refers to the "Uruguayan riddle," the "Colombian riddle," and the "Argentine riddle." Most scholars have concluded that these "riddles" constitute "exceptions" to an unspoken rule.[9] In contrast, the following chapters question the "exceptional" status of these countries and suggest that they follow comparable and recognizable patterns of nation building.

Civil Society, Parties, and the State

As in every discussion of state formation, one must inevitably say a few words about the concept of civil society. Unlike state-centric theories, such as the one offered by Skocpol (1979), the cases examined in this book point to the weight of social forces. Although institutions are not merely a mirror of these forces, the analysis suggests that social forces strongly shaped the state and were key agents in consolidating different types of regimes.[10] This should not come as a surprise, given that at early stages of state building, movements, cliques, and political organizations are usually very influential; even institutionalists such as Terry Moe (1990:236) have acknowledged that these forces cannot be eliminated. Although state growth in most of Latin America during the 1940s and 1950s somewhat blurred the relevance of civil society, its downsizing in the 1980s and 1990s has again revealed the active role civil society can play in changing government institutions.

Is "civil society" the same as the "political system"? This question is reminiscent of the critique of predominant state-centered approaches offered by modernization theory.[11] Yet the theory did not entirely resolve the problem of overlapping definitions of civil society and political system. It eliminated the rigidity of state-centered theory but made the political system identical to civil society, thus embracing virtually every single manifestation of collective action and "interest articulation."[12] In an effort to avoid similar problems, I adopt here the term "polity formation" to refer to the process by which the state, the army, movements, and political parties developed into an orderly body of institutional practices and regulations. Although still problematic, this conceptualization allows for the incorporation of party activity and the institutionalization of the military as independent factors of state formation. Therefore, whereas this book focuses on state building, unlike interesting work on the formation of bureaucracies and their evolution, it does not necessarily dwell on the construction of state agencies or examine in detail their rationale and objectives.[13] Instead, it focuses on the inter-action among parties, movements, the state, and the military.

A distinctive feature of the Americas is that parties and movements became state makers even to the point of becoming synonymous with the state. For example, in Colombia and Uruguay, we find a situation similar to Richard Bensel's (1990:3–4) portrayal of periods of "un-mediated party rule" in the United States, when the state and a political party were virtually one and the same. Venerable work on North American parties, such as that by William Nisbet Chambers (1969), has long stressed the identification of parties with government. It is not surprising that Samuel Huntington (1968, 1991) strongly argues that political parties played the most important role in the creation of modern political systems. While the cases examined here confirm the crucial role of parties as state makers, however, they do not support Huntington's claim that party politics is a clear sign of modernity.[14] Less modern Uruguay and Colombia created party systems, but more European and modern Argentina did not.

The definition of political parties I adopt here follows the well-known tradition of Robert Michels (1949), in which the degree of party orga-nization is directly proportional to the development of a party hier-archy that can secure the allegiance of the rank and file. Parties differ from other groups seeking political power in terms of four familiar criteria: (1) regular connections between party leaders at the center and local cadres and activists in the localities; (2) coordinated efforts to win popular support in order to gain influence and control of public policy; (3) a durable base of mass support, either by active militancy or by voting; and (4) a set of consciously shared beliefs or perspectives. As we shall see, this last trait is problematic for our main cases because at several points in their history, shared beliefs united members of dif-ferent parties and at the same time were not enough to unite factions within the same party. Nevertheless, I retain this characteristic because party members themselves used it as a criterion to define membership.

Periods and Cases

The current analysis starts at the critical juncture marked by the wars of independence (circa 1810), includes their confusing aftermath (from the 1830s to the 1860s), and ends with the consolidation of these states in the 1880s and 1890s. In some cases, the analysis extends into the first decade of the twentieth century. To assume the notion of "critical juncture" means to establish analytical boundaries to separate "periods."[15]

Following Arthur Stinchcombe (1968:120–22), this book assumes that established patterns reproduce themselves without the repetition of the original cause, and that once a set of institutions is established, power holders will attempt to perpetuate them because—among other things—this represents the least expensive option in terms of social and political costs.

I join others in suggesting that the wars of independence and their aftermath provide a critical juncture that started out an innovative period of institution building. For the most part, the study of this period has remained the domain of historians,[16] including some who have placed these cases in comparative perspective.[17] Among social scientists, however, only a handful have compared institution-building experiences during the postindependence period.[18] Most have contended that the years between 1870 and 1914 were the most relevant, searching that period for the key to explain the political or economic trajectory of these states.[19] These years have become the favorite testing ground for theories stressing the impact of the world economy and export expansion on power centralization.[20] This book instead suggests that earlier events in a "premodern" period, established the institutional design that was consolidated in the later part of the nineteenth century, molded state expansion, and helped to explain the formation of the so-called "oligarchic states" of the early twentieth century and their radical transformations after the 1930s. In a sense, this study contributes to the explanation of what Collier and Collier (1991) in their study of critical junctures have called the "incorporation period."[21]

Why compare Uruguay, Colombia, and Argentina? The rationale takes to heart the suggestion of the small-n comparative approach: in-depth case analysis renders better comparative results. In other words, purely deductive explanations based on a set of well-known assumptions and brief historical sketches create inaccurate descriptions and lead to incorrect conclusions. The result is poor theorizing and scarce counterintuitive propositions. On the first page of a delightful piece on the "miracle" of European development, Michael Mann (1988a:5) states that "there are two main types of explanation: the comparative and the historical." In this book, no major contradiction arises between these two "types." Further, the following chapters suggest that a marriage between comparative and historical explanations offers a most promising avenue to comparative inquiry.

Table o.1 depicts the salient characteristics of the three main cases and outlines their institutional and regime differences, presenting the comparative puzzle that this book attempts to solve. Basically, whereas the differences between Argentina and Uruguay were institutional, the gap that separated Uruguay and Colombia was fundamentally structural and cultural. To reduce variables, I have taken a slightly unorthodox route and juxtaposed two classic methods guiding comparative analysis. On one hand, Arend Lijphart (1975) and Arthur Stinchcombe (1978) have advocated the selection of a few extremely well matched cases, or a method of "deep analogy." On the other hand, Adam Przeworski and Henry Teune (1970) have pointed to the advantages of a "most different" system design, where cases must be as diverse as possible but present specific and fairly analogous developments that the analyst wishes to explore. Each follows one of the two well-known options that John Stuart Mill opened to comparative research, the method of difference and the method of agreement.

Uruguay, Colombia, and Argentina provide an opportunity to pair cases following *both* these methods. Whereas overall similarities between Argentina and Uruguay make them an ideal comparison in terms of the "deep analogy" system design, Uruguay and Colombia present more-than-suitable grounds for an application of the "most different" system design. The simple diagram in figure o.1 illustrates this point. At both ends of the diagram, Argentina and Colombia display alternatives that would otherwise be difficult to pair. I am able to draw comparative conclusions by contrasting them using Uruguay as, so to speak, a nexus case, and making this country a central comparative instance. Given the relative scarcity of available data on rural insurrections in Colombia during the nineteenth century, I am compelled at times in chapter 3 to draw more from the logic of this comparison than from actual hard figures on rural unrest and their effects on political leaders.

Comparisons following this rationale show the limits of some of the

Table 0.1. The Three Major Cases, circa 1800–1900

	Argentina	Uruguay	Colombia
ECONOMY	Pastoralist	Pastoralist	Coffee dominant
Use of labor	Extensive in agriculture	Extensive in agriculture	Intensive in agriculture
Labor relations	Ranching predominant, wage labor and European indentured labor	Ranching predominant, primarily wage labor	Various: slavery, sharecropping, and wage labor
Level of development	Higher[a]	Lower	Lower
Grain sector	Larger	Smaller	Minimal
Peasantry	Small to minimal	Minimal	Larger
Mining enclave	Not present	Not present	Present
Economies nationally owned	Yes	Yes	Yes
POPULATION			
European immigration	High	High	Low
Ethnicity	Predominantly white Europeans in urban centers. Also large numbers of them in the countryside. Smaller indigenous population.	Predominantly white Europeans in urban centers. Large numbers of them in countryside. Smaller indigenous population.	Not as many Europeans. Large Creole population by time of state expansion. Larger indigenous population.
TYPE OF POLITY	Weaker parties and no party system	Strong parties and party system	Strong parties and party system
Colonial state strength	Weaker	Weaker	Stronger
Military intervention	Frequent	Scarce	Scarce
State corporalist tendency	Pluralism with more corporatist practices	Pluralism with less corporatist practices	Pluralism with less corporatist practices
Nature of professional military	Stronger	Weaker	Weaker
Rural labor	Less mobilized	Highly mobilized	Highly mobilized

[a] This applies mainly to the province of Buenos Aires.

most popular theories of state formation and regime outcomes often applied to Latin America. Let us start with the first pair shown in figure 0.1, Uruguay and Argentina.[22] Geographic, structural, and cultural similarities make Argentina and Uruguay as comparable as cases can be. First, Uruguay and the province of Buenos Aires shared much

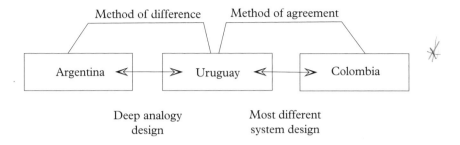

Figure 0.1. Methods of Agreement and Difference

geographically. Their capitals at Buenos Aires and Montevideo operated ports on opposite banks of the River Plate and enjoyed a privileged situation that led to a virtual monopoly of maritime trade. Second, they shared much structurally. Both countries were part of the so-called informal British empire and depended on the same markets. They largely exported the same products (with the only exception being wheat, which Argentina exported and Uruguay did not) and borrowed from roughly the same international sources of financing. Both cities grew as forward linkages of livestock production. Both countries used labor extensively in cattle and sheep raising, and in both, wage labor and similar forms of tenancy became predominant in the rural areas. The differences were in the pace, rather than in the type, of economic development.

Third, in terms of their cultural makeup, Uruguay and the province of Buenos Aires also were very much alike. Both were lands of recent settlement that received large numbers of European immigrants from the same countries roughly at the same time. One can argue that the notion of nationality that emerged in these countries responded to similar cultural constructs, and that—borrowing Benedict R. Anderson's (1983) conceptualization—both Creole and non-Creole "imagined" that they belonged to very similar "communities."[23] Therefore, geography, structure, and culture do not suffice to explain the different paths of state making taken by these two countries.

Surely there were differences in size and pace of development that could provide an explanation for the political differences separating Argentina and Uruguay. After all, by most accounts, Uruguay until the late 1830s was just another rebellious province struggling to establish independence from growing Buenos Aires. Indeed, Uruguay's loss of territory in 1815 was Argentina's gain, with differences in size leading to distinct relations between capital cities and hinterland. Yet although the following chapters indicate that size and the pace of development were important factors shaping state making, they do not fully explain the differences we observe between these two countries. It is the addition of Colombia to the comparison of Uruguay and Argentina that makes this point the most apparent.

Whereas in terms of their economies, trade patterns, culture, and geography, Argentina and Uruguay provide a strong "deep analogy" comparison, the Colombia-Uruguay pair offers an ideal "most different systems" exercise. As table 0.1 shows, the two countries developed similar institutions of government but differed in virtually everything else. In Colombia, as in Uruguay, competition between two parties shaped the polity. By about the late 1880s, these two parties had established mechanisms of cooperation under civilian hegemony. Both the Uruguayan and Colombian militaries lost political space vis-à-vis the political elite, and the institutions almost had to reconstruct themselves at the end of the century. In both cases, generals acted as partisans, ruling in the name of their parties and paying close attention to their political constituencies. In these two countries, the state confronted serious obstacles to the centralization of authority and remained for the most part weak during the period under consideration.

How different were the contexts in which these similar institutions grew and developed? Patterns of urbanization and the characteristics of social life and culture in cities, important variables in accounting for party formation and activity, differed greatly in Colombia and Uruguay. Uruguay developed only one major urban center: the "Europhile" city-port of Montevideo, whose demographic growth placed the country among the most urbanized societies of the time. No urban center among the many that emerged in Colombia shared these characteristics. Moreover, rates of urbanization in Colombia remained rather humble, with most of the population living in the rural areas. In Uruguay, the predominance of Montevideo contributed to a sharp urban-rural cleavage that characterized party competition and political struggles well into the twentieth century. No cleavage of such intensity developed in Colombia, where small and medium urban centers engaged in various trade circuits, preventing one city from dominating linkages with the international economy.

Therefore, Uruguay and Colombia followed similar patterns of state building in very different geographic, demographic, and physical contexts. Table 0.1 shows that Colombia, unlike Uruguay, was home to several ecosystems and rural economies that, at times, did not even connect with one another commercially, much less socially. As a result, Colombia created complex systems of labor relations virtually unknown in Uruguay. The rural workforce in Colombia ranged from wage laborers and slaves in mining or agriculture to cowboys, sharecroppers, peasants, farmers, or tenants of various kinds. These countries were culturally very different as well. Explanations of the cultural and organizational influence of European immigrants on party building, largely stressed by the scholarly literature on Uruguay, have problems in Colombia, where the number of European foreigners who established residence in the main cities remained scattered and small. Although they could be found in sizable numbers in Bogotá and the Antioquia region, Europeans' cultural importance and social influence in Colombia cannot be compared to that in Uruguay. In addition, Colombia was the site of a rich ethnic and cultural mélange that differed greatly from the more homogeneous ethnic and cultural landscape of Uruguay.

In terms of the pace of power centralization in relation to geography, culture, and territorial size, these three cases, along with Venezuela and Paraguay, lead us to question commonly accepted assumptions. In Colombia, the process of power centralization was slow, and scholars have traditionally argued that a major reason was the cultural diversity and rough geography.[24] In Uruguay, thus, one may reasonably predict that state makers in this small, rather homogeneous area, dominated by a single urban center, would face fewer problems when centralizing power. Yet Uruguay experienced a delayed process of state building. This puzzling correlation between size and state formation is confirmed by Argentina, the largest of the three and the one that, under Juan Manuel de Rosas, centralized power first.[25]

In addition to delving more deeply into the central argument, chapter 1 briefly contrasts the breakdown of colonial rule in Latin America and its postindependence experience with Europe, China, and the Ottoman Empire. Chapters 2, 3, and 4 provide case studies of Uruguay, Colombia, and Argentina. To facilitate comparisons, I have organized the presentation of the cases by variable so that individual cases can be read directly into the book's overall argument. Each chapter starts with a review of current theories about the case and a synopsis of the argument advanced in that chapter. Although some comparative work is available on nineteenth-century Colombia and Argentina, chapter 2 offers one of the very few discussions of polity formation in Uruguay and, to my knowledge, the only comparative treatment of the case. Chapter 5 discusses Paraguay and Venezuela. Throughout the book, the reader will also find tangential references to other instances of state formation in Latin America and succinct references to the United States that are meant only to clarify and illustrate. In particular, the process of nation building in America provides an opportunity to elaborate on the importance of industrialization and larger domestic markets in state making.[26] It also suggests the advantages of redirecting the inquiry to include comparisons involving all of the Americas, a direction long neglected by comparative literature.

1

The Argument:

War, Polities, and the Rural Poor

Once a development path is set on a particular course, .
the network externalities, the learning process of organizations,
and the historically derived subjective modeling of the issues
reinforce the course.—DOUGLASS C. NORTH, *Institutions, Institutional
Change, and Economic Performance*

Before delving into the book's main thesis in detail, we must place Latin
America in a broader context of state making. Good reviews of literature on the state do exist, and it would be redundant to repeat them
here.[1] Literature on Europe, Asia, and the Middle East has correctly
defined state formation as the process by which state makers overcome
entrenched opposition from their populations and subdue regional political bosses.[2] The challenge from a comparative perspective is to explain differences in the timing of the centralization of power, to spell out
the conditions under which state makers succeed or fail, and to detect
the rationale behind more democratic or authoritarian outcomes.

1.1. Lessons from Europe and the Empires

Perhaps the first and most logical place to go for comparative clues is
Europe, which enjoys a wealth of theories on state formation. Some of

the most widely used variables to explain types of states and authoritarian or democratic outcomes include the commercialization of agriculture, the rise of a bourgeoisie, the formation of the working classes and their incorporation into politics, the growth of the industrial sector, the preexistence of medieval forms of "constitutionalism," labor relations under feudalism, and even the pervasive influence of "Roman law" in Western Europe.[3] Most of these theories have a structural or, to a lesser extent, an institutional leaning.

Which of these theories best illuminates the paths we observe in Latin America? Some seem of little relevance, for while the dynamics of class alliances were similar, the class actors and the international contexts of state making differed. Latin America lacked an entrenched nobility, confronted very different international pressures, underwent no industrial revolution, formed a rather weak and late industrial bourgeoisie, held no colonies, and experienced colonial rule. To these, one must add differences in demography, culture, and factor endowments. But it is precisely these contrasts that both mark the limits of theories emerging from the European experience and contribute to a sharper picture of state making on both sides of the Atlantic.

Many, including John A. Crow (1992:255–63), have found a strong conceptual linkage between theories of state making in Latin America and Europe in the strong "feudal" character of Latin America.[4] Crow's application of feudal categories to Latin America remains one of the most convincing; nonetheless, Crow ends up admitting that feudalism in the new world remained very "different" from the European variety. The degree of difference remained quite unyielding, and the concept-traveling unresolved.[5] Although structurally one could detect some "feudal" features in the new states, politically and institutionally the new nineteenth-century republics did not resemble feudal Europe. Moreover, there was really a world of difference between the accepted notions of the two feudalisms. Those who saw feudalism in Latin America perceived it as a sturdy obstacle to democratic practices. Those who studied feudalism in Europe, however, saw it as a predecessor to the industrial revolution and, for all its dark features, also as a noble precursor of capitalism and democracy.

The chapters on Uruguay, Colombia, and Argentina show that the "feudal" characteristics of rural life that can be detected in these societies, however defined, are poor predictors of state making. More-over, culturally, politically, and institutionally, one finds little resemblance between the historical evolution of these Latin American cases and the European varieties of feudalism. In the new world, reasons other than feudalism explained the hardy predominance of some "feudal" features, such as the preponderance of agricultural enterprises with low technology requirements, limited access to credit, poor communications, and frequent wars.[6]

Although ideal for comparing long historical processes, mode-of-production arguments about Latin America are of dubious value when explaining the rise of new states after independence.[7] If mode-of-production explanations do have some relevance, it is in a sense somewhat similar to Perry Anderson's (1974:421–22) interpretation of the rise of the absolutist state in Europe. He claims that the political, institutional, and juridical transformations that accompanied absolutism were not preceded by substantial reorganization of the feudal mode of production: "Contrary to all structuralist assumptions, there was no self moving mechanism of displacement from . . . [the feudal] to the capitalist mode of production, as contiguous and closed systems." Indeed, Anderson's argument about Europe seems less contentious when applied to Latin America, for although most scholarly literature agrees that in Latin America structural transformations were minimal, an analogous consensus has not been reached regarding Europe.

Comparing Europe and Latin America, we come to the conclusion that although the pace of economic development and differences in factor endowments undoubtedly affect state formation and influence democratic or authoritarian outcomes, to stress these variables alone does not necessarily facilitate the formulation of a more encompassing theory. Factors related to war and conflict resolution, on the other hand, seem to create an easier and more common ground for comparison. All theories suffer from a margin of error, yet when purely structuralist or institutionalist variables make up the theoretical picture without including factors related to conflict resolution and collective action, that margin of error significantly increases. The following chapters, among other things, show how different types of conflict shaped phenomena that most other theories have associated exclusively with structural changes. Conflict and the concomitant collective action determined access to the means of production, altered property relations, created new classes, and displaced old monopolies in land and trade. North's (1981) argument about the importance of property rights, prices, and transaction costs in state formation is well taken, but I take more to heart his insistence that customary economic models do not suffice.[8] Huntington's (1968:6) conclusions that economic development and political stability remain two separate and independent goals, and that progress toward one does not necessarily lead to the other, fit the cases studied in this book quite well.

Conflict and State Making

Michael Mann (1993) and Charles Tilly (1990) have suggested that European states tried to secure territories through war, and that war facilitated class alliances, either strengthening or weakening the state.[9] In Europe and elsewhere, wars shaped two related but different efforts at state making. First, conflict influenced the control of resources, taxation, and the construction of a central army. Second, conflict to a great extent determined the different ways by which ruling coalitions achieved political power, and how they constructed viable regimes.

Tilly (1990:30, 1993:31–32) has submitted a useful categorization to explain different routes to state formation. Three modes resulted from war and the relation between coercion and capital. All of them converge in the contemporary nation-state. In the process, both Tilly (ibid.) and Mann (1986:vol. 1) observe a continuum from coercion to capital-intensive modes.

The first mode, the "coercion-intensive" route practiced by Brandenburg-Prussia and Russia, remained largely alien to Latin America. In this mode, states—driven by the requirements of war—were able to increase revenues and enlarge their bureaucracies by forcing taxation on their rural populations. This pattern was dominant in regions that featured few cities and where direct coercion played a major part in agricultural production. After the wars of independence, no state in Latin America was able to enforce taxation efficiently, cities were coming to dominate rural areas, and direct labor coercion was not always possible.[10] Indeed, the emerging Latin American nations rapidly evolved into an area of many cities and commercial predominance, which placed them closer to the capital-intense regions described by Tilly (1990). Even in Argentina, the strongest state among our cases, the central power found it extremely difficult—and at times even undesirable—to rely on revenue extraction through coercion. In most of the region, states depended heavily on customs duties because the states were ineffectual at taxation, making them extremely sensitive to disruptions in the prices of exports and imports. If tariffs were too high, the government could succumb to plain smuggling; if they were too low, income plummeted. As we shall see, in countries such as Colombia and Uruguay, the state was only one among many competing organizations trying to extract resources and loyalty from the population. This brings these cases perhaps closer to picture of the nineteenth-century Ottoman state drawn by Resat Kasaba (1988, 1994) than to European states.

Like some European monarchs, the Latin American state more often than not was forced to borrow heavily from the merchant and landowning classes to build its army, wage war, or perform the basic business of state making. The state customarily acknowledged and lamented its dependence on local capital. A major difference from Europe, however, lay in the availability of external resources, for Latin American state makers could and did resort to external sources of funding. The history of the "great" loans taken from European and, shortly thereafter, American banks, is well known. Borrowing, however, did not seem to help power centralization or contribute to more efficient management. Rather, a disturbing and increasing external debt contributed to a worrisome balance of payments and fiscal crises, which further weakened the state. To satisfy its domestic creditors (and sometimes its international creditors as well), the state tried to reduce its liability through land grants and light taxes, pensions, or appointments to influential posts in the central bureaucracy.

One could argue that toward the second half of the nineteenth century, some states took the second route Tilly (1990:51–66) defined for Europe: a capital-intensive path, in which state makers and capitalists basically exchanged resources for protection. These agreements applied to city-states, city-empires, urban federations, and other forms of fragmented sovereignty. The Southern Cone region in particular, with its large degree of urbanization and thriving cities, seems to come close to this mode. Moreover, at least in the cases considered here, the availability of external loans allowed state makers to import capital to a degree unknown in Europe.

Yet the resemblance is not complete. Merchant classes and rural capitalists usually enjoyed the necessary control of resources to strike a bargain with the state, but the state often lacked the means to provide adequate protection. Most owners of capital had to organize their own militia to enforce property rights and defend their assets, contributing to the formation of militias outside the state's control. Moreover, capitalists did not always agree with the developmental goals of the state and, when they did, asked for much more than protection. Of our three main cases, Argentina—because of its wealthy landed upper classes and more organized military—possessed the ingredients needed for such an alliance, and indeed, it came the closest to this route. Nonetheless, the contribution of rural capitalists to the state remained, overall, quite modest. In fact, as Schwartz (1989) has shown for Argentina, in the second half of the nineteenth century, landowners managed to relinquish responsibility for the increasing foreign debt and transfer it onto the state's shoulders. Often the state could not, or did not want to, subordinate local magnates and enforce central taxation. As we shall see, the ineptitude of the state to do one or the other largely depended on its inability to resolve domestic conflict.

In Tilly's classification, Latin America falls more easily into a third form of "capitalized coercion," in which state makers used both coercion and capital to centralize power. Coercion and capital in Latin America were used unevenly, however, for coercion was brutal but inefficient, and scarcity of capital remained most often the rule. We must also include other caveats. In the New World, the sources of capital were not necessarily under state control; nor did this capital generate a dynamic economy as in Europe. A major difference, of course, was that Latin American states built no colonies to support their state-making activities, and in part because of that, they were often unable to curb market forces to increase their revenues.

Among our cases, Argentina again best fits the model. One can argue that given the large degree of local autonomy and the strength of provincial power networks, the Latin American states used coercion and capital in a way more reminiscent of France or England than Russia or

Prussia. Still, there are important differences. The route taken by France does not completely fit the Americas. For the most part, state makers in Latin America were not able or willing to mobilize their populations into a centralized military and a strong bureaucratic administration as France did. In terms of the incorporation of the upper classes, Latin American states also could not subjugate the social classes that resisted state penetration, as happened in France. The states that by the end of the nineteenth century resembled France somewhat more closely, Venezuela and Paraguay, did so only in regard to the strong weight they placed on the military. They remained unable to create an adequate, much less a strong, bureaucracy. And again, none of them created an efficient system of central taxation.

Despite a fairly good mechanism of taxation that went far beyond customs, England presents a better analogy. Especially in terms of the relationship between the state and the classes that resisted its growth, a number of Latin American countries—Colombia, Costa Rica, Chile, Uruguay, and Argentina—came closer to England, where royal power was limited. There, the creation of Parliament as the joint representative of landowners and bourgeoisie limited the monarch's power; in Latin America, local *caudillos* (political bosses) and Congress did. Structurally, however, the limitations of the analogy are marked by two basic differences: in Latin America, the bourgeoisie was much weaker, and the availability of domestically generated capital to state makers was much more restricted.

The foregoing comparisons contribute to our understanding of state making on both sides of the Atlantic but tell us that the paths taken by Europe apply only partially to Latin America. The limits are marked by serious structural and cultural differences. At the same time, one can find similarities in the process of institution building, and despite different contexts, one can certainly argue that both European and Latin American state makers relied heavily on war and coercion. More importantly, one can argue that different types of war shaped different types of states.

Recurrent guerrilla warfare and army wars in South America gave birth to confusing lines of authority that compare well with the *vendee* in France, for instance, or other similar European conflicts. However, there are also telling differences in terms of the type of conflict associated with state making on both sides of the Atlantic. These differences allow us to draw an even sharper picture of the process of nation building in Latin America. For instance, the frequent wars among European monarchs have no direct parallel in the New World. After independence, the major armed confrontations over power centralization took place within fairly geographically confined territories. Compared with the European experience, in which neighboring states fought each other for prolonged periods of time, one may think that Latin America did not fight enough wars. The question, however, is not the number of wars fought but rather war's impact on crucial periods of nation building. Latin America did fight numerous wars, and they had as much of an impact on institution building as wars in Europe. But the type of war and the resulting states differed. In the New World, state makers fought guerrilla wars, usually more short-lived and domestic. As we shall see, conflict led to a different kind of civil-military relations and ruling coalitions. As in Europe, the Latin American states underwent foreign invasions and engaged in territorial disputes, but most of the conflict remained domestic, characterized by intense civilian participation.

A clear lesson to be drawn from the contrasting experiences of Europe and Latin America is that conflict seems inherent to state building: it contributes to shaping states and regimes, and the collective action that it generates sets the scenario for coalition formation. This can be argued about other areas of the world as well, such as the East and the Far East. China, through the exhausting but successful seventeenth- and eighteenth-century period in which the Qing Dynasty was able to tighten central power and incorporate new territories, demonstrates that the consolidation of imperial power cannot properly be understood without examining the character of conflict.[11] As in Europe or Latin America, whether the state was able to recruit the nobility and secure its support made a great difference in the timing and character of class alliances and the development of state bureaucracies.

The wars between the central government and the so-called Three Feudatories, for instance, offered a lesson familiar to state makers in Latin America: the failure of the rebellious nobility to coalesce against the central power accelerated power centralization.[12] A second, less obvious, but still important lesson was that the geographic location of

the war effort mattered. When nobles were defeated in their own domains, the central government centralized power faster. In Uruguay,
Colombia, and Argentina, the geographic site of wars also had great
consequences for state formation. If conflict involved the site of the
central government and its close hinterland, a slower pace of power
centralization unfolded. If battles were fought on distant frontiers, the
central state and its hinterland usually enjoyed a better economic situation and, in turn, could devote more resources to the construction of a
central army. Chapters 2, 3, 4, and 5 testify to the explanatory power of
this simple finding. State making in Europe, as well as in Asia and the
Middle East, also points to the importance of the collective action of the
lower classes.

State Making and Rural Rebellions

To the European specialist, the overall picture that emerges in Latin
America is quite conventional. Local barons, magnates, or caudillos
either struck alliances with the population under their control to oppose
the central power or allied with the state to subdue the revolting lower
classes. Most literature has pictured power centralization as a game in
which three major actors—the state, the upper classes, and the lower
classes—coalesced or clashed, determining the relationship between the
state and civil society and influencing the institutional design finally
adopted.[13]

A shared finding of Mann (1986, 1993) and Tilly (1990) is that state
and nobility worked together in state building, but that not all emerging
states—including Prussia and Russia—were able to consolidate an association between the two. Frequent unrest from below provoked deep
concern in the monarchy and set the conditions under which state and
local barons allied. As in Latin America, antistate (rather than antifeudal) rebellions formed part of the landscape of institution building in
France, England, and Spain. Rural unrest also shaped the imperial
state in China, which offers an example of one familiar type of alliance:
peasants and local lords against the central power. Particularly when
tax collectors were also state officials, rebellions tended to be antistate,
and in many cases, local lords supported the rebellion. But in other

instances, the lords were perceived as the enemy, and windows of opportunity for alliances between the state and the peasantry emerged. This gave the central power a chance to reach the rural populations directly and to increase its strength vis-à-vis the noble classes. Peasant-state alliances took place even when not only the nobility but also the state supported the extractive policies that caused the conflict in the first place.

Like Europe, China illustrated that much of this rural mobilization depended on who, in the eyes of the population, implemented tax policy. In nineteenth-century Latin America, central taxation did not play such a central role in rural rebellions, and alliances between the central power and the rural populations did not materialize.[14] The main motifs for rebellion were land property rights and friction between rural labor and local landlords, but above all, the rural populations revolted against central authority. Local political bosses and community leaders played an important role in these rebellions, which more often than not reinforced clientele ties between labor and the local elite. Indeed, caudillos recurrently encouraged rebellion against the central power or the neighboring political boss in order to strengthen those ties. Promises of social betterment and enrichment played a strong incentive for revolt as well. Unlike what frequently happened in Europe or China, the alliances between the state and the regional elites did not necessarily translate into a coordinated policy of taxation. Nor did these linkages between local elites and central power always represent a joint, much less coherent, policy of exploitation of resources and labor. Consequently, rebellions rarely expressed a coordinated effort against *both* the central power and local lords. Local elites remained powerful, and ties between the state and the regional caudillos were loosely dependent on political favors and patronage rather than on a serviceable bureaucracy.

In terms of the character and frequency of rural rebellions, the Latin American and European experiences of state making find their most stark contrast in the Middle East. Consideration of this region points to the importance of the role of the army in the mobilization of the lower classes, a component of state making to be treated in more detail shortly. There, Ottoman state makers managed to build the state efficiently while provoking a minimum of antifeudal or antistate revolts.[15] Such an accomplishment owed much to a bargain between the state and "bandit-mercenary troops," which points to an alternative process of army building.[16] Comparing the Ottoman empire and seventeenth-century France, Karen Barkey (1991:699) has concluded that the major difference in state making lay in the strong peasant-noble alliances that characterized France.

These contrasting scenarios of rural insurrection beg further treatment of at least three key questions about state making in Latin America. The first is, Why were alliances between the central power and the lower classes so infrequent? The second and related question is, Why did local landlords and the rural poor tend to develop warring associations at the national level, with enormous consequences for party formation? The third is, Why were these rebellious alliances almost always alliances of class groups from very different sectors of the economy that, at times, obtained part of their strength from the urban middle class?

More Lessons from the Empires: The Balance between the
State and Civil Society

To consider rebellions from below as a causal factor of state making inescapably leads us to the role of civil society in nation building. As with other scholarly literature, that on the Latin American state has struggled to find the balance between the state and civil society. The picture, however, is still blurred. One accepted depiction of nineteenth-century Latin America portrays weak states with ill-trained bureaucracies, struggling with limited resources to centralize power in the face of powerful opposition and a prevailing antidemocratic culture.[17] At the same time, and somewhat contradictorily, this literature also depicts the postcolonial state as a centralist, corporatist institution, strong enough to provide a foundation for twentieth-century centralist and corporatist policy making. One could conclude that the emerging states were weak and powerless in terms of capacity or autonomy while at the same time centralizing and corporatist. This is puzzling.

To bridge these contradictory aspects of the emerging Latin American states, once may conceivably resort to culture. It is always possible to claim that despite their weakness, these states pushed toward centralization driven by their strong Spanish colonial heritage. Perhaps feeble institutions could not accomplish centralization, but culture could. This assumes that culture constituted a powerful engine of policy making and societal discipline, if it could generate centralized and corporate forms of authority in civil society despite the state's weakness. How a weak state and scarcely developed bureaucracy could be defined as successfully centralist and corporatist, however, still needs explaining. To be sure, the following chapters show that despite apparent traces of the centralizing ambition of the old colonial state, these republics remained rather decentralized. Argentina and Paraguay, the most centralized of all the cases, still did not resemble the picture portrayed by most literature. Part of the solution to this contradictory finding may come from accepted customary notions about the state, culture, and the relation between the state and civil society.

Contrasting scenarios of state formation drawn from the Ottoman and Chinese empires help to unravel the puzzle. State strength is usually measured against the strength of civil society. If one is strong, the other is usually assumed to be weak, and vice versa. From the shifting balance of power between the state and civil society in the Ottoman Empire, and especially from its evolution during the nineteenth century, however, we learn that this "classic" dichotomy may not be fully reliable.

By the fifteenth and sixteenth centuries, the Ottoman Empire had centralized authority and constructed an efficient system of taxation. Paul M. Kennedy (1987:10–12) tells us that the Ottoman Empire, like China, had grown larger and turned "inward." A striking difference from colonial and postcolonial Latin America was that the sultans were able to build a central army, control land property, and monopolize coercion.[18] By the end of the sixteenth century, this strong state faced collapse, and the balance between state and civil society changed in favor of the latter, which grew stronger and entrepreneurial.[19] By the 1800s, however, Ottoman state makers regained strength. They expanded the state bureaucracy and restructured the army. Yet civil society did not weaken, and both state and civil society remained strong.

Groups acting in nonstate arenas had acquired considerable social influence, and at that point they could not, or did not wish to, penetrate the state. Civil society continued to control activities that usually have been regarded in the West as prerogatives of the central power.[20] Private organizations retained influence over the regulation of market activities and actively shaped public policy without interfering with the state. A sort of division of labor was reached. Groups outside the state "spread . . . [their] . . . snares" into activities traditionally attributed to government, and the military-bureaucratic elite concentrated on professionalizing the army, diversifying the bureaucracy, and levying taxes more effectively.[21]

Many differences between the Ottoman and the Spanish empires may account for their divergent evolutions, their resilience, and their collapse. My focus is on the development of state-civil society relations in both cases, which requires a reexamination of our conceptualization of this equation in preindependence and postcolonial Latin America. A different balance in the equation was reached in the New World. Like the Ottoman state, most of the Spanish Indies during the late seventeenth and eighteenth centuries experienced a sort of symmetry between state and nonstate actors. That symmetry, however, stood as a mirror image of the Ottomans'. A balance was reached between state makers and groups of Creole or indigenous peoples who had forged a power base in the nonstate arena but were unable effectively to penetrate the state. The polarization between civil society and the Latin American colonial state represented a balance between weak partners and therefore opposite to the Ottoman situation.

This contrast reveals the European roots of the traditional dichotomy between strong state and weak society. To an extent, the dichotomy also finds solid precedents in the literature on the United States that has traditionally emphasized the strength of civil society.[22] My suggestion here is that preindependence Latin America gained a sort of stability during the nearly three centuries in which the institutions of the state never fully penetrated civil society. Regional differences were too sharp, and institutions too dependent on local notables and distant Spanish authorities. At the same time, collective action external to the state, stemming either from ruling cliques of notables and their allies or from the lower classes, gained strength but did not fundamentally threaten the stability of the empire.

No doubt the colonial state, despite its weakness, was able to exclude

groups from policy making. Yet because the state remained weak, ex-
clusion affected almost exclusively the lower classes; as mentioned,
alliances between the state and the lower class rarely materialized. This
remained a defining feature of the state after independence. And precisely because civil society remained weak, it did not develop the vigor
that Alexis de Tocqueville observed in the United States. Most group
action was targeted at obtaining favors and services from a weak government, services that only the state was perceived as able to provide.
When, as often happened, the state did not effectively respond, these
groups took justice into their own hands. On one hand, for the upper
classes, barriers to entry in government affairs were low; therefore most
sectors of the upper classes achieved representation in the state. On the
other hand, as a general rule, the colonial state was unable to meet
demands for protection or settle property rights disputes. The balance
between weak state and weak civil society meant that the empire was
not seriously threatened from within. Not until the 1760s did rural
populations and small towns—particularly in Quito, Peru, New Granada, and Mexico—rise in revolt against local authorities, some of them
appealing to the absent king for land redistribution and social justice.[23]
Yet Anthony McFarlane (1995:313) points out the rarity of "rebellions
of sufficient scale and duration to challenge colonial governments directly." The same may be said of the Ottoman case, where both state
and civil society were strong.

Independence broke the balance in the equation. In our cases, and
in most of Latin America in general, wars favored societal forces over
the state. One important achievement of the wars of independence was
the empowerment of civil society. Yet this empowerment, especially in
relation to grassroots organizations, was slow in coming and confronted many counterrevolutions, affecting the social capital and the
self-determination of civil society in the emerging republics. For most
of the period of state building, because the state and civil society remained weak, neither was able to generate reliable spheres of economic
and political activity from which to gain strength. In Colombia and
Uruguay, state institutions remained frail until the beginning of the
twentieth century. Civil society organized but gradually lost momentum. State capacity was strongest in Argentina but still remained highly
dependent on the owners of the export economy. The active civil so-

ciety that backed the May Revolution there seemed to be in decline immediately thereafter.

By the twentieth century, the balance of power between the state and civil society, reminiscent of the Ottoman case, shifted in favor of the state. Much of the history of the first sixty years of the twentieth century tells the story of a state buildup. Unlike in the Ottoman case, however, in the smaller states of Latin America, the strength gained by civil society during the convulsive period of independence and its aftermath was almost lost. Groups emerging from civil society decreased in numbers and importance. One way or another, most of them developed clientele ties with the state; thus the image of a corporatist arrangement depicted in some of the scholarly literature. At the same time, however, this so-called "corporatist state" did not necessarily gain enough power to dominate groups that it supposedly controlled.

In our negative cases, Venezuela and Paraguay, independence broke the balance in a different way. In Venezuela, it tipped in favor of military-caudillos and the military rather than in favor of the broader category of "civil society." In Paraguay, the colonial balance shifted in favor of the state. Both, like Argentina, saw the army rise to the forefront of state making. And in both, somehow similar to what occurred in the Ottoman Empire, the army provided a direct linkage between the state and the rural poor.

More Lessons from the Empires: Bandits and the Army

State autonomy in each case examined here remained directly tied to aspects of army recruitment and composition, and to the construction of lines of authority between officers, parties, and state makers. More powerful and centralized armies did not always facilitate state autonomy. An example is Argentina. In the following chapters, we shall see how mechanisms of incorporation of the rural poor and excluded groups (mestizos, blacks, and Indians) into armies and parties, as well as the connections between the army and the political elite, contribute to explain paths of state making.

Army building in the Ottoman case helps us to detect aspects of the role of the army in state making in Latin America that are not customarily considered in most of the literature. In particular, the contrasts help to explain why alliances between the army, the central power, and the rural poor remained rare. Barkey (1995) writes that in the seventeenth century, the Ottoman state relied on the service of mercenary bandits. Banditry was, of course, also common in Europe and China. Ottoman rulers, however, differed in that "vagrants turned into mercenaries and became organized along state military lines. It is difficult under these conditions to see the bandit as a rural product; instead, it is necessary to accept the role of the state in the production of this new social type."[24] There was a problem of control with this strategy, however, for to produce banditry is easier than to control it. The sultan resolved this by both creating and repressing banditry. In responding to peasant complaints against bandits in the localities, the state often achieved legitimacy by crushing the very bandits whom it had employed.

Like Ottoman state makers, Latin Americans also struck flexible deals with local patrons and militias who occasionally played the role of bandits, not in the romantic style of Eric J. Hobsbawm (1981) but more in the crude sense described by Barkey (1995). Army building included the flexible absorption of dissident "generals" who often resorted to banditry to maintain their militias, but who were opposed by the central power—whenever convenient—in order to defend property rights and the safety of the local population. Unlike the Ottomans, however, the state often lacked the resources to suppress the activities of local bosses it had hired. Therefore, the rural poor remained under the control of local caudillos and revolted more frequently against the state. No state in Latin America came close to accomplishing alliances with the peasantry or the rural working classes that compare to successful populist cases in Europe, such as Sweden, which is often cited as a unique alliance of king and peasant through a citizens' army.[25] Only in the twentieth century were some of the Latin American states able to galvanize popular support and establish a direct linkage with the lower classes, including Argentina, Brazil, Mexico, Uruguay, and, to a more limited extent, Venezuela.

We shall see in the following chapters how the state struck bargains with alternative centers of militarism (the bandits) to build its central army. State makers used caudillos who often harassed, as bandits, neighboring villages and pueblos that opposed the central government.

Similar to Barkey's argument in the Ottoman case, but unlike what Elizabeth J. Perry (1980) suggests for China, political bosses in the rural communities developed strong clientele ties with the distant state and the parties in power. Somewhat reminiscent of Barkey's claim, local caudillos for the most part were not exclusively the product of rural life and circumstances; rather, most of their backgrounds show ties with the colonial military elites and the urban merchant classes, all of which facilitated the caudillos' access to the central power. Despite the influence of a European military ideology that stressed the advantages of a strong central army, after independence, the Latin American cases studied here deviated from that model. As in the Ottoman case, power centralization took place "mostly through negotiation and [the] incorporation" of armies that had emerged in revolts during prior attempts at centralization, going back to the late eighteenth century.[26]

1.2. State Formation in the Americas: Parties and Armies

The Parties

Although political parties provided the distinguishing feature of state making in the Americas, from 1810 to 1900, one can also find a similarity between these infant parties and bandits in the Ottoman Empire or the civil-military units called "Banners" in China.[27] Clientele lines of authority and flexible ties with the central power were similar. Banditry also structured selective incentives strongly associated with party activity and party wars, from looting and robbery to the temporary use of haciendas as hideouts, or the plundering of crops and livestock. Reliance on militias under the supervision of loyal leaders remained an often viable and cheaper administrative alternative to monopolize coercion and impose order.[28] More than in any other area, however, parties in the Americas contributed to outlining the limits of citizenship and nationhood, and to building the army. For the most part, Latin American militia activity remained attached not to the state or to mercenary bands but to parties.

Parties formed alongside the state and became state makers; at the same time, party organizing became the most common form of regional resistance to the state. The Americas differed from Europe in the timing of party formation in relation to state building. In Europe, parties arrived later on the political scene, when states were already strong and consolidated, which places North America and Latin America closer together in the larger picture of state formation. To be sure, a large body of literature has viewed the emergence of the American republic as an experience unlike any other precisely because of the formation of parties at early stages of state building.[29] In all of the Americas, parties played the role of state maker and provided linkages between the state, the army, and civil society.[30] As Richard Bensel (1990) notes regarding the United States, state makers in Latin America also officiated as party makers, so that partisanship divided the state. Political parties tried to attract a somewhat contradictory clientele; they claimed to defend the interests of both the upper and lower classes vis-à-vis the state while at the same time they claimed to represent the state's interests in the hinterlands. The following chapters tell the story of why and how parties developed into durable organizations and party systems in some countries, and why parties could shape the state in some countries but not in others. An important part of the answer lies in the competition that developed between parties and the military in mobilizing the rural poor.

The Army

The army and the parties prevailed as the most important vehicles of incorporation. Unlike in Europe, where monarchs frequently hired foreign mercenaries, in our cases, the army recruited almost exclusively from the local poor, in a context of labor scarcity. Contemporaries testified that soldiers of fortune—British, Dutch, Italian, French, North American, Spanish, and German—did enlist in the armies in our three main cases but noted that these were exceptions. Argentina and Paraguay were able, for different reasons, to professionalize their armies before the end of the nineteenth century, but the overall picture is one of states forcing both foreigners and Creoles to enlist. At times, even the families of forced draftees were held hostage to guarantee their permanent service.

If one leaves the parties aside, military buildup and the correlated timing of state formation in Latin America come closer to that in Europe than in Asia. Brian M. Downing's (1992) argument about the European experience establishes a useful contrast. He finds the origins of European democracy in the relationship between military organization and state strength. Based on his (brief) comparison with Asia, Downing submits that the key difference between East and West "seems to be the relative power of the state . . . [in Asia] . . . at the outset of the military benefice system" (1992:53). Stronger state power at the time of the formation of the central army yielded "a more centralized system of military benefices, without contract, without immunities, and without constitutional support," while by contrast, weak monetary resources and weak state power in Europe gave rise to a "contractual military feudalism."[31] Both Europe and Asia used land grants to build their military establishments, but whereas Western military organizations remained decentralized and loose, those of the "Shogun and the Tsar" did not.[32]

Latin America followed the contractual route. This is not surprising, given the weakness of the state. Some of the entitlements granted to the military endured, such as the *fuero militar,* a controversial privilege granted during the colonial period that exempted officers from the official system of justice, and that, with slight modifications, was maintained after independence.[33] An important distinction about Latin America was that, at least in the cases examined here, the military emerged at a time in which the nation-state was embryonic, and a powerful gentry was not in place. In Europe, similar cases can be found. But whether there existed a powerful urban or rural gentry at the time of the military's formation, and whether the two coalesced, made a great difference. In terms of this important aspect of state making, the cases analyzed in this book more closely resembled England and Poland than countries like France. The comparison helps to explain why the rise of absolutist forms of state making were not viable in Latin America.

Wars in England in the Middle Ages, or even during the Tudor period (approximately 1485–1609), required low levels of resource mobilization; indeed, the army, by and large, was composed of a large loose infantry (militia). In France, however, the army was formed in the context of a stronger state and gentry, which came to control army de-velopment. The outcome in France was the rise of absolutism. There-fore, in Latin America, absolutism could not flourish. Absolutism fea-tured states and armies growing hand in hand, both of them highly institutionalized, both of them strong. One must add that in this and other aspects of state formation, France somehow escapes the Euro-pean context, coming closer to China and the Ottoman Empire than to the rest of Europe or the Latin American cases considered here.

As elsewhere, land grants were crucial to the growth of the officer corps. They tied the military to a state that remained, in theory, the largest landholder—if only as holder of *baldios* (unused land). How the process of land grants and army building unfolded, however, made a difference for the type of polity. In Uruguay and Colombia, officers and war heroes received land grants for their military merit, but military men were also able to access land because of their performance as party leaders. Political parties granted their loyal generals state pensions and benefits as well, which progressively tied them to the party machine and a state run by civilians. By the 1890s, retired officers in Uruguay who were receiving pensions from the party in power (usually the Colorado Party) largely outnumbered their active counterparts and, in some bat-talions, even the rank and file. The same can be argued for Colombia. As a result, the central army was weakened and lost autonomy during the process of state formation. In Argentina, a similar system of land grants characterized army formation, but the grantor of favors re-mained, for the most part, the state. It was also the government, rather than the major political parties, that took the lead in granting pensions and benefits to retired officers. In Paraguay, and also in Venezuela, the wars of independence and subsequent struggles favored land control in the hands of the state as well. There, by the end of the century, a system of land grants had above all favored officers and military caudillos, with the state and its generals remaining one of the largest, if not the largest, landholders.

1.3. The Argument

While consensus exists that the period from 1810 to 1900 in Latin America was one of political disorder, there is disagreement about the

cause of the conflict. Frank Safford (1992:96) contends that three prevailing interpretations have characterized the literature on state building. One stresses the characteristics of Spanish American culture, a second points to structural economic problems, and a third argues for the
importance of conflicting ideologies and fear of the lower classes. The
argument submitted here acknowledges all these factors but offers still a
different explanation of causes, state building, and regime outcomes.

State Formation and Revolutions

The different timing and dissimilarity of the revolutions of independence expressed a variety of conflict types. Jorge Domínguez (1980)
has emphasized the different speed and determination of the revolutionary movements. Whereas Cuba and Peru did not seriously question
Spanish authority, and it took more than a decade before Mexico reso-
lutely joined the revolutionary movement, cities as distant and different
as Buenos Aires and Caracas demonstrated an early determination to
become independent. When one looks into individual cases, it is clear
that despite a common reaction against Spanish domination, the different timing of independence responded to a complex set of local
factors.[34] This book views the period of independence as a time of
political revolutions that set different scenarios of institution building.[35]
In other words, state formation can be understood as a process of
postrevolutionary reconstruction.

This view of independence is not without controversy. Although the
war for independence in North America has almost invariably been
considered a "revolution"—even by scholars who have ignored the effects of war or structural theories of revolution such as James A. Morone (1990) or Gordon S. Wood (1972), or by those who have expressed a more critical view of democracy in America such as Charles
Beard (1913)—much the opposite has been true of the literature on
Latin America. The disagreement hinges largely on whether the heritage of the colonial state determined the path taken by the new states.
The debate is well known and need not be repeated here.

The comparative references examined in the first part of this chapter, and the case studies that follow, submit persuasive evidence that by
the 1850s, the ongoing conflict had destroyed the most important traits

of the colonial heritage and had triggered new political alliances, institutions, and styles of leadership and organization. During the nineteenth century, the growing dependence of the Latin American economies on international markets controlled by Europe, and later the United States, changed institutions; but it was war that changed them the most. As John Lynch (1992:82) writes, the wars of independence were not short conflicts "followed by the departure of the soldiers and the entry of civilians." Rather, these wars involved five, ten, or fifteen years of fighting, so that "institutions were out of place."[36]

Only a few of those who were in power before independence remained in positions of influence, and many who belonged in the middle and lower ranks of colonial society jumped to the top of the social ladder. The new states stood in sharp contrast to their colonial predecessors. The only entrenched institutions, the military and the Catholic Church, underwent rapid transformations. Bureaucratic tasks became simpler and, as Tulio Halperín Donghi (1989b:140) has observed, more subordinated to politics. Again, although at the onset of state formation a "centralist tradition" may have been strong in the minds of state makers, in practice, centralization remained feeble.[37]

Four Claims and a Thesis

Some, such as Blainey (1973:18), note that it remains a mystery why "unusually long eras of peace" characterized the nineteenth century in the West. A large part of the West, however, seems to pose no enigma. In that century, Latin America fought ferocious wars. If in the early twentieth century, the death of more than seven hundred men and women remained a criterion to differentiate small skirmishes from war, then one can argue that most of Latin America experienced almost constant war during the entire nineteenth century.[38] Miguel Centeno (1997) has found that the death toll in the Latin American civil wars of the nineteenth century reached extremely high levels. If these wars are placed in a relative context of land-population ratios and demographic growth, one could even argue that their effects on society came close to that of European conflicts. The region was also involved in several instances of international conflict. Table 1.1 shows their frequency and length. Some of these incidents, in turn, triggered civil wars, not represented in table 1.1. Instances of the participation of U.S. forces in these conflicts remain, in most cases, trivial; nonetheless, they are included because they indicate a modestly active United States in Latin America during the nineteenth century, and because they offer a comparative reference to assess U.S. intervention after the 1880s.

Tilly (1990:11) argued that "many different kinds of states were viable at different stages of European history"; an analogous argument can be made for Latin America. As in Europe, no country set up a model of power centralization that was followed by all others.[39] To explain their differences, this book offers four specific but interrelated claims.

URBAN OR RURAL WARS AND TYPES OF POLITY

The first claim suggests that the power and autonomy of the military, and thus the degree to which regime outcomes turned out more democratic or authoritarian, are partially explained by whether the locus of the revolutionary wars was supported by the city or the countryside.

Whether the central army formed under the tutelage of an urban center made a great difference for its development and its linkages with the political elite. Before the early nineteenth century, armed Spanish contingents played the role of "official" forces in urban centers, the core of decision making and commercial activity. These cities incarnated a loose notion of a state. Starting with the wars of independence, things changed dramatically—in particular, the relationship between the military and the ruling elites. Independence, in many ways, represented the "ruralization" of the polity; cities remained militarized, but they were forced to share military power with rural areas. In our cases, we can identify two distinct patterns. When the recruitment of militias and the formation of the army decentralized the power of the city, the military tended to develop a loose sense of autonomy and did not necessarily identify with the central power. The state grew weaker and the parties stronger, as in Uruguay and Colombia. When the army retained some degree of autonomy, and military power remained associated with the urban gentry, the state grew stronger and the parties weaker, as in Argentina.

Table 1.1. Nineteenth-Century Wars of Independence, External Wars, Foreign Invasions, and Foreign Blockades of Latin America

1804	1824	Wars of Independence
1810	1816	Argentina
1810	1825	Bolivia
1810	1818	Chile
1810	1822	Great Columbian
1810	1821	Mexico
1810	1826	Paraguay
1810	1826	Peru
1810	1828	Uruguay
1810	1820	Venezuela

EXTERNAL WARS, FOREIGN INVASIONS, AND BLOCKADES

From	To	Invasion or Blockade
1825	1829	Cisplatine War: Argentina and Uruguay versus Brazil
1829		Mexican war with Spain
1833		United States lands forces in Buenos Aires
1835	1836	United States lands forces in Callao and Lima
1836		Texas War, Mexico
1836	1839	Peru-Bolivian Confederation versus Chile
1836	1852	Argentina versus Uruguay
1836	1839	Chile versus Bolivia
1837		Pastry War, Mexico versus France
1838	1850	Guerra Grande-Plata
1838	1840	Blockade of Argentina by France
1841		Peru versus Bolivia
1845	1848	Blockade of Argentina by France and Great Britain
1846	1848	Mexico versus United States
1851	1852	La Plata
1852	1853	United States lands forces in Argentina (two occasions)
1853		United States lands forces in Nicaragua
1854		United States lands forces in Nicaragua
1855		United States lands forces in Uruguay
1856		United States lands forces in Panama
1857		United States lands forces in Nicaragua
1858		United States lands forces in Uruguay
1859		United States display of naval force in Paraguay
1860		United States lands forces in Panama

(*continued*)

From	To	Invasion or Blockade	(*Table 1.1 continued*)
1861		Tripartite intervention in Mexico: Great Britain, France, and Spain	
1861		French occupation of Mexico (1864–1867 empire of Maximillian)	
1861	1865	Reoccupation of Santo Domingo by Spain	
1862	1867	Franco-Mexican War	
1863		Ecuador versus Colombia	
1864	1866	Peru versus Spain	
1865	1866	Spanish-Pacific War	
1865		United States lands forces in Panama	
1865	1870	War of the Triple Alliance: Brazil, Argentina, and Uruguay versus Paraguay	
1868		United States lands forces in Uruguay	
1868		United States lands forces in Colombia	
1879	1883	War in the Pacific: Chile versus Peru and Bolivia	
1885		United States lands forces in Panama	
1888		United States lands forces in Haiti	
1890		United States lands naval forces in Buenos Aires	
1891		United States lands forces in Haiti	
1891		United States lands forces in Chile	
1894		United States lands naval forces in Rio de Janeiro, Brazil	
1895		United States lands forces in Colombia	
1896		United States lands forces in Nicaragua	
1898		United States lands forces in Nicaragua	
1898	1899	United States–Spanish-Cuban War	

Sources: Bannon and Dunne 1958; Centeno 1997; Small and Singer 1982.
Note: Refer to chapters 2–4 for detailed accounts of the three main cases.

Argentina offers the strongest example of the early consolidation of an alliance between the economic elites and the professional military in an urban setting. Unlike the other two cases, Buenos Aires was able to launch aggressive military campaigns to dominate the hinterlands. State and army developed a close partnership, which ultimately encouraged more frequent military intervention and the formation of movements rather than parties. In Uruguay, the revolutionary movement was primarily rural based, and the wars extended from the countryside to the city; civilian governments and parties found it easier to dominate in the long run. Colombia largely fits into the same pattern, although the country did not breed a rural-based populist movement comparable to that in Uruguay. In chapter 5, I suggest that conflict in Venezuela and Paraguay weakened civilian control of the military.

TYPE OF COALITION AND TYPE OF INSTITUTION

The second claim argues that the correlation between type of coalition and type of institutional arrangement (or type of polity) is not symmetrical. Although the characteristics of economic development and the type of export economy remain good predictors to explain the composition of ruling coalitions, they do not render the same service in explaining the type of institutional arrangement. Table 1.2 illustrates the correlation between the type of coalition and the type of institution. In the cases I examine, my efforts to correlate a certain type of coalition with a certain type of institutional arrangement led to frustration. The impact of conflict and subsequent collective action were more persuasive in explaining why similar institutional arrangements remained under the domination of very different coalitions, and vice versa. This simple point has attracted limited attention in current theories of coalition formation and regime development.[40] Chapters 2, 3, 4, and 5 show that coalitions that differed in terms of composition acted in a similar way, hence achieving similarities in institutional arrangements. The opposite is also submitted to be true.

My point is apparent in table 1.2. It shows that in Colombia, coalitions of coffee growers, mine owners, small farmers, and landless peasants, organized politically in ways very similar to alliances of landless rural laborers and the less entrepreneurial sectors of the landed elites in Uruguay; both coalitions adopted party organizations and competition. However, similar alliances of cattle-raisers and wool producers organized and acted differently in Argentina and Uruguay.

DEVELOPMENT AND DEMOCRACY

The third claim suggests that higher levels of economic development do not necessarily favor the rise of more inclusive, democratic regimes. This begs the question of whether the term "democracy" even applies to nineteenth-century Latin America. For some, democratic rule emerged under a specific set of circumstances associated with early capitalist development, circumstances that were not to be repeated for later industrializers.[41] Even a champion of democratic theory such as John Stuart Mill (1991:122–43) found representative government in many respects problematic, and much more so in societies with lower

Table 1.2. Coalition Type and Institution Type

Country (circa 1810–1890)	Composition of Ruling Coalition	Type of Polity
URUGUAY	Livestock sector[a] 　Cattle raisers 　Sheep raisers Urban merchants, mostly 　exporters and importers Grain growers Politicians	Two-dominant-party system Weaker state Weaker military Lesser military intervention Weaker corporatism
COLOMBIA	Large coffee growers[a] Mine owners Plantation owners[a] Urban merchants Mid-size landholders Politicians	Same as Uruguay
ARGENTINA	Livestock sector[a] 　Cattle raisers 　Sheep raisers Urban merchants, mostly 　exporters and importers Grain growers Politicians	No party system Stronger state Stronger military More frequent military 　intervention Stronger corporatism

[a] Dominant sector within the coalition.

levels of "civilization." Nonetheless, if one follows the standard criteria offered in the introduction, neither in Latin America nor anywhere else in the nineteenth century can one find full-fledged democratic regimes. Participation was limited to the few in mid-nineteenth-century England and the United States, and things were not much better in German and Italian states. In terms of the extension of suffrage, Argentina in the 1820s ranked higher than Europe and the United States in the same decade, and by the second decade of the twentieth century, Uruguay would rank as high or higher in comparison. The point is that despite frequent instances of corruption and clientelism, Latin American "democracies" resembled the liberal democratic model more than any other.

In the most developed of the three main cases, Argentina, the political outcome was not more democratic. Rather, the expansion of the export economy encouraged the consolidation of an alliance between the military and the upper landed gentry, which, during state building, reacted negatively to democratic reform. In Uruguay and Colombia, much slower economic development and constant turmoil contributed to the weakness of coalitions between landlords and the military, which encouraged political competition through party organizing. The ample degree of freedom that characterized levels of agrarian development and the type of ruling coalition can be illustrated further by comparing Argentina with the much less developed Paraguay, which bred similar alliances between the military and the landed elite.

Did the expansion of commercial agriculture affect democracy? The timing of the switch toward commercial agriculture was a crucial factor in Barrington Moore's model. Rueschemeyer, Stephens, and Stephens (1992:8) have emphasized even more strongly the empowerment of the subordinate classes as a necessary factor for democracy in Latin America and Europe, arguing that the working class was the most "consistently pro-democratic force" and much more "insulated" from the hegemony of the dominant classes than the rural lower strata. These authors' strong emphasis on the switch merits a quote: "If no significant export expansion occurred, no movement towards democracy occurred either, and if expansion started late, movement toward democracy was delayed. . . . Democracy depended on the sequences of social structural and political institutional developments set in motion by export expansion."[42]

I find plain historical timing to be a major problem with this thesis. Uruguay, Colombia, and Argentina indicate that the foundation of institutions that contributed to democracy materialized *before* the switch toward commercial agriculture, during what may be called the premodern period. The cases here offer a good opportunity to assess the switch's influence on regimes and institutions, for in each of them it differed in its intensity and the consequences of its development. It was, after all, backward Uruguay—where the switch occurred painfully and late—that emerged as the champion of parliamentary democracy. In Colombia, the kernel of a party system already existed before the 1870s and 1880s, when the switch toward coffee as a major export commodity took place. And the 1880s and 1890s, or even the early 1900s, were not

exactly democratic years in Colombia. Argentina, the most economically developed of the three main cases, ended the century under the
Orden Conservador (Conservative Order), its booming export economy
notwithstanding. In all of our major cases, the switch changed the composition of coalitions, but not necessarily the prevailing institutional
arrangement, and the new coalitions that emerged were not invariably
more democratic. Furthermore, in Venezuela, when agricultural exporting developed early in the nineteenth century, it supported different types of semiauthoritarian regimes; when the major switch took
place in the later part of the century, it ended up consolidating military
rule. And in Paraguay, the various stages of the switch backed benign
dictatorships and military rule.

Europe taught us a similar lesson: conflict and political developments
before the switch to commercial agriculture determined outcomes.
Moore himself pointed out that this was particularly true of France.
Like Russia or Asia, France had a strong state bureaucracy and a robust
peasantry that had actively carved a niche in a revolution that changed
France's institutions before the country became fully commercialized.
Thus in many ways the French Revolution could be considered—in
terms of its effects on democracy—a substitute for the commercializa-
tion of agriculture, which never gained the intensity that it did in
England.

Last, to accept the equation of economic development and democracy as it has been accepted in current literature means to hold civil-
military relations and army building constant. Such a strategy may
seriously distort our conclusions. While it stands to reason that higher
state revenues tend to speed up the process of power centralization, it is
also true that this depends on whether state makers can, or wish to,
invest their income in strengthening the central army. In Argentina,
they did; given army growth and prior civil-military relations, the outcome was not democratic. Conflict, rather than economic development, may force governments able to extract adequate revenues in a
different direction, away from a military buildup. For example, starting in the 1870s, the commercialization of coffee in El Salvador in-
tensified three- and fourfold; most income went to the landed elite,
but a considerable part went to the state.[43] Nonetheless, well into the
twentieth century, the state had still not invested in a central army and

relied instead on militias under the control of local landowners. States with modest incomes that experienced no spectacular switch could go different ways as well. Although limited by a slow-growing economy, Paraguay placed major resources into the construction of the military and thus centralized power faster; the outcome was not democratic. Meanwhile Uruguay, also a state with humble income and an unpretentious switch, invested very little in the construction of its central military. The state centralized power much slower, and democracy emerged.

THE INCORPORATION OF THE RURAL POOR

The fourth and final claim is that the mode of incorporation of the rural poor into war and politics substantially shaped institutions and the type of resulting regime. Labor was scarce in the agrarian societies of Argentina, Uruguay, and Colombia, creating a situation in which the allegiance of the rural labor force was essential, not only for economic development but also for political control. Unlike in Eastern Europe, a second serfdom remained an impossibility, and unlike in Western Europe, a growing industrial sector did not upset labor relations. When relations of production changed, they changed most often in response to conflict, rather than to overall changes in the mode of production. An analysis of who took the lead in mobilizing the rural lower classes, and what institution recruited them into war and politics, contributes to a better understanding of the outcomes. I identify at least three types of mobilization, as represented in table 1.3.

In column 3, the scope of mobilization is ranked in terms of the dominant role played by the central army, the parties, or armies other than the central army. The rankings are, of course, only relative to the other cases and have no absolute value, given problems of real measurement with the available data. Additionally, all countries represent a mix of these mobilization types.[44] Argentina, for instance, fits into categories 1 and 3 but, as column 3 indicates, fits more in category 1 than in category 3. The suggestion is that in the wake of civil wars, international conflict, or local rebellions, the rural poor were often drafted by one of three major means: (1) an army that responded to the central government, (2) a party or parties, or (3) caudillo armies not directly

Table 1.3. Mobilization of the Rural Poor, 1800–1900

Type of Mobilization	Country	Scope of Mobilization
Mobilization through central army	Paraguay	Highest
	Argentina	High
Mobilization through a party of parties	Uruguay	High
	Colombia	High
Mobilization through caudillo armies	Venezuela	High
	Argentina	Medium

connected to the central government or to a party. Banditry also played a role in the formation of the militias but was of lesser importance. Thus which group or institution did the dominant drafting affected the outcome.

Control of the countryside and fear of rural mobilization influenced state making. As we shall see, fear of revolution from below was more acute in Uruguay and Colombia than in Argentina. Although there can be no certainty that ruling elites felt a "shared fear," or that if they did, it determined their behavior, both Guillermo O'Donnell's (1979) notion of "perceived levels of threat" and Carlos Waisman's (1987) similar argument to explain economic decline in Argentina are illuminating.[45]

Contrary to the evidence shown in the following chapters, some literature has argued for a correlation between the use of labor and perceived level of fear.[46] In labor-extensive systems, the threat seemed less intense; in labor-intensive ones, the "perceived level of threat" seemed greater. Argentina, however, strengthened army building and mechanisms of rural repression in the context of a labor-extensive economy and a lower perceived level of threat, at least in the province of Buenos Aires. Uruguay, which also had a labor-extensive economy, nonetheless experienced intense rural mobilization throughout the whole of the nineteenth century; there, the perceived level of threat seemed as high as in labor-intensive Colombia, or even higher. Additionally, the cases examined here show that rebellions and coalition formation during the process of state building remained rather unrelated to the intensive or extensive use of labor, or the dominant relations of production in the rural economy.

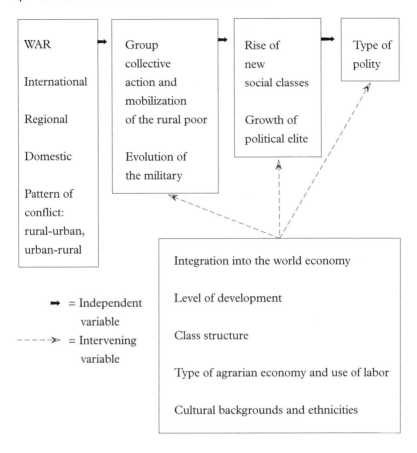

Figure 1.1. Independent and Intervening Variables

The four claims presented can be condensed into a thesis: *In agrarian postcolonial societies, types of war and the type and scope of mobilization of the rural poor during state formation shaped institutions, civil-military relations, and regime outcomes.* Figure 1.1 links our independent variables (types of wars and conflict) to the scope of mobilization of the rural poor, the formation of the military, and the rise of new social classes and the political elite in explaining outcomes, in that order. Other important factors are incorporated as intervening variables.

Within the type of war (e.g., army versus army wars, guerrilla wars), we include the role of urban centers and the direction (i.e., rural-urban or urban-rural) in which the conflicts unfolded. Figure 1.1, however,

Table 1.4. Type of Polity and Regime Outcome, circa 1810–1900

CASE	COUNTRY	WARS OF INDEPENDENCE AND THEIR AFTERMATH					OUTCOME		
		Mobilization of Rural Labor through Parties	Mobilization of Rural Labor through Central Army	Frequency of Party Revolutions	Frequency of Civil Wars	Strength of Central Army during State Formation	Pace of Power Centralization	Type of Institutional Arrangement	Type of Regime
Main	Uruguay	Higher	Lower	Higher	Higher	Lower	Slower	Weaker state, stronger parties, weaker military	Competitive and less restrictive
Main	Colombia	Higher	Lower	Higher	Higher	Lower	Slower	Weaker state, stronger parties, weaker military	Competitive and restrictive
Main	Argentina	Lower	Higher	Lower	Higher	Higher	Faster	Stronger state, weaker parties, stronger military	Less competitive and more restrictive
Negative	Paraguay	Lower	Higher	Lower	Lower	Highest	Faster	Stronger state, weaker parties, stronger military	Restrictive
Negative	Venezuela	Lower	Higher	Lower	Higher	Medium	Slower	Weaker parties, stronger military, stronger state	Restrictive

does not show the correlation between causes and particular country outcomes. This is done by table 1.4, which includes specifics about types of rural mobilization, the strength of the army, the pace of power centralization, and the frequency of conflict. Civil-military relations are, as the following chapters make clear, directly connected to types of war and mobilization. The same applies for the pace of power central-ization. Table 1.4 also distinguishes between the frequency of party revolutions and the frequency of civil wars and suggests that at least in these cases, the frequency of civil war is not directly related to the outcome. Except in Paraguay, all the cases experienced frequent civil wars, but outcomes differed; what made the difference was the type of mobilization of the rural poor, and whether parties or the central army led the war effort. We now turn to the evidence needed to support this argument.

2

Gauchos, Ranchers, and State Autonomy

in Uruguay, 1811–1890

During the period of state formation from 1811 to 1890, the *Banda Oriental* (Eastern Bank) is best described as a backward pastoral society ravaged by wars, violence, and personalism—a society that only dreamers or idealists could have predicted would become a model of democracy. Starting in the second decade of the nineteenth century, Uruguay and Buenos Aires were intermittently at war. In 1816 Brazil invaded, and in 1820 Uruguay was officially incorporated into Portugal as the *Provincia Cisplatina.* In 1825 a liberation movement supported by Buenos Aires ended Brazilian rule, and the conflict with Buenos Aires resumed. In 1828, supported by Britain, the small country of 74,000 inhabitants finally gained independence. Yet independence did not mean stability. Another war followed almost immediately, the *Guerra Grande* (Great War) from 1839 to 1851, during which Montevideo was besieged by an alliance of Argentine forces and dissident Uruguayan militias. After that, the country continued to be ravaged by constant domestic conflict that abated only in the early twentieth century.

By the 1890s, however, civilians fully controlled the state. By 1920, Uruguay had gained international recognition as a democratic paradise, and in the early 1920s, it became one of the first American welfare states. Some scholars have argued that Uruguay evolved not into a democracy but rather into a corporatist or neocorporatist state.[1] Yet it did not develop the mechanisms of interest intermediation that characterized corporatist arrangements in Europe or Latin America, particularly *à la* Argentina or Brazil.[2] Rather, despite growth in its public sector and the populist policies of reformers, scarce linkages developed between labor and the state. Organized labor remained autonomous.[3]

The rise of democracy in a context of war and violence, and the dismal experience of most of Uruguay's neighbors with early democratic reform, encouraged both scholars and policy makers to picture the nation as an exception, not only to Latin America but to the world, much as the literature depicts the United States. By the 1950s, most Uruguayans, on both the Right and the Left, accepted their exceptional nature as a matter of course. Its most radical expression was articulated by the so-called *neo-batllismo* movement that dominated politics during the 1950s and early 1960s.[4] At that time, Uruguayan society perceived the country in the terms frequently preached by schoolteachers and others: "*Como el Uruguay, no hay*" [There is no place like Uruguay].

A short list of these "exceptional" qualities perhaps suffices to explain this enthusiasm. Uruguay was the first Latin American country to have a ministry of labor and industry, and the first to adopt the eight-hour day and additional labor legislation, which many countries in the area then emulated. The 1917 constitution sanctioned divorce and gave women the vote.[5] After 1910, legislation protected the rights of illegitimate children, providing a novelty and an example to the world.

Most literature dates Uruguayan democracy to 1911, when both Congress and the president were chosen by popular vote. Democracy was consolidated during the second presidency of the foremost Uruguayan reformer, José Batlle y Ordoñez. The founder of a reform faction (the Batllistas) within the Colorado (Red) Party, Batlle was president from 1902 to 1906 and again from 1911 to 1915.[6] His administrations were characterized by a number of "progressive" social and economic policies with an energetic populist bent, which dominated Uruguayan political life until the 1960s.[7] During his second administration, Uruguay extended the vote to all males and adopted the secret ballot.

Puzzled by the rapid pace and depth of these reforms, most scholars have emphasized the importance of Batlle's first presidency.[8] The striking difference between the chaotic process of nineteenth-century state building and the model democracy of the early twentieth century has shocked most students. As José Pedro Barrán and Benjamín Nahum

1. *Army Maneuvers in Military Camp No. 1* (1929). Departamento de Estudios Historicos, Archivo Central de las Fuerzas Armadas, Montevideo, Uruguay.

2. *Battalion of Engineers, Division of Telephone Communications* (1918). Departamento de Estudios Historicos, Archivo Central de las Fuerzas Armadas, Montevideo, Uruguay.

3. *Gaucho* (1904). Photo
Archive, Intendencia
Municipal de
Montevideo.

(below) 4. *Family group in
Campana* (1910). Photo
Archive, Intendencia
Municipal de
Montevideo.

(above) 5. *Army Battalion*
(1918). Photo Archive,
Intendencia Municipal
de Montevideo.

(right) 6. *Urban Housing*
(1920). Photo Archive,
Intendencia Municipal
de Montevideo.

(1967–1978:vol. 4:18) put it, "How great an abyss existed between the Uruguay we find toward the end of the Guerra Grande . . . and that which was born in 1900!" They argue that the state's high level of autonomy explains the Batlle reforms.[9] This is correct, but it is precisely the source of this autonomy that needs explaining, particularly when, in terms of capacity, the state remained relatively weak, involved in costly wars, and narrowly dependent on customs duties.[10] Indeed, shortly after the Guerra Grande ended in 1851, a journalist expressed the opinion from Rio de Janeiro that "some European Government must assume the protectorate of Uruguay, for though Brazil could do this more easily than any other power, the Spaniards would never consent to it, such is the hatred they bear the Portuguese. . . . Financially, Uruguay is hastening to her ruin. Her weak Government frightens away immigrants, and how she is to recover herself is past ordinary human foresight."[11]

By the 1870s, the central power remained unable to penetrate the countryside and depended almost completely on the parties and their local political chiefs for basic lines of communications and the enforcement of government ordinances. The military, as a professional establishment responding to the executive, existed only on paper. State capacity remained minimal, with the state controlling no natural resource except the port.[12] A recognizable state bureaucracy did not exist until the late 1870s, and even then both the military and the state resembled a loose group of agencies with scarce coordination.

To answer this puzzle, one must not focus exclusively on the Batlle presidencies. Long before his victory in 1886, civilian control of the military was consolidated, and the state already showed signs of unusual autonomy. Civilian control, except for a short period of military intervention in the 1930s, secured governments run by civilians until 1973.[13] As Carlos Quijano (1949:292) puts it, the late 1880s marked a time in which "the coach carrying [the country's] fortune changed horses." This chapter seeks to explain this "change in horses" by examining the earlier period of independence and its aftermath.

Examination of that period shows a feeble professional military establishment with little political clout. Conflict had undermined the power of a pro-military coalition, weakened important landed sectors, and strengthened the urban political elite, facilitating state autonomy.

One can conclude that in this case, an important precondition of democracy long identified by Barrington Moore (1966) may also help in explaining the Batlle welfare state; that is, that landowners failed to form a "reactionary configuration." The following pages make clear, however, that the reasons for the weakness of this "configuration" were not necessarily structural but rather related to the characteristics of war and problems of collective action within the agrarian sector (see section 2.4).

The deep changes that transformed chaos into a welfare state occurred in the context of minimal shifts in institutional design.[14] The constitution spoke little about welfare or democracy and was far from reflecting that unshakable faith in the goodness of human nature that provoked Victor Hugo to comment, when revising one of the Colombian constitutions, that it was a "constitution for Angels." In other words, changes in the polity cannot be attributed to constitutional reform, at least until the reform of 1917. Although constitutional reform remained a touchy issue, frequently leading to rancorous legislative debate, this chapter argues that frequent foreign invasions tilted the balance in favor of those who opposed reform.[15] The notion of nationality was at stake, or so thought most state makers. They feared that reform bills would undermine an already weak notion of nationality, and that this, in turn, would work against mobilizing the population against invaders.[16]

The constitution became strongly identified with "the nation."[17] Some built-in features also contributed to its endurance, such as the complex mechanism of consensus required for its reform, and the fact that it favored a centralized structure of power with the president at its apex, encouraging the party in power to oppose reform.[18] The constitution also discouraged lobbying by excluding the right of citizens to organize into associations. Therefore, and not surprisingly, for most of the nineteenth century, the governing Colorados generally supported the original 1830 design, while the opposition (the Blancos, Principistas, Constitutionalists, and at times the military) called for reform.

Although the constitution tried to discourage factions and partisanship, civilian control was channeled through two major parties that monopolized most instances of collective action: Batlle's Colorado Party and the Blanco (White) Party. Their catchall character poses a problem for class analysis; thus the scholarly literature has focused more on leadership and ideology. Some have identified psychological and semireligious sentiments as the basis of party formation. Roberto Ares Pons (1967:41) claimed long ago that "in his unconscious search for a father image, the gaucho finds the caudillo, and in his search for God, the Motherland or *La Divisa*. Both loyalties are related [which] . . . explains the irrational adherence . . . to banners and causes that means nothing to analytical thinking." Likewise, Martínez Lamas (1946:115) submits that the parties embodied "sentiments" rather than ideas, and that they were the product of emotions rather than rationality. Some have definitely seen ideology as the glue that held parties together.[19] Almost identical to arguments presented in the next chapters on Colombia and Argentina, others stressed that liberal and "progressive" ideas imported from Europe found better reception in Uruguay than elsewhere.[20] The Colorados were identified as liberal modernizing reformers, and the Blancos as more traditional, rural-based conservatives.[21] These arguments suggest that the final triumph of the Colorado Party, and its ability to establish hegemonic periods during the nineteenth century, secured liberalism's predominance and the consolidation of democracy in the 1900s.

Although one can count more liberals among the cosmopolitan Colorados than among the Blancos, it is also true that by the 1870s, as Juan A. Pivel Devoto (1956:vol. 2:137) puts it, liberalism "commanded all the acts of the legislators" in both parties. Ideological cleavages between the parties, in fact, remained blurred for most of the process of state making. Powerful groups within both parties wanted a noninterventionist state, with both protesting the creation of the national bank, which they considered an encroachment on the private sector.[22] Although the Blancos remained more nationalistic, rural based, and conservative, and though the personal beliefs of leaders at times differed, one can argue that on issues of participation and political democracy, the parties were similar.

What was it that kept the parties as separate organizations? The answer lies in rural Blanco mobilization against a city dominated by the Colorados, foreign occupation, party wars for the control of the regions, and the types of settlement reached. Independence and, later, party wars carved a profound urban-rural cleavage and made the Blancos the traditional party in the opposition, while the Colorados could retain control of government if—and only if—they negotiated with the Blancos. As the century came to an end, the influence of intellectuals in the incipient parties grew, but the major engine of party building remained largely dependent on guerrilla war and rivalry over the control of resources. Other parties, of course, also emerged. In the 1870s, for instance, urban lawyers and *doctores* (physicians and accountants) strongly embraced liberal ideas and organized the *partidos de ideas* (parties of ideas), whose major goal was to challenge caudillo leadership in the parties.[23] These parties were united by a common platform, *principismo,* which aimed to impose new rules on the existing political game, particularly regarding vote counting and the importance of elections.[24] These parties helped secure civilian control over the military, but they could not survive independently because they did not control the rural party militias. Instead, they ended up merging with Blancos and Colorados and thereby modernizing the old party machines.

Section 2.1 of this chapter offers a review of current literature on nation building in Uruguay, points to crucial gaps in these explanations, and prepares the terrain for my own interpretation. In addition, it reviews some of the most salient structural and political features of the small republic. Section 2.2 discusses the impact of war on the state and parties, with special attention to the mobilization of the rural poor. Section 2.3 is devoted to a brief analysis of state autonomy, one of the salient features of state making in Uruguay, and an important development to explain democracy. Finally, Section 2.4 explores the evolution of civil-military relations and civilian control over the military.

2.1. Uruguay, the Exceptional Democracy

Farmers, Peasants, and Democratic Rule

Scholars have long claimed that the existence of a farm economy favors democratic outcomes. The literature has cited the examples of the United States, Canada, and France. It has also assumed that "small rural producers" generated a similar effect in Latin America; for example, in Colombia or Costa Rica. Uruguayan democracy, however, has few small rural producers.[25] Beginning in the 1850s, Uruguay estab-

Table 2.1. Structure of Exports in Uruguay, 1829–1842 and 1862–1920 (in %)

Period	Cattle Hides	Horse Hides	Tasajo	Fats	Horse Hair	Wool	Other Products
1829–1830	67.6	12.3	13.0	—	—	—	7.1
1840	59.8	1.2	23.3	6.2	2.4	3.6	3.7
1841	62.8	1.3	22.7	5.3	1.3	2.6	4.0
1842	68.2	1.5	15.2	3.0	1.5	4.5	6.1

Period	Hides	Wool	Tasajo	Frozen Meat (1)	Meat Total (2)	Other Livestock Products (3)	All Livestock Products
1862	35.8	10.7	11.6	—	11.6	25.6	83.6
1872–1875	41.9	22.7	11.7	—	13.1	12.8	90.5
1877–1880	33.0	19.3	16.0	—	20.3	13.5	86.1
1881–1885	31.1	26.6	14.9	—	20.6	12.0	90.4
1886–1890	28.6	38.2	15.7	—	21.0	1.0	88.7
1891–1895	25.9	29.1	15.7	—	22.6	14.6	92.1
1896–1900	22.2	35.7	17.6	—	23.0	10.7	91.6
1901–1905	28.1	32.7	19.0	0.1	19.4	12.1	92.2
1906–1910	24.0	40.2	9.8	1.4	15.8	11.3	91.3
1911–1915	19.9	43.6	6.1	14.4	25.0	4.3	92.7
1916–1920	20.8	36.9	1.9	15.7	32.5	6.9	97.1

Sources: Kleinpenning 1995:171, composed from Millot and Bertino 1991 and Rial Roade 1983.

lished so-called colonies of agriculturalists in the south and southwest, but they attracted few immigrants and brought no real change to the rural economy, which was dominated by livestock production. Notice the scanty contribution of small-farm production to exports in table 2.1. The table shows the structure of exports from 1829 to 1842, and from 1862 to 1920.

From 1872 to 1875, wool rose to prominence. Although its position later declined, in 1884, wool represented 27 percent of the value of exports.[26] Small producers, however, remained a minority among sheep raisers. Few immigrants settled in the countryside, and large and small grain farmers remained a tiny minority. Uruguay also lacked artisans; hence the argument that a strong artisan sector favors democracy (as in Colombia) does not apply here, either.[27]

Perhaps the "classic" argument about the negative effects of peasants on democracy could find some ground in Uruguay, for Uruguay had no peasantry.[28] Two caveats come to mind, however. First, the line between peasant and small producer in Latin America is really a thin one. Second, countries with a peasantry still developed competitive systems, such as Colombia.

Perhaps one can argue that similar to England, the land enclosures forcefully put into effect in the 1870s, along with the subsequent decline of both small producers and the gaucho lifestyle, were all positive steps toward modernization and thus democracy in Uruguay. After all, this was the view of contemporaries, as expressed in the 1860s by Argentine president Domingo Faustino Sarmiento. The comparison with England, however, points to the apparent impact of the industrial sector on democracy. Moreover, and perhaps more significantly, Sarmiento's native Argentina subdued the gaucho first, modernized first, and enforced even stricter land enclosures. The outcome, however, was not democratic.

Entrepreneurs, Modernization, and the Political Elite

In Uruguay, a party system emerged before the country switched slowly toward commercial agriculture. Modernization took a hesitant pace; landowners hardly reacted to government incentives to invest in manufacturing, answered languidly to international incentives in the beef and wool markets, and, for the most part, did not put much energy into improving the competitiveness of agriculture. Table 2.1 indicates the modest share of frozen meat exports vis-à-vis other livestock products; overall, the livestock sector did not respond readily to market incentives. Table 2.2 shows that these exports acquired real importance in the first decades of the twentieth century. Even during the brief bonanzas of the late nineteenth and early twentieth centuries, landowners rarely adopted crossbreeding and remained cautious regarding new commercial ventures. As many sources point out, the rural elites' entrepreneurial drive lagged behind their counterparts' in Latin America and elsewhere.[29]

As late as the mid-1860s, regional trade with Brazil and dry-beef

Table 2.2. Uruguayan Exports of Frozen Meat, 1904–1915

Year	kg	Year	kg	Year	kg
1904	13,309	1908	6,914,274	1912	20,342,473
1905	2,399,577	1909	5,680,929	1913	49,563,614
1906	1,710,224	1910	9,398,660	1914	69,407,781
1907	5,472,301	1911	7,680,868	1915	95,247,704

Source: Kleinpenning 1995:170.

exports to the slave economies of Cuba and Haiti still kept most of the landed class in business.[30] Many producers indeed mistrusted and re-sisted an integration into a frozen-beef trade dominated by British and Argentine capital. Some modernization materialized in the expansion of sheep farming under the control of European immigrants. In the 1860s, the so-called wool revolution definitely linked the country to European markets; but even then, landowners invested more in pur-chasing new land than in technological innovation.[31] When the Asocia-ción Rural del Uruguay rose in 1871 as a modernizing force, it really represented a small number of entrepreneurs from the South and the Littoral, among whom Uruguayans were a minority. The landowners' behavior was not irrational. Land remained the most reliable long-term investment compared to what they perceived as being volatile oppor-tunities. In section 2.3 of this chapter, we shall see how frequent wars and foreign invasions shaped their market preferences and their politi-cal behavior.

Modernization's highest achievement was the relatively intense ur-banization of Montevideo. Argentine president Sarmiento's aspiration to eliminate barbarism with urbanization (or John Stuart Mill's argu-ment about the good influence of urban life) was put to a test in the small republic. In 1830, 18.9 percent of Uruguayans lived in the capital city, rising to 25.7 percent by 1852. When one includes the agricultural belt that surrounded the city, 37.2 percent could be classified as urban. Barrán and Nahum (1979–1986) have pointed out that most of these urbanites still lived a rural lifestyle, but the fast pace of urbanization is undeniable. As the authors recognized, by 1908 about half of the total population of the country could be classified as urban, culturally and occupationally.[32] Real de Azúa suggested that Uruguay's uniqueness lay in the city's quick conquest of the countryside. By 1887, even a newspaper in rival Buenos Aires acknowledged the charming features of the competing city, believing it to be superior to Buenos Aires: "Comparisons are not detrimental when there is a need for them. Montevideo, the Plate's Queen, surpasses Buenos Aires in about one hundred years. . . . Really, Montevideo makes the Plate River proud. . . . There is nothing in Buenos Aires that can be compared with Montevideo's streets . . . since [they] rival Sackville Street and other European cities."[33]

But the countryside had not been conquered. It seemed empty and detached but remained an important locus of political mobilization, able to threaten the city up until 1904. What did happen was that rural and urban areas "became two worlds apart," culturally and politically.[34] Rural war, in fact, contributed to urbanization, especially to the augmentation of the urban political elite, simply because it ruined landowners. By the end of the Guerra Grande in 1851, for instance, many bankrupt *hacendados* established permanent residence in Montevideo and turned to politics to exercise influence. Their sons became lawyers or physicians and also pursued political careers. The brotherhood of notables, a feature of urban politics under the *cabildo* system and a group that at midcentury organized under the aegis of the Colorado Party, merged with these professionals and contributed to a growing body of full-time politicians. This group forged close ties with the merchants of Montevideo; together, they formed the modernizing urban *patriciado* (patricians), or *doctores*.[35]

Structural Theories of State Making

Nation building in Uruguay has often been explained by economic structures and markets.[36] Emphases differ, even among the same authors. For example, Barrán and Nahum (1967–1978) see state building as the product of sluggish modernization.[37] In another collection (1979–1986) devoted, in part, to explaining state autonomy, the same authors add to their structural argument a behavioral-Weberian framework mixed with some dependency theory and neoclassical economics.[38] Individual and class actors calculated transaction costs and made the choices that best satisfied their material interests.[39] *Ganaderos* (cattle raisers), especially, resisted technological innovation as a rational response to the nature of markets.[40] My point is that despite their emphasis on economics, a careful reading of Barrán and Nahum's (1967–1978:vols. 1, 2; 1989) encyclopedic work reveals that economic factors alone cannot explain state making. When accounting for government institutions, the logic of war and problems of collective action faced by parties seem to take priority even for them.

One can say something similar about Lucia Sala de Touron and collaborators (1986–1991:vols. 1–2; 1970:especially vol. 1:17–23, 47–72; vol. 2:224–45), who, within the framework of Marxism and dependency theory, give great weight to the economic aspects of state formation and focus on the role of merchants as nation builders. A wealthy class of urban merchants rendered the state weak by making the government dependent on loans; thus they controlled much of the state. No sign of Barrán and Nahum's autonomous state is detected in the state making studied by Sala de Touron and Rosa Alonso Eloy (1986–1991:vol. 2:315–33). They argue that the mild protectionist laws passed in this period responded to growing competition with the port of Buenos Aires rather than to pressures from domestic protectionist groups.[41] The state clearly emerged as a product of class struggle and economics, and as a free-trader coalition. They also stress the importance of regional conflict in state building.[42] Touron and Alonso, however, rely too much on the mode of production as an interpretative category.[43] Second, they attribute too much influence to dependency to explain poor economic development and state institutions.[44]

Cultures, Immigration, and Democracy

Some have argued that as in the United States, Uruguayans' innate love for freedom and life in the open spaces favored a weak central government and democracy. After all, Uruguayans were "born" fighting foreign invaders and authoritarianism.[45] The more conservative Blanco party claimed to incarnate this "political culture."[46] In the late 1960s and early 1970s, the radical Left—the National Liberation Movement

(MLN), or Tupamaros—argued likewise.[47] As in Argentina, the rebellious and free character of the gaucho had forged a democratic ethos in Uruguay.[48] As in Argentina or Australia, a Rousseauian notion of incorruptible natural freedom and a celebration of the *bon savage* in the gaucho emerged from the romanticism of the 1930s and 1940s.[49] From this standpoint, rather than an asset, modernization represented deprivation and foreign intrusion, an obstacle to Uruguay's "natural" development. Much later, and more systemically, dependency theory echoed these ideas.

Somewhat opposite to these notions, others stressed European immigration and cultural heritage to explain the emergence of a democratic ethos. Close to the literature on Argentina, Europeans were perceived as the promoters of democracy in a wild frontier. After all, the country was part of the "privileged" group of recently settled lands that Adam Smith believed to be more prone to develop democracy than those in which colonizers had to exploit the labor of a preexisting society.[50] Like Frederick Jackson Turner's (1920) description of the United States, or H. A. Innis's (1933) study of Canada, Uruguay lacked both an indigenous labor force and a strong colonial background.[51] Many claimed that for all practical purposes, the rural areas provided the equivalent to the American frontier.[52]

Immigration comprised such an important part of this society that it merits a few paragraphs. State makers themselves regarded European immigration as a crucial ingredient of liberalism.[53] Although not all foreigners were European—by the 1860s, Brazilians formed the largest group—available figures on immigration support the view that European culture strongly shaped urban society and some of the *departamentos* (provinces or localities), even before 1867, when huge immigration waves of Spaniards and Italians arrived. Table 2.3 shows census figures for 1860, by department.

Table 2.3 indicates that in Montevideo, Italians were a majority.[54] Almost twenty years later, in 1879, the Italian consul Ippolito Garrou reported that according to a recent census, Spaniards outnumbered Italians in the city only by four hundred.[55] French cultural influence also seems to have acquired some prominence. In 1843 a French observer concluded that there were more French residents in Montevideo than in Algeria, a country under French domination since 1830. By the

Table 2.3. Division of the Population of the Departments in Uruguay by Nationality, 1860

Department	Brazilian	Spanish	Italian	French	Argentine	African	British
Canelones	116	5,942	438	372	92	200	22
Cerro Largo	5,885	516	36	107	123	207	10
Colonia	56	551	638	474	868	—	177
Durazno	691	232	75	131	125	70	34
Florida	532	572	117	222	116	134	57
Maldonado	332	727	154	38	25	90	6
Minas	705	544	86	147	68	133	18
Paysandú	?	?	?	?	?	?	?
Salto	5,714	642	390	390	1,526	44	22
San José	100	836	421	421	202	90	50
Soriano	149	564	410	410	696	41	58
Tacuaremó	4,391	127	71	71	155	29	11
Interior	18,671	11,253	2,783	2,783	3,996	1,038	465
Montevideo	767	7,811	6,141	6,141	2,366	1,352	603
Uruguay	19,438	19,064	8,924	8,924	6,362	2,390	1,068
%	26.0	25.5	11.9	11.9		3.2	1.4

Source: Censo de 1860; see also Puiggrós 1991; Kleinpenning 1995:229.

1860s, the total percentage of foreigners in Uruguay was 21.6 percent, but in Montevideo, it reached 46 percent. By 1867, the city's population had grown to almost 130,000, of which 75,000 were foreign-born. When one adds to these figures the cultural influence of a first generation of Uruguayans who were raised in their parents' European traditions, the societal-cultural fiber of Montevideo was clearly European. Moreover, until the 1920s, the proportion of foreigners there tended to increase because of two immigration patterns: Europeans favored Montevideo, whereas Creoles who had established residence in the city but could not make a decent living tended to migrate toward the countryside.

The Spanish consul optimistically reported in 1887 that the small republic had demonstrated a strong "propensity" to democratic rule, resulting from its emptiness and the overwhelming majority of Europeans who had made the country a land of promise:

Portuguese	German	Other	Unspec.	Total foreign	%	Total Uruguayan	Total pop.
68	26	27	—	7,303	15.5	13,165	20,468
71	34	22	—	7,011	14.9	10,464	17,475
77	131	53	—	3,025	6.4	9,544	13,349
20	16	21	—	1,415	3.0	7,558	8,973
33	37	24	—	1,844	3.9	10,326	12,170
24	14	1	—	1,411	3.0	12,344	13,755
41	7	16	—	1,765	3.7	11,087	12,852
?	?	—	5,048	5,048	10.7	9,153	14,201
81	54	50	—	9,001	19.1	6,820	15,821
44	20	34	—	1,954	4.1	10,573	12,527
63	85	42	—	2,478	5.3	11,660	14,138
23	21	14	—	4,920	10.4	4,673	9,593
545	445	304	5,048	47,175	100.0	117,367	165,322
511	235	306	—	27,674	—	30,190	57,916
1,056	680	610	5,048	74,849	—	147,557	223,238
1.4	0.9	0.8	6.7	100.0			

The European population exceeds 300,000 souls among whom 60,000 were Spaniards. . . . [the country] enjoys a happy and prosperous condition which contributes to the prosperity of the Peninsula. . . . Because these countries are empty, they must encourage foreign populations to establish residence and therefore they must also establish democratic principles of government, conditions of equity that shall please the foreigner who . . . comes to these lands to find a better tomorrow.[56]

Therefore, unlike those who have portrayed Spanish culture as an obstacle to democracy, immigrants and Creoles alike stressed the democratic ethos of the Spanish immigrant. According to Julio Martínez Lamas (1946:86–88), the major difference between North and South America was not in the cultures and habits of their colonizers (they were, after all, all white Europeans) but in natural resources and the distances that separated the colonizers from Europe.[57]

Thus one can conclude that on one hand, native Uruguayans (Indians, mestizos, and Creoles) struggling against both modernization and Spanish, French, British, and Portuguese invaders forged a culture of freedom and equality that favored a weak state and a democratic outcome. On the other hand, the growth of the city and the influence of European culture brought democracy and modernization to an uncivilized reality that, left to itself, could never have created democracy. Are these contradictory statements? Some have argued that democracy resulted from the mix of these two ethos; others, that it kept them separate. Our comparative exercise may help. The comparison with Colombia suggests that party systems and political competition can emerge in the absence of a strong European culture. The comparison with Argentina suggests that as far as party politics and the emergence of "method" of democracy goes, a strong European cultural heritage may not suffice.

Skillful Leadership

Similar to what is found in the literature on Colombia and Argentina, a powerful and popular claim is that the extraordinary qualities of Uruguayan political leadership explain democracy. For the most part, this "exceptional leader" hypothesis was designed to account for the statesmanship of José Batlle y Ordoñez.[58] The first, and most popular, version combines Batlle's exceptional leadership with the economic prosperity of the first two decades of the twentieth century. Basically, favorable terms of exchange with Britain both allowed state expansion and persuaded economic elites that they could afford democracy. The president was able to strengthen the state and make rapid democratic reforms. Yet the "bonanza" of the early twentieth century was not that impressive, and it is dubious that this modest prosperity "convinced" elites to go along with the reforms pushed by the Batllistas in the Colorado Party.[59]

Other versions of the exceptional leader thesis add the rise of an early proletariat, which helped Batlle. With the establishment of slaughterhouses as part of the expansion of the beef industry, Montevideo attracted many workers—and foreign labor and arrivals from the coun-

tryside backed Batlle's agenda. Those who stress the populist or socialist aspects of batllismo, and those who criticize Batlle as a demagogue,
have endorsed this position.[60] Some claim that entrepreneurial landowning elites, who perceived future gains in industrialization, supported Batlle as well.

These are rich but problematic propositions. First, rather than a
"bottom-up" reform based on working-class support, from 1903 to the
first serious effort at industrialization (circa 1930), what we really
find is a democracy imposed from above. No evidence shows that labor
and Batlle had a tacit agreement, or that labor leaders partook in his
agenda.[61] Working-class support for the first presidency was confined
to a few unions and cannot explain the emergence of the welfare state.
Second, the size of the industrial workforce was relatively small. Industrial establishments—mainly associated with the beef and wool trades—
employed many workers, but they were not numerous enough to constitute the main force behind political reform. The workers' support for
the Batlle initiatives came later, during his second administration, and
cannot explain how Batlle reached the presidency in his first term.
Moreover, many workers were disenfranchised foreigners, and given
their modest participation at the polls, the popular mass-support thesis
cannot even explain Batlle's second term. Although by his second presidency, direct popular suffrage increased support for Batlle, less than
half of the urban citizenry in fact voted.[62] Finally, other versions based
on the combination of the rise of an industrial bourgeoisie and Batlle's
outstanding personality also seem inadequate. Julio A. Louis (1969:9–
11, 64–88), Javier Bonilla Saus (1981), and others have interpreted
democracy as the expression of a "democratic bourgeoisie," but even in
the 1940s, industrialization was too limited to create such a bourgeoisie.

Handwritten marginalia: Batlle imposed democracy from above... It wasn't so much poor fighting 4.5 it.

2.2. Wars, Parties, and the Rural Poor

War and the Economy

Before discussing the impact of wars on institutions of government, we
must say a few words about their enormous effect on the economy. I
wish to make the point that ongoing conflict, rather than structural

constraints, contributes to an explanation of the poor economic performance of the country. State making took place in a situation of economic scarcity, in which war disrupted both city and countryside. In 1832, just two years after the approval of the first Uruguayan constitution, Montevideo merchants estimated that the final destination of almost 90 percent of the ships and freighters entering the River Plate was Buenos Aires; they believed that war in the Banda had worked to their disadvantage.[63] And they were right. Despite structural similarities, the province of Buenos Aires was always richer, and no strong structural difference can fully explain why the Banda lagged so far behind.

Although Uruguay did not possess the same resources as Buenos Aires, it controlled excellent pastures and a first-rate port. Compared to Buenos Aires, "the city . . . benefits from navigation and commerce. . . . Its port is more secure and comfortable."[64] By the late 1820s, however, Buenos Aires expanded its maritime trade, and very soon the landed elite engaged in a profitable partnership with Britain in the hide, wool, and beef trades. Nothing comparable happened in Uruguay. A similar story can be told in terms of livestock production. Despite an encouraging performance in the years after 1810, ten years later, war in Uruguay caused Buenos Aires to rise to the forefront. Barrán and Nahum (1967–1978:vol. 1:267–70) remind us that the Guerra Grande (1839–1850) reduced livestock production to levels below those of the colonial period. "Rivalry between the parties and chronic civil wars" had been largely responsible for the weakness of the state and skyrocketing external debt.[65] By 1874, the executive reported that from 1860 to 1874 alone, public debt increased about thirty times; war was a major and constant drain on the economy.[66] According to Oscar Oszlak (1985:49), when neighboring Argentina in 1870 experienced "profound changes in economic developments that generated growing expectations of material progress," the British chargé d'affaires in Montevideo wrote:

The consequence of this wretched state of [war] . . . is that the peons . . . are taken from the estancias, the flock of the different proprietors mingle . . . and [that] . . . the men who cultivate either their own bits of land . . . are forced to join the military service of one of the other of the [party] leaders or to seek refuge in the woods. . . . I believe my Lord that no political change could make the conditions of this country worse than it now is, and which old inhabitants declare to be the more deplorable than it was in the 9 years war ending in 1851.[67]

Wars and Parties

During the first half of the nineteenth century, two major parties emerged as a product of war, becoming powerful crafters of the state. Despite his emphasis on ideas to explain party cleavages, most of Pivel Devoto's (1942:12, 63–71, 75, 86, and especially vol. 1:chap. 3) findings point to the impact of invasions from Brazil and Argentina to explain party activity. The same can be concluded from Sala de Touron and Alonso Eloy (1986–1991:vol. 2:112, 152). The nation, which began as a military outpost, emerged from a peace treaty between Buenos Aires and the Portuguese.[68] The treaty was preceded by the Artigas rebellion and several other guerrilla wars. Table 2.4 represents wars and *revoluciónes de partido* (party revolutions) from 1811 to 1904, and the length of these conflicts. The most important wars in table 2.4 are analyzed in some detail hereafter.

The intention behind the creation of Uruguay was to develop a sort of neutral ground between Brazil and Argentina that would, among other things, facilitate the penetration of British commercial interests. With the creation of the country emerged two *bandos,* or protoparties: the *abrasilerados* (pro-Brazilian factions), and the *aporteñados* (pro-Buenos Aires factions). Brazil and Argentina remained military and logistic bases for revolutionary forces, who tried almost constantly to subdue the incumbent government in Montevideo. By the early 1830s, when the issue of independence had been settled, two identifiable organizations directly linked to Argentina and Brazil gathered around two war heroes, José Fructuoso Rivera (founder of the Colorados) and José Antonio Lavalleja (founder of the Blancos). The Colorados seemed more liberal because they "embraced the dogma of liberty . . . although this was, most of the times, a different name for anarchy."[69] Meanwhile, the Blancos wanted a government *á la española,* with a stronger bureaucracy and more centralization.[70] Foreigners and Creoles perceived foreign influence as the source of party strength.[71]

Table 2.4. Wars and Revoluciónes de Partido: Uruguay, 1811–1904

Duration	Wars and Revoluciónes de Partido
1811–1820	José Gervasio Artigas's rural-based revolution.
1816	Portuguese invasion.
1825	Liberation Crusade supported by Argentina, or Los 33 Orientales' Crusade.
1836–1838	Revolución de partido—war between Colorado leader Rivera and Blanco leader Oribe.
1839–1851	Guerra Grande and siege of Montevideo by Uruguayan and Argentine forces. Colorado leaders remain in Montevideo, Blanco leaders in the hinterland. To a large extent, this was another revolución de partido.
1863	Revolución de partido—Colorado Venancio Flores uprising against Blanco government of Bernardo Prudencio Berro.
1865–1870	War of the Triple Alliance, or Paraguayan War. The Colorados took a more active role in this war than the Blancos.
1870–1872	Revolución de partido—insurrection of Blanco leader Timoteo Aparicio, or Revolución de las Lanzas (Revolution of the Spears).
1875	Exiles organize an insurrection from Buenos Aires against the government of Pedro Varela, or Revolución Tricolor. They are defeated by the army in the battles of Guayabos and Palomas.
1897–1898	Revolución de partido—insurrection of Blanco leader Aparicio Saravia against interim Colorado president Lorenzo Batlle.
1903–1904	Last revolución de partido—Blanco leader Aparicio Saravia is defeated by Colorado government of José Batlle y Ordoñez.

Regional alliances, therefore, facilitated the survival of the opposition party. Both the Portuguese and Argentines attempted to undermine the Uruguayan state by war or conspiracy and in the process strengthened the parties. Tulio Halperín Donghi (1989b:67–80) reminds us that the revolutionary junta in Buenos Aires held the domination of the Banda, or the "war in the East," as a priority. The same can be said of Brazil, which regarded the possession of the Banda as vital for its regional hegemony. Uruguayan presidents during the nineteenth century were forced to confront foreign invasions, mutinies, and territorial disputes. Frequently, they gained office by war as well; although elections were important, conflict often settled party rivalry. All of the revoluciónes de partido represented in table 2.4 concluded in an agreement that established quotas of representation for both parties in government.[72]

The Guerra Grande established Colorado dominance in Montevideo and left the countryside in the hands of the Blancos. After that, the revoluciónes generally expressed the dissatisfaction of Blanco leaders with their assigned quotas or the violation of prior agreements. The Venancio Flores insurrection of 1863, supported by Brazil, and the Paraguayan War (1865–1870) further consolidated the control of the Colorados over the army. Blanco caudillos reacted with the Revolución de las Lanzas, or Revolution of the Spears (1870–1872). This revolution closed what I see as a first period of polity formation, since it resulted in the Paz de Abril (April Peace) of 1872, by which Colorados and Blancos agreed on a geographic distribution of influence that reinforced the rural-urban cleavage. The Colorados still retained control of Montevideo, and the Blancos gained control of a number of departamentos. In 1897, another compromise between the parties was reached, which further consolidated the parties' division of power in government. The last Blanco revolt, led by Aparicio Saravia (1903–1904), and put down by the Colorados under Batlle y Ordóñez, was triggered by disagreements over the 1872 and 1897 pacts. Saravia's revolution succumbed when confronted by a Colorado Party that had been able to build a more professional central army. This ended the mechanism of fixed quotas of representation and the use of revoluciónes as a means to compromise on the degree of power centralization.

While the Blanco Party became part of government, it never ceased to challenge the Colorados. Colorado predominance in the presidency of the country during the process of state building can be seen in table 2.5.[73] Many presidents tried to end party wars and even to dismantle the parties. After the Guerra Grande, three presidents defined themselves as *fusionistas;* that is, they wanted to either combine the two existing parties, create a new encompassing party, or eliminate them altogether.[74] Their efforts failed, and the ongoing conflict further reinforced Colorado predominance. Even the leaders of the three military governments shown in table 2.5 were Colorado sympathizers or Colorado Party members. Colorados in power, then, and Blancos in revolt demanding participation, quite accurately describes the process of power centralization. After the Blanco interim presidency of Anastasio Aguirre, the Blancos did not return to office for ninety years. Similar to the situation in Colombia, yet unlike that in Argentina, a professional

Table 2.5. Presidents of Uruguay, 1830–1903

Dates	President	Party Affiliation
November 1830–February 1835	General José Fructoso Rivera	Colorado
March 1835–October 1838	General Manuel Oribe	Blanco
March 1839–1951	General Fructoso Rivera (governed through the Guerra Grande)	Colorado
March 1852–September 1853	Juan Francisco Giro	Fusionista
March 1854–September 1855	General Venancio Flores	Colorado
March 1856–March 1860	Gabriel Antonio Pereira	Fusionista
March 1860–March 1864	Bernardo Prudencio Berro	Fusionista
1864–1865	Anastasio Aguirre (interim president)	Blanco
March 1868–March 1872	General Lorenzo Batlle	Colorado
March 1873–January 1875	José E. Ellauri	Colorado
January 1875–March 1876	Pedro Varela	Colorado
March 1876–March 1880	Colonel Lorenzo Latorre	Military government
March 1880–February 1882	Francisco Vidal	Colorado
March 1882–March 1886	General Máximo Santos	Military government
March 1886–November 1886	Antonio Vidal	Colorado
November 1886–March 1890	General Máximo Tajes	Military government
March 1890–March 1894	Julio Herrera y Obes	Colorado
March 1894–August 1897	Juan B. Idiarte Borda	Colorado
March 1899–March 1903	Juan Lindolfo Cuestas	Colorado
March 1903–March 1907	José Batlle y Ordoñez	Colorado

army was absent in the wars represented in table 2.4. In comparison, Uruguay had fewer conflicts, but they were lengthy and consequential. As shown in table 2.4, the country enjoyed few years of peace after independence. Indeed, until after 1910, Uruguayans perceived war as a "natural" feature of political life. In a system in which no armed group could gain hegemony and the central power remained feeble, negotiation became key for survival; this, more than anything else, explains the party system and the relative coparticipation in government. By the 1870s, the high human and material costs of war had consolidated mechanisms of arbitration as a routine practice, with the two parties using intimidation and informal mediation to avoid further war. By the early 1900s, an observer reported that the common objective of the parties was "apparently to avoid fighting and sending the usual bombastic reports to the head of their respective factions."[75]

The Founding War:
The Artigas Revolution and the Rural Poor

Historical circumstances made Montevideo an important bastion of the royal Spanish forces. Independence was fought from the rural areas to the capital city, and José Gervasio Artigas and his gaucho militia led the first battles for independence. Therefore, independence became a rural-based movement, mobilizing most of the rural population of the province. From 1810 to 1816, the war was fought against two major but very different enemies: the Spanish authorities in Montevideo, and the independence movement headquartered in Buenos Aires, which wanted to annex Uruguay. At the end of the Artigas period, Brazil occupied the Banda (1816), and the struggle for independence had to be fought against a third enemy as well (see table 2.4).

A contemporary described José Gervasio Artigas's followers as a group of "gauchos transformed into field marshals."[76] He was right, for a large majority of gauchos, Indians, and mestizos fought the 1811 "revolution," which can be called a revolution from below—a grassroots, armed, mass-based movement that challenged the government and set the basis for an alternative regime. This revolution benefited the rural poor by attempting to replace the old elite and enforce changes in the access to the means of production. Therefore, from the standpoint of the rural poor, nation building started with the struggle that spanned the years 1810 to 1820. These guerrilla wars established *la patria vieja* (old motherland)—also called the *protectorado*, a federalist system that aspired to form a *liga* (league) of provinces—to challenge the hegemony of Buenos Aires and the influence of Montevideo. It demanded open trade and access to maritime ports that until then had been controlled by both cities.

One of the revolutionaries' main objectives was to take Montevideo.

Unlike in Colombia, in which the revolutionary effort involved the complicity of Venezuela and Bogotá, plus the close collaboration of the regions within the future Colombian territory, in Uruguay the revolutionary wars were fought almost exclusively by a rural coalition under the leadership of Artigas and other caudillos.[77] This revolutionary movement took land redistribution seriously. Despite the extensive character of agriculture and the small population of the country, during the colonial period, large numbers of "free but miserable men" had populated the countryside, partially explaining the support for the Artigas crusade.[78] To be sure, by the late eighteenth century, the *alcalde* (mayor) of the cabildo of Montevideo acknowledged the need for land redistribution: "The grandsons and sons of the original settlers do not possess an inch of land to cultivate or raise cattle. . . . it cannot be conceived that the cause for this state of affairs is land scarcity; rather, it lies in a few hacendados who occupy more land than all the others put together . . . all in detriment of [our] industry and population."[79]

Therefore, this so-called "empty" land of recent settlement experienced high rural unemployment and offered a limited frontier for colonization.[80] Invasions of large *estancias* (ranches) and conflicts over evictions became more frequent as the century's second decade approached, particularly in the South and the Littoral. We can learn a lesson here about the structural conditions of collective action: the extensive characteristics of this economy perhaps made for a higher rate of mobilization among the rural dispossessed. Problems of land distribution and unemployment were at times even more acute than in a more complex agrarian setting such as Colombia. Pastoral Uruguay lacked a peasant economy, Indian villages, or sharecropping systems that could contribute to absorbing some of the rural unemployed. Thus, contrary to common belief, this labor-extensive system was more prone to mobilization than labor-intensive economies.

With the encouragement of landowners, the unemployed and the rural poor in general came to perceive the city as an evil and parasitic economy, depriving the countryside of its share of the nation's wealth. Strong antiurban sentiment was only aggravated by absentee landowners residing in Montevideo. Therefore, Artigas's war against the Portuguese and Buenos Aires found propitious supportive grounds; it focused not only on expelling invaders but on reforming the prevailing system of land tenure. Somewhat paradoxically, the war waged by the patriots attempted to restructure an economy that had already been modeled by prior wars and invasions. Large *latifundia* ranching was not only the product of structural circumstances and "Spanish feudalism." The main reason for large land grants along the country's borders was the need for border defense. Colonial authorities, fearing Portuguese invasions through an uninhabited frontier, opted for large land grants as a means of creating some border control. Landholders at the borders were expected to defend their property militarily, using their labor force as a militia.

Artigas thought that he must accomplish two things to establish his federation of "free provinces": break the monopoly of the ports in Montevideo and Buenos Aires and eradicate large latifundia in the Banda. The second objective was to be achieved by creating a group of small livestock farmers. The struggle for independence gained momentum from 1811 to 1816 as the Artigas forces of Indians and mestizo gauchos gained some military victories over the Spanish, the *porteños* (natives of Buenos Aires), and the Portuguese.[81] The active role of rural grassroots leaders in the guerrilla movement frightened some of Artigas's lieutenants. Not surprisingly, the growing populism of the Artigas crusade also alarmed large hacendados; thus in 1814 they allied with the porteño invader and, in 1817, with the Portuguese. By 1814, Artigas himself complained of the scarce number of upper-class elements among his troops.[82]

Popular support for the Artigas crusade was truly overwhelming. During the siege of Montevideo in 1811 and the so-called "exodus of the Oriental people," entire populations migrated, following Artigas and his movement, abandoning land, family, and employment. The "mobile character" of the rural population facilitated the exodus.[83] All sources agreed with the leader himself, who, in a letter to L. Galvan, wrote: "All the Banda Oriental follows me massively. . . . some burning their houses and the furniture that they cannot carry with them, some on foot . . . because they have exhausted their horses . . . old ladies and weak old men, innocent children . . . march [with me] in the midst of unimaginable deprivations."[84]

On 26 February 1815, backed by the northern Argentine provinces, the Artiguista militia finally gained control of Montevideo. Legislation passed at that time reflected an old aspiration of the rural poor. Land was going to be taken from "those who left the motherland, bad Europeans, and worse Americans who without justification claimed property rights over their old possessions . . . [land was going to be given to] men who deserve it, under the condition that those who are the most humble will be the most privileged." The measure was drastic regarding the abolition of racial and cultural barriers and spoke of the mixed ethnic character of Artigas's following: "Negroes, mixed-bloods of this class, Indians, and poor Creoles, all must be awarded haciendas so that with their work and goodness they will contribute to their own happiness and the greatness of the Province."[85]

In terms of class formation, the Artiguista wars made possible the rise of the so-called *minifundio ganadero,* ranchers who prospered under the protectorado and engaged in livestock production on a small scale. Frequently, these ranchers possessed no land at all; somewhat nomadic, they used haciendas as temporary grazing areas. They quickly declined with the fall of the protectorado. The same can be said of small farmers, who also started to multiply in the immediacies of Montevideo and cities in the Interior, somewhat changing the character of the countryside. The advent of Portuguese rule after the decline of the Liga made it hard for these farmers to survive; the Portuguese tried to restore land to old landowners, and to augment the number of Portuguese-owned haciendas in the Banda.

Independence, therefore, became a conflict about the redistribution of land and wealth.[86] Even more than the confrontation with Spain, the war against the *directorio* (directory) in Buenos Aires, and later Brazil, created a sense of the collective and a notion of nationality that advocated the right of lower classes to participate politically and economically.[87] Artigas's final defeat at the hands of the Argentines and the Portuguese was perceived as a frustrated revolution, the ruin of those who, in Artigas's words, had been considered "the most humble" and therefore the "good orientales." From the standpoint of the rural poor, the destruction of the Liga and thus the first phase of state formation meant the victory of foreign powers and urban doctores. The class tensions created by the wars of independence characterized the state long after formal independence was reached in 1828. Among other things, the sharp rural-urban cleavage that distinguished Uruguayan political history found a strong precedent in the clash between Artiguismo and the cities. After all, the main enemies of Artigas's army remained powerful urban merchants, international traders, and manufacturers engaged in the jerked-beef industry.

More than anything else, the legacy of the Liga Federal expressed a tradition of collective action and rebellion in the countryside. The Portuguese invasion exacerbated a strong sense of relative deprivation among small rural proprietors and gauchos who had benefited during the Liga. Tellingly, the fall of La Cisplatina (the regime that followed Artiguismo under Portuguese control) resulted from another insurrection headed by one of Artigas's lieutenants, José Antonio Lavalleja, in the mid-1820s. This so-called Cruzada de los 33 Orientales (Crusade of the Thirty-three Orientals) was started by Uruguayan exiles in Buenos Aires and, as its name expresses, counted at first only thirty-three volunteers. Arriving secretly from Buenos Aires, the leaders organized a resistance movement against the Portuguese and succeeded in allying rural and urban interests, sharply divided after Artiguismo. The outcome was Uruguayan independence in 1828, with the help of British diplomacy.[88]

The now independent state, however, started as a divided nation, as a pact between two legendary lieutenants who had fought under Artigas and founded the two major political parties: Rivera (Colorado Party) and Lavalleja (Blanco Party).[89] They divided the country in two captaincies: one controlling the city, the other controlling the countryside.[90] Lavalleja, leader of the Cruzada de los 33 Orientales and the first caudillo to control the central state, in reality controlled only Montevideo. Even before the ratification of the first constitution, Lavalleja and Rivera had split the country into two political and geographic spheres following the Artigas tradition: city and countryside. In November 1830, Rivera became the first elected president of Uruguay, but politics long remained a function of the established urban-rural cleavage.

The Rural Poor and the Constitution after Independence

After the signing of the constitution, state makers made economic development and power centralization their priorities, but they confronted serious problems, especially in the rural areas. One problem was that the populist movement had encouraged fuzzy lines of authority in the countryside, and a culture of resistance to central authority. State makers had indeed inherited the urban-rural cleavage created by the wars, and many argued that the document expressed an urban view divorced from the reality of the rural areas.[91]

A second problem affecting rural Uruguay was confusing, and at times contradictory, property right claims—also a heritage of land redistribution under Artiguismo. Still another problem was the caudillos, and a migrant or unemployed labor force that could instantly be transformed into militia. For livestock to prosper, the system demanded a watchful staff that could ensure that herds could expand and alleviate the threat of cattle rustlers. Thus labor control was badly needed, and this became the watchword of the landed and commercial elites throughout the process of state formation. The wars of independence, however, had shown the unruly character of the rural population and its revolutionary potential.

Peons, migrant laborers, and vagrants became a source of serious concern for modernizers. Having survived the Artigas period and the Cruzada de los 33 Orientales, state makers had been exposed to another source of concern: the clear ethnic and cultural differences that separated the urban elites and the rural population. A shared fear of rural insurrection was reflected in the first constitution. This constitution, like the first and second Colombian constitutions, intended to end the "rural threat," that is, to control the impoverished militias who had fought the wars of independence under Artigas and other caudillos. Barrán and Nahum (1967–1978:vol. 1:560) have shown that the Asociación Rural (Rural Association) lived in permanent fear of a serious revolt and believed that it would be best for the country to convert nomadic gauchos into farmers or small agriculturalists.[92] Many members believed that European events would inspire insurrection at home, where the lack of both an indigenous bourgeoisie and a strong state made matters much worse.

Among other things, rural mobilization was fueled by rural unemployment, the refusal of gauchos to seek permanent occupation, and the noncompliance of small producers who refused to give up their land to larger hacendados. This situation remained almost constant for most of the nineteenth century. Although the Artigas League had somewhat alleviated the problem, old hacendados regained control of their land after the Brazilian invasions and the Cruzada de los 33 Orientales. This helps to explain successful party recruitment under party banners after 1830, increasing the fear of rural rebellion. In 1832 a contemporary reporting on the so-called Convencion de Rivera (Rivera Convention) described the readiness of mobilization: "Orders had been given to the [Colorado] political bosses of different Departamentos to rally their forces. . . . [they] have responded with incredible celerity. The *jefe* [boss] from San Jose arrived to the meeting point with 207 men . . . Major Santa Ana with 70 from his [departamento] and Captain Benito Ojeda with 122 from his area. Much more are expected in the following days."[93] Barrán and Nahum maintain that the enclosures of the estancias during the 1870s fueled mobilization even further. Enclosures forced small and medium proprietors to sell, and gauchos and renters to leave the haciendas, augmenting the unemployed and the available militia.[94]

Carlos Real de Azúa (1984b:28) claims that the 1830 constitution had two main objectives: to demobilize the rural masses, and to make a "political outcast of the military establishment." This chapter agrees. State makers soon perceived, however, that to accomplish both objectives led to a somewhat contradictory policy. One way to try to control the unruly rural poor was to draft them into a professional army. Yet this meant precisely the strengthening of a central army, a move that provoked much uncertainty among civilians who wished to control the state. The other possible option was to empower loyal landowners to control their labor force in the localities and repress banditry. The obvious disadvantage of this option was that these local political bosses could, in turn, challenge the state. It was this second option that won the day; still, the constitution did its best to ameliorate the negative consequences attached to this choice.

Both to please loyal landowners and to weaken caudillos, the constitution withheld the franchise from most of the "vagrant" rural population. This was common in Latin America, but in an economy based on migrant labor, most of the workforce fit into the category of "vagrants."[95] In the country that would be the first to adopt welfare reform, more than in our other cases, enlightened elites strongly rejected the incorporation of mixed-bloods in the political system.[96] The men who had participated in the wars of independence remained, as Pivel Devoto (1956:vol. 2:72–76) wrote, "neither electors nor elected." These measures, however, backfired. Oral voting meant that caudillos could monitor allegiances. Literacy and property requirements reinforced the caudillos' towering influence, for they strengthened the role of political chiefs as intermediaries between the state and those who had no political rights.[97] The constitution also tried to curb the power of rural political bosses within the Colorados and Blancos by discouraging party bickering. Therefore, hoping to undermine the parties, the 1830s Asamblea Constituyente (Constituent Assembly) managed to impose a nonpartisan foreign governor, José Rondeau, as president.[98] Rondeau lasted a short time as governor, however, and was soon replaced by Artigas's lieutenants.

Constitutional measures intended to limit popular participation remained in place until the 1900s, when the welfare state emerged. But in reality, war and negotiation imposed power sharing. Still, toward the end of the century, populism and rural militias were perceived as a problem—the main reason that the country could not get back on its feet. As late as 1876, liberal Juan Carlos Gómez rejected universal suffrage and direct elections because "they mean the artificial symmetry of what in reality is asymmetrical and a route to mediocrity. . . . If the Yankees would want to escape the predominance of mediocrity . . . in the great Republic, they ought to eradicate both things at the same time, things that have been introduced in the political world with more originality than discernment."[99] In the country that would turn into a welfare state in the early 1900s, only 5 percent of the population was able to cast ballots by 1887, and in the countryside, only 1 percent enjoyed citizenship rights.

The Guerra Grande and Revoluciónes de Partido

In 1850, almost at the close of the Guerra Grande, representative Luis Melian Lafinur characterized the *cámaras* (lower and upper houses) as sophisticated sites of political debate housing intellectuals whose brilliant speeches and debates "did not correspond" to the country's basic needs.[100] The war had isolated Montevideo, and state making had developed divorced from the rural areas. Lafinur reminded the senate that a project of state building unbound to the countryside remained wishful thinking. He was reflecting on the effects of the Guerra Grande.

This war, more than any other, sharpened the urban-rural cleavage, encouraged party building, and further divided the state. During the first revolución de partido after independence, from 1836 to 1838 (see table 2.4), the Colorados and Blancos had already gained a differentiated profile, but the Guerra Grande stood as the most prolonged and consequential conflict for party building and state making. Briefly, the cause of the conflict was Argentina's invasion of Uruguayan territory with the complicity of the Blancos. Under Juan Manuel de Rosas, Argentina pursued a policy of expansion in competition with Brazil; most literature agrees that this confrontation between the two largest countries of South America had lasting consequences for Uruguay and its institutions.[101]

Incidents that led to the war began in October 1838, when the Blanco Manuel Oribe was deposed by the Colorado Rivera. Rivera had developed a strong alliance with Brazil, and in fact, evidence shows that part of his army was on the Brazilian government's payroll.[102] Once in control of Montevideo, Rivera tried to lessen his strong ties to Brazil by breaking his alliance with the insurrectionist movement of Río Grande (southern Brazil) while opening communication with Rosas in Argentina. This last move was unsuccessful; Rivera could not undermine the already consolidated alliance between Rosas and Oribe. In 1839 Rivera—with French help—rejected Oribe's allies in a series of small battles and skirmishes.[103] In February 1843, with the support of Rosas, Oribe and seven thousand men began a siege of Montevideo, where they remained until October 1851. President Rivera sought the help of the Argentine Unitarists and the French. Thus the city became the focus of anti-Rosas resistance and the refuge of anti-Rosas exiles.

Montevideo became known as La Defensa (The Defense), while the pro-Rosas forces controlled a nearby small port next to El Cerrito (the Little Mountain). El Cerrito sought to establish its own administration and considered itself an alternate state. Given Rosas's campaign against foreign commercial interests, all foreign powers involved in the conflict supported Montevideo and vigorously opposed El Cerrito.[104] Fewer than 4,000 men defended the city, among whom only 400 were Uruguayan born; indeed, according to the United States and Brazilian consulates, nationals numbered between 200, by the former's estimates, and 100, by the latter's.[105] The Spanish consul in Montevideo reported that in view of imminent civil war in Uruguay, "emigration has augmented enormously, 15,000 persons having left the country in a very short period of time."[106] As a result of this prolonged siege, in the city, "demoralization prevails amongst the larger portions of the inhabitants, particularly the soldiery. . . . assassinations have taken place, some in broad daylight . . . [and] the disaffection . . . in the garrison has been unbearable."[107]

If this was the situation in Montevideo, things were not much better in the countryside.[108] If plunder and pillage by loose bands of gauchos was not alarming enough, direct, exorbitant taxes were imposed on merchants and landowners, both nationals and foreigners, to finance the war effort. For instance, the Spanish consul reported that President Rivera forced small and medium businesses in the small town of Melo to give the state a loan

> of 12,000 duros, which he reduced to 4,000 afterwards. . . . [The Colorados] threatened that . . . they would be expelled from the country . . . their property confiscated, and in 40 days they would have to clear their houses, during which time they could not conduct business. . . . 17 Spanish merchants, one French and one Argentine, were in fact taken outside the villa before General Rivera, who ordered that they be transported to Brazil without farewell from their families . . . riding horses that other neighbors felt compelled to provide out of compassion.[109]

Newspapers frequently reported on the appalling situation of the rural economy: the scarcity of labor, the lack of resources, depopulation, and diminishing herds.[110] Two years after the struggle, lawyer and politician Pedro Bustamante wrote that only "sky and grass . . . awaits the traveler who wants to cross from Minas to Maldonado. In 16 leagues of terrain I have not been able to count more than 400 heads of cattle and horses. There are estancia owners who live off rice and dry beef, and those who can afford to offer you an *asado* cannot be labeled poor."[111]

Although this remained a low-combat, low-intensity war, it had enormous consequences for institution building. The siege deepened the gulf between the city and the hinterland and dismantled what remained of the central bureaucracy. It provided the Colorados with captured constituencies in Montevideo while leaving the Blancos free to dominate the rural areas. Foreigners who lived in Montevideo joined the Colorados and even became leading members of the party, giving the organization a rather cosmopolitan outlook. All of this shaped two political subcultures separated by the walls of the citadel, identified with the Colorados and Blancos. Not surprisingly, the Colorados elaborated a more urban liberal platform and became identified as pro-European and modern, while the party of El Cerrito, led by Oribe, came to be considered the stronghold of national "indigenous" interests. Indeed, in 1848, the most widely read newspaper of El Cerrito claimed that the assault on Montevideo was justified as an attack on Europhiles and other antinationalists.[112] One can conclude that rather than the typical ideological split between conservatives and liberals over the church or free trade, the most important cleavage separating the parties stemmed from the characteristics of the Guerra Grande.

Sala de Touron and Alonso Eloy (1986–1991:vol. 2:320) claim that the end of the war initiated a new phase in the formation of the nation-state, a phase that made it more dependent both on the parties and on the British trade network. The war ended with an accord between the parties, a "ni vencedores, ni vencidos" (neither winners nor losers) formula, which allowed for power sharing in the national legislative assembly. The preconditions for a party system were henceforth in place, and it was on these premises that the process of state formation continued. Both elites and the subordinate classes wished peace, and the state made efforts to eradicate party rivalry; for example, the fusionistas' postwar efforts. Yet to the disappointment of many, parties and caudillos increased their power while the state weakened. A clear indicator of the parties' strength was their influence on the army, which became more partisan: soldiers who identified with either party adopted La Defensa or El Cerrito as their cause. State autonomy increased, since merchants, manufacturers, and landowners were part of the ruling coalition but depended on parties they did not completely control; and the state's capacity remained low.

By the end of the war, the government, however, seemed optimistic:

"The situation in the country is hopeful, pacification is complete, and this peace will be long lasting. . . . atrocities committed in the past will not be repeated."[113] Yet peace was short-lived, for in the early 1860s, the state was to be shaken by war again.

Revoluciónes de Partido after the Guerra Grande

Almost ten years after the end of the Guerra Grande, state makers, unable to resolve a "permanent" state of war, considered several "schemes" to stop party revolutions. In desperation, they were willing to change the original intent of the founding fathers and the design of institutions radically. Some of them wished Uruguay to become an Italian protectorate, others a British protectorate. Others proposed that the Banda seek protection from a combination of European powers. And still others wanted the country to become a monarchy under an Italian or British prince, or even a monarchy under the aegis of Brazil.[114] For the most part, this expressed urban-based initiatives, and some even concluded that it would be more desirable if "Montevideo could be neutralized as a free Port, like Hamburg, the interior of the republic being left to manage its own affairs as best it can."[115]

The revoluciónes that triggered their concerns were led by politically active hacendados who partook in power by rallying militias. Loyalties, however, shifted, and gauchos often defied landowners' rule and either joined the enemy next door or remained in hiding during war efforts. Therefore, in the second half of the nineteenth century, landowners were still forced to put a lot of time and effort into cultivating the loyalty of their following. The 1860s, a remarkable decade of state formation, witnessed the consolidation of Colorado Party rule with the triumph of the Venancio Flores revolt against Anastasio Aguirre in 1865, and the growth of the professional military as a consequence of the Paraguayan War (1865–1870). At this point, the political system looked like a one-party-dominant system, with a party in opposition that more often than not refused to participate in national elections but set the limits of Colorado power.[116]

The alliance between Flores and Brazil turned out to be troublesome and contributed to a growing sense of xenophobia. By 1865 there were clear signs of popular dissatisfaction with the administration's pro-

Brazilian bias. Apprehension increased when Brazilian troops were permanently stationed in Montevideo to control army mutinies. When Brazilians rose to importance in the Flores administration, the government's prestige declined to its lowest point, since the Brazilians "[devoted themselves to] plunder and public robbery, a development that was formerly unknown."[117] Foreign diplomats shared the Uruguayans' antipathy toward these measures, and from Brazil, newspapers reported that the hope that "the government of General Flores would enter on a legitimate course of conduct . . . and avoid frequent upheaval . . . proved deceptive."[118]

The war against Paraguay added to the political equation that deposed Flores.[119] Uruguay's participation in the Paraguayan War provoked radical changes in the polity because it built up the military establishment. Under Flores, the army had remained divided; when strengthened by the ongoing war, battalions revolted. This made the Colorado Party even more eager to consolidate linkages with army officers, and it did so successfully. As the army gained strength, so did Colorado influence among its ranks. The Colorados actively campaigned among officers, starting with its central headquarters in Montevideo; in a few years, the Paraguayan War had become a Colorado war. In contrast, although they also counted on the support of a few professional military men, the Blancos kept operating mainly on the basis of voluntary rural militias.

Thus the Paraguayan War transformed the Flores presidency into a regime that represented the growing partisan commitment of army generals to the Colorados. The Flores regime also tightened power centralization, using unmediated party rule with army support. Tax collection and the penetration of the countryside, however, remained almost unchanged, with party machines providing the only vehicle used by the state to reach into the rural areas. Moreover, because the Blancos were able to galvanize support in most rural areas during the Guerra Grande, the Colorado governments of Flores and Batlle faced stronger resistance in the countryside and were forced to negotiate with the Blancos, who were almost constantly rising in revolt.

During the last decades of the century, at least two of these revolts are worth mentioning. The first was the Timoteo Aparicio rebellion, the Revolución de las Lanzas (Revolution of the Spears) of 1870 to 1872, which seriously challenged the state. As usual, neither party was able to definitely dominate the other militarily. The Italian chargé d'affaires reported on the stalemate between the two parties: "Hundreds of people died on both sides, among whom were large numbers of Spaniards and Italians but . . . [after a while] things came back to be exactly as they were before . . . [namely] the Blancos are not able to take the city over and the Colorados are not able to push the Blancos away from the city limits."[120] Aparicio, nonetheless, forced the Colorados to negotiate quotas of participation in government in the Paz de Abril. The two parties agreed that the Blancos were to be given control of four out of twelve departamentos. With this agreement, they obviously sanctioned electoral fraud and divided the parties regionally, as the results of elections in Blanco- or Colorado-controlled departamentos were highly predictable. Some intense rural migration followed the agreement, since the rural population sought residence in the departamento under the protection of the caudillo of its choice.

Hence, the importance of this revolution was that it further consolidated the parties geographically and culturally. It also modified the parties organizationally, for among other things, it provided for a more comfortable alliance between doctores and caudillos in the Colorado Party. The Blanco Party suffered the most radical transformation because the revolution made the party into a more modern organization, contributing to the consolidation of the party system. Until that time, the party had operated exclusively on the basis of rural insurrections and guerrilla warfare, but after 1872, partially through the partidos de ideas, it made a conscious effort to reinforce its civilian urban wing and to work on party doctrine and discourse.[121] Blanco caudillos who under the new pact desired to reconstruct their party found receptive ears among doctores Principistas who defended the right of political minorities to representation. Intellectuals who feared the authoritarian consequences of Colorado hegemony now detected an opportunity to transform the Blanco Party into something closer to a partido de ideas. The experiment did not fully work, but it enlarged the party's intelligentsia and triggered a similar reorganization in the other party as well. Alliances between doctores and caudillos within both parties after the Paz de Abril meant that party platforms looked even more alike, both favoring similar versions of liberalism.[122]

In terms of state formation, the war allowed for more power centralization, but after the Paz de Abril, the parties of caudillos still controlled the state, especially when they remained the undisputed mediators of state authority in the rural areas. Because the revolt had strengthened the Blancos, it therefore eroded the possibility of a one-party Colorado system backed by the professional military. In 1897 Blanco Aparicio Saravia, dissatisfied with the quotas of representation obtained in the Paz de Abril, staged his own revolt; but he could not count on the full support of his party, since a number of Blanco leaders did support the Paz de Abril. Party modernization also worked against him; still, Saravia and his allies were able to impose new quotas of participation on the government. In 1903 Saravia revolted again against Colorado president José Batlle y Ordoñez. The effect was to tighten the Colorado-army alliance that had begun under Flores.[123] This was the last revolución de partido and the final rural revolt, because it strengthened the coalition of the Colorados with a much more powerful urban environment and triggered cross-party alliances between Colorados and dissident Blancos. Most important, it allowed for the unification of loose party guerrillas and army battalions into a central army under Colorado control, contributing to the centralization of power and the consolidation of the nation-state. All these developments, especially the sound defeat of the alternative army of Saravia, guaranteed only weak opposition to the president's reform program. Batlle's success at establishing the welfare state owed much to a pattern of conflict that had rendered a feeble "reactionary configuration." Thus a few words must be said about the relationship between the state and the conservative coalition.

2.3. State Autonomy and the Conservative Coalition

Conflict within the livestock sector worked against the consolidation of a solid conservative coalition. The next chapter shows that economic elites in Colombia, in the framework of a similar party system and a state as weak as Uruguay, nonetheless united into a more unified conservative alliance under the aegis of the conservative party. In contrast, by the end of the Guerra Grande, revoluciónes de partido and different ties with Montevideo had divided Uruguayan landowners basically into three groups.

The first group consisted of large *estanciero*-caudillos of Creole origin who by and large owned estates in the northern, central, and western regions of the country, closer to the Brazilian border and further from Montevideo. They developed close ties with the Brazilian market, often trading contraband cattle across the border. International trade via Montevideo was also a possibility, but as a result of their refusal to crossbreed (which lowered the competitiveness of their cattle) and their traditional mistrust of urban intermediaries, these landowners generally avoided the urban market. Rather than increasing their influence by improving the quality of their livestock or devoting part of their lands to agriculture, they did so by acquiring or conquering more land, controlling more men, and actively participating in war and politics. The spoils of war remained an important source of revenue for these estancieros, and as war veterans or active "generals," they were eligible for generous state pensions. Because they were perceived as a threat to the state, government was more often than not willing to grant favors to these landowners. After almost all revoluciónes de partido in the late nineteenth century, in fact, the state granted land and pensions to war heroes belonging to both parties.

The loyalties of this group often shifted between Brazil and Argentina, and most of them opposed the city. For example, during the Brazilian-Portuguese struggle of 1816, landowners in regions close to the northern border and the central plains chose to ally with Brazil, fighting Montevideo under the Colorado banner.[124] During the Guerra Grande, most of them shifted their allegiance to Argentina and consolidated positions as leaders of the Blanco Party. Yet Flores was able to recruit successfully among this group for his Brazilian-backed Colorado crusade as well. Leaders of the revoluciónes de partido, they and their sons reacted aggressively to the encroachment of doctores within the leadership of the parties. Because the estancieros participated both in the army and in the parties, they became an important link between the two institutions. From the Flores revolt in 1863 to the Saravia uprising in 1904, officers predominantly came from this group.[125]

Very close politically to these estancieros and often depending on their patronage was the second group, the minifundio ganaderos. Between 1830 and the late 1870s, these landless hacendados prospered. Some even became opulent cattle owners. When the government attempted to enforce the rural code and started land enclosures in the 1850s, the ganaderos strongly opposed the state and became further alienated from the more entrepreneurial estancieros tied to urban business.

In contrast to these two, a third group of landowners, who formed the Asociación Rural, was anxious to promote state centralization and modernization. These landowners established close links with the urban upper classes, were reluctant to participate in the revoluciónes de partido, and adopted new breeding methods for cattle and sheep to meet the demands of the promising Atlantic market. The association became an important lobby in financial and political circles. Many members shared ownership in land and industry. In short, this third group, which included many foreigners, embodied the familiar urban-rural coalition.[126]

British, French, and German sheep ranchers belonged to this group. In the 1850s and 1860s, they modernized the rural economy, particularly in the Littoral region near Montevideo—the departamentos of Soriano and Colonia. By the 1860s, the foreign hacendados represented 10 percent of the ranchers in these regions and the departamento of Río Negro. At the close of the century, the percentage of foreign estancieros in the country was impressive; by 1900, the censo ganadero (livestock census) indicated that Uruguayan-born ranchers constituted hardly 64 percent of the ranching elite and controlled only 45 percent of livestock production. Foreign estancieros represented 36 percent of the landed elite and possessed 55 percent of the cattle.[127]

These numbers are rather significant for state making because most foreign-born estancieros refused to participate in the parties, remaining aloof from politics, which weakened the linkages between the most modern sectors of the rural elites and the state. They retained their native citizenship, regarded party politics as a corrupt and backward practice, and showed no interest in getting involved in a political career that would require them to become Uruguayan citizens. Citizenship would mean higher taxes and the loss of a number of privileges that only foreigners enjoyed (including free use of the port for shipment, and no taxes), not to mention the dreaded military draft. Indeed, foreigners perceived their respective embassies and chargé d'affaires, rather than the nation-state, as their real government. They found par-

tidos de ideas and principismo much more palatable than the traditional parties, but overall, they refrained from joining party politics.
Foreigners.

2.4. The Outcome: Civilians Controlling the Military

In part because of a lack of data, and in part because of the literature's focus on the economy or the parties, no treatment exists of the evolution of the Uruguayan military and its relationship to both the state and the parties. This is paradoxical in scholarship that has focused so much on explaining democracy. Furthermore, until the turning point of the late 1880s—more precisely, March 1890, under the presidency of Julio Herrera y Obes—the Uruguayan government remained under the strong influence of caudillos who were military men as well.[128] In a country permanently at war, the government comprised an unstable mix of military men and civilians, and as such, there was no guarantee that a civilian political elite would prevail.

From the 1830s to the late 1880s, generals and colonels were active in politics, yet a crucial difference from the other cases was that during state making, it would have been difficult to distinguish between the Colorado militias and the professional military, or between Blanco militias and soldiers. Officers joined both parties, and generals and military heroes publicly expressed their party affiliation.[129] We have already seen how the Guerra Grande tied parties and soldiers, and during the Flores administration, alliances between the military and doctores also became noticeable.[130] War developments and other things enabled the Colorados to retain the strongest influence over the army. From the October Peace of 1851 to the April Peace of 1872, the majority of officers leaned toward that party.[131] In the early 1870s, the struggle against the Blanco revolt of Timoteo Aparicio continued the professionalization of the army under Colorado influence, which reached its highest point during Saravia's last insurgency.

This army contributed little to state making, and its recruits had been for the most part a residue of the parties' militias. At several points, the state wished to recruit soldiers but was forced to use gaucho cavalry under the leadership of local caudillos instead. Foreigners were at times forced to join the army, but more often than not, parties enforced the draft. During the Flores rebellion, Spaniards, Italians, and some British citizens were coerced in the name of the Colorado Party into serving in the Colorado-Brazilian army of Flores; even "Greek citizens [were] . . . forced into serving and carried to the barracks."[132] During the Guerra Grande, Basque soldiers were forcibly recruited by the Blancos to serve as Argentine-Blanco troops, and in 1870, during a Blanco-led "revolution" organized in Buenos Aires, the Blancos recruited mercenaries mainly of Italian nationality.[133] The growth of the military during the Paraguayan War helped to create the first military government in the country's history under Colonel Lorenzo Latorre (1876–1880), but militarism did not prosper. The same can be said of the two military governments that followed, the administrations of Máximo Santos from 1882 to 1886 (see table 2.5), and Máximo Tajes from 1886 to 1890. These military regimes were tied to the Colorados and recognized the Blanco Party as the legally organized opposition.

Modernization and state building came in the fashion of a military government allied with the entrepreneurial sector of the landed elites and urban business; that is, the Latorre administration—which has traditionally been considered "the" state maker.[134] The equation seems simple enough. The parties had to become weaker for the state to grow stronger and thus be able to modernize the nation. Business groups that experienced trouble finding a voice in government found a reliable ally in the officers who had returned from the Paraguayan War. They also resented the government; in the war's aftermath, officers came to resent party control and a system of promotions that rewarded party loyalties and benefited the old heroes of revolucións de partido rather than career officers. This coalition brought Latorre to office, and from 1876 to 1880, he furthered the interests of urban business, factions of the military, and entrepreneurial estancieros. Compared to prior regimes, this was a rather homogeneous coalition, with a majority of entrepreneurial self-made men—such as the colonel himself—who despised both "traditional society" and politicians of illustrious origins such as the principistas. Latorre's followers, as Barrán and Nahum (1967–1978:vol. 1:484) have suggested, were pragmatic men inspired by a strong work ethic. His very ascension to power, as described by a notable and outstanding member of the ganadero elite, is telling: "The people of Montevideo have gathered yesterday in a General Assembly *called by both national and international commerce,* and have acclaimed as Provisional Government the ex-Minister of War and Marine, Colonel Lorenzo Latorre. Responding to the call of his fellow citizens, he has accepted such a demanding appointment until the first of March of 1877."[135]

The "call" came from a paralyzed and stagnant country. Under the hegemony of Great Britain and the ascendancy of the United States, market opportunities had triggered serious modernization in Argentina and Chile, but Uruguay remained at the margins. During the Pedro Varela presidency (see table 2.5), the country faced one of the most critical economic depressions in years. By the mid-1870s, the British embassy accurately reported the reasons for the "prostration" of the "unfortunate" country: "The principal causes I believe to have been the lavish waste of public money immediately succeeding a four year civil war on the advent of General Flores to power, the . . . license afforded to Bankruptcy and every sort of speculations upon fictitious capital . . . [and] complete neglect and oblivion of every interest in the interior of the Republic."[136]

Latorre proved a remarkable state maker.[137] By most standards, his coalition achieved most of the prerequisites of state building.[138] He promoted educational reform, imposed social order, balanced the budget, made remarkable progress toward monopolizing coercion, enabled the state bureaucracy to provide services and carry out public works, improved the transportation system—the railway in particular—and communications, such as the telegraph and mail. The enforcement of property rights in the countryside became a priority for Latorre, who reformed the rural code and expanded the Supreme Court of Justice's scope and power in rural areas.[139] Additionally, the government set in motion a vigorous policy of enclosures.[140] Indeed, Latorre argued that the most important tasks for the state were to populate the *campaña* (countryside) with Anglo immigrants and to eliminate the gaucho.[141] The state budget was finally balanced, and during the colonel's tenure, the government actually increased its revenues.

Montevideo merchants benefited greatly, particularly the wealthiest members of that community. Meanwhile, the Asociación Rural also obtained state help. In addition to reforming the rural code, the government dispatched the *reglamento de policías* (police regulations and rules) to augment the rural police force. One can argue that even the common citizen gained from the orderly peace imposed by Latorre, for the regime acquired a high degree of popularity. The "dictador" was popular among ethnic minorities as well. Influenced by populist Colorado leaders, Latorre transformed the characteristics of the draft, raising the Colorados' popularity among the African Uruguayan and mestizo populations. As in most of the continent, the racially excluded perceived the army as a means of social mobility but experienced discrimination and mistreatment. Latorre abolished compulsory draft for people of color and tried to eliminate the abuse they received in the army. As he put it, "It is a matter of honor for my government to abolish this abusive procedure that until the present has condemned citizens of color to an imposition that not only contradicts the Fundamental Law of the State that demands equal rights for all, but also the democratic principles to which we adhere."[142]

Despite the popularity of the regime, the army could not organize a coherent power bloc under Latorre. Rather, the Colorado Party received the credit for Latorre's success. The customary interpretation of the Latorre period denies the influence of parties, but informally both parties cooperated with the regime. The Blancos opposed Latorre's push to centralize power but collaborated with the government in exchange for direct access to the so-called council of advisers.[143] And while the reform of the rural code weakened the banditlike Blanco caudillos, it also benefited large Blanco landholders and did not threaten landowners' control over their rural labor force and gaucho militias. Indeed, unlike Argentina—but very much like Colombia—during the most intense phases of power centralization, Uruguay did not impose a compulsory draft in the rural areas and left landholders in complete control of their clientele. As for the Colorados, they regarded Latorre as a party member and an ally who would, in time, turn a more orderly government back into their hands.

Thus state expansion under this regime did not result in a state run by a professional military but, instead, one in which the parties were active participants in the process of power centralization. Real de Azúa (1969) points out that Uruguay's first military regime was neither praetorian nor completely authoritarian.

Indeed, this military regime reduced the army, which to some extent explains Latorre's success in balancing the state budget.[144] Under pressure from the parties, particularly his own, Latorre resigned to the general assembly barely four years after accepting his mandate. During the two military regimes that followed, the state showed more strength, but the bureaucracy was still unable to perform basic tasks, relying on *jefes políticos* (political bosses) and partisan governors to connect with the regions. In the localities, the official representative of the state, the *juez de paz* (justice of the peace), remained a delegate of the Supreme Court but was by no means immune to party politics. The same held true in issues of taxation. The dominance of livestock production made efficient collection difficult because of the movable character of cattle and sheep. Thus, by the 1880s, governments customarily still courted the political loyalty of landowners and relied on local jefes políticos to persuade the elites to make contributions. Colorado governments tended to tax Blanco ranchers and traders more aggressively, and Blanco governments operated in a similar fashion with Colorado businessmen and landowners. In the urban areas, a large part of the urban merchant and entrepreneurial classes remained an elastic portion of the tax base as well, because they used party affiliation as an exemption.[145]

The strongest political actor remained the Colorado party. Reminiscent of socialist and communist regimes, state makers supported the idea of a Partido Unico (Only Party) and argued that an alliance of party and army would best defend the popular interests. The military regime of President Máximo Santos, who subscribed to a soft populist credo, strove to create the Gran Partido Colorado (Great Colorado Party). The army would function as the party's armed wing. In part to achieve these ends, Santos increased the number of rank-and-file soldiers to about three thousand and created both the military code of 1884 and a more technologically oriented military academy.[146] At the peak of his military regime, he adopted the title of Jefe del Gran Partido Colorado. Another military regime under Santos's successor, Maximo Tajes, did likewise and kept cultivating a close relationship between the Colorados and the army. The intermeshing of politicians and officers who shared party loyalties helps to explain why it took so long for the military to emerge as an autonomous force. Most presidents turned out to be former generals who kept in close contact with the barracks and consulted openly with party leaders. Parties (especially the Colorado) monitored the system of military promotions and appointed numerous military men to the state bureaucracy.

Although a pro-Santos, pro-military coalition did exist, by the time of the Herrera y Obes presidency from 1890 to 1894 (see table 2.5), the state had fallen under complete civilian, Colorado, control. When Herrera y Obes campaigned for the 1890 presidential election, he encountered feeble resistance from the military, perhaps because of his reputation as an "extremely astute politician, whose political position is to go to extremes in order to support the Colorado Party."[147] Civilians retained control of the state for most of the twentieth century, and the two military coups that occurred expressed alliances between the military and the Colorado Party.[148] One can conclude that the so-called era of militarism during state formation (1876–1886) represented instead the defeat of militarism as an option of state formation. In the 1890s, Blancos and Colorados returned to sharing power through quotas of representation, and presidents were elected by indirect voting. Therefore, it was not hard for Colorado president Batlle y Ordoñez to reinforce a preexisting Colorado-army alliance and defeat the Saravia rebellion. And when Batlle put forward social and political reforms, he encountered weak opposition from conservatives, who failed to form a bloc. Thus, a few years after his rise to power, the reformer Batlle was, in fact, reforming; his ambitious platform was fairly complete by the end of his second term. As we shall see in the next chapters, few Latin American leaders encountered as favorable circumstances to impose democracy from above.

3

A Weak Army and Restrictive Democracy:

Colombia, 1810–1886

Like scholarship on Uruguay, work on Colombia has also considered the country an anomaly, and for good reasons. With a labor-intensive economy frequently ravaged by rural violence, a low level of economic development, slow urbanization, a deficient communication system, enclaves of slavery, and a strong conservative landed elite associated with a powerful church, nineteenth-century Colombia seemed more prone to militarism than to civilian control. Civilians, however, managed to control the military. The emerging regime, though less inclusive than its Uruguayan counterpart, elected citizens to a bicameral legislature and a presidency that, despite its powers on paper, was forced to operate within a limiting federal system.

   Colombia fought wars of independence from 1811 to 1822, in a long and inefficient effort to gain control of a territory that was disputed by both Spain and Venezuela. From 1810 to 1816, during the period called the *patria boba* (foolish fatherland), the state and army failed to centralize power and form a recognizable state. The regions fought among themselves instead and failed to provide a united front against Spain; thus the strength of the Spanish reconquest (1816–1819). As part of an alliance with Venezuela, Gran Colombia (Greater Colombia), which also included Ecuador, was created in 1819 but lasted only until 1830; its dissolution reduced the country to Nueva Granada (New Granada). Therefore, in the early 1830s, the state was able to retain control of a smaller territory (present-day Colombia). Yet serious difficulties in centralizing power, remained a defining feature of state making until the twentieth century. It was not until the last decades of the nineteenth century that the country experienced an intense process of power centralization and army building under the Conservative administrations of President Rafael Núñez (1877–1889), the leader of La Regeneración (the Regeneration).[1] This movement spanned the years from 1869 to 1900, but for all its importance, it neither eliminated party rivalry nor created an independent central military. Among other things, this chapter seeks to explain why La Regeneración succeeded in centralizing power and why the military remained under civilian control.

Two major parties, Conservadores and Liberales, crafted the Colombian polity. Given the predominant role of these parties, most literature has focused on party formation and competition. Like Uruguay, Colombia provides an example of unmediated party rule. Recognizable party machines emerged in the period before the 1849 election when, for the first time, the labels "Liberal" and "Conservador" were formally used during a political campaign.[2] However, the cliques and groupings that formed the two major parties went back to the period immediately after independence, a phase much less studied. The origin and evolution of those cleavages is still at issue.[3] Party rivalry remained the dominant mechanism to resolve disputes and determine institutional design, but why and how regional party associations evolved into larger alliances, and why other parties did not proliferate and consolidate, remain unclear. In light of the available data, especially in the regions, theories on party formation in Colombia must stand only as approximations. Mine is no exception. The logic of the comparison with our other cases, however, supports the suggestions I make in this chapter.

Given the importance of several urban centers, the country more closely resembled Italy—where rival city-states controlled their hinterlands and clashed with one another—than Uruguay. Federalism in Colombia (1858–1885) seemed to express the unstable equilibrium reached by these mini-units. Lacking a central institution with a monopoly on coercion, the elites in each of these *estados* were forced to resolve issues of property rights and distribution of power within the confines of their region without much external help. A first suggestion I want to make, however, is that help came in the form of party affiliation.

(handwritten margin notes) Centralizing Power / Big Problem / Columbia until 20th Cent.

Interregional alliances among elites under the Conservative or Liberal labels stemmed largely from the repeated need to resolve regional strife with external military assistance. In the context of a weak army and a weak state, small-town and rural elites often sought the support of neighboring caudillos and their militias. This both tied regional elites together under loose party labels and cemented clientele ties between leader and followers.

Undoubtedly, other issues—particularly the church's influence in government, and the institutional and ideological support it could deliver—contributed to create nationwide cleavages and helps to explain the duality of the party system. Much more than in Uruguay, the defense of the Christian faith, the federation, and the presence of more differentiated subcultures added incentives for regional collective action and party building.[4] One could argue that this wider mosaic of incentives for collective action somewhat substituted for the sharp rural-urban cleavage that characterized Uruguayan politics.

A second suggestion is that the pattern of conflict found in Colombia is very similar to that in Uruguay; thus the construction of a similar polity with a similar party system. Like the Uruguayan Colorados and Blancos, the Colombian Liberales and Conservadores formed loose coalitions of relatively autonomous leaders who recognized the advantages of a collective party label. Long before the landmark 1849 election, rural caudillos and urban politicians had come to understand that their capacity to serve their constituencies and maintain power in the regions would be enhanced in the long run if they could act collectively for electoral purposes. This allowed them to control and later divide the spoils without really threatening the stability of the system they came to dominate.

A third suggestion is that a key engine of party building is to be found in collective action and armed struggle in the regions. Although Bogotá-based groups and their struggles in the capital city remained important, strong party organizing shaped the parties from the localities and cantons. Despite scarce information on coalition formation in the regions, we do have some important data on Bogotá, Cundinamarca, and other areas that support this point.[5] That most nineteenth-century Colombian presidents came from small towns, for instance, is a good indicator of the importance of party activity in the regions.[6]

As in Uruguay, war helped party cohesiveness, both horizontally and vertically. Frequently, alliances between the parties, or the creation of poles within the Liberal and Conservative parties, were responses to conflict settlement or fear of imminent war.[7] Issues of development such as the construction of roads and railroads, access to markets, and the use of natural resources were often solved by the threat of armed struggle and party mediation as well. Competition for power in the regions enhanced the power of family and clientele networks; political changes almost always comprised the downfall of some families and the rise of others with different party connections. The picture that emerges is one in which local elites, to undermine the power of rival regional groups, competed for the support of cliques that shared similar interests outside their region or in Bogotá. This provided for organizational networks of support (protoparties and parties) and facilitated the escalation of local struggles into national conflict. Parties furnished a vehicle to launch group demands at the national level and to articulate interests in state-building projects that emerged (and perished) in Bogotá. Connections with Bogotá brought these groups closer to bureaucrats and intellectuals who, in the capital city and some small towns, were active in elaborating the parties' ideological platforms.

Colombia differed from Uruguay, however, in the degree of state autonomy and the openness of the regimes that emerged in the early twentieth century. The state enjoyed less autonomy, and the regime was less inclusive. This supports the positive correlation between state autonomy and democracy that we found in the last chapter. In Colombia, the economic elites exerted considerable pressure through more powerful interest groups, and the state became clearly dependent on the upper sectors of the landed gentry. By the early twentieth century, for example, the prestigious Coffee Growers Association played a prominent role in Colombian politics.[8] The Asociación Rural in Uruguay never reached such a level of influence. A strong conservative coalition, closer to Moore's "reactionary configuration," did emerge, articulating its interests through both parties, particularly the Conservative Party.

A Weak State and a Weak Military

The most common reason why the state and the military have occupied a secondary place in the analysis of Colombia is the minor role they

(above) 7. *Signature of Revolutionary Constitution, Bogota,* and (below)
8. *General Francisco de Miranda in Ceuta Prison.* Academia Colombiana de
Historia. Album del Sesquicenternario. Daniel Ortega Ricuate Editores,
Bogota 1961. Library of Congress.

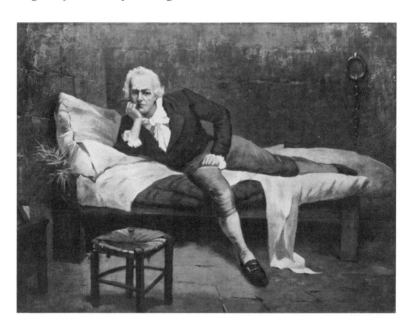

played during state building. For most of the nation-building period, the state remained unable to reach down into the rural population, but the parties could and did. In terms of army building, both in the regions and in Bogotá, political bosses maintained direct contact with officers and the army rank and file. As in Uruguay, the army became partisan. As we shall see in section 3.4, the political chiefs were army men, had relatives in the army, and used their laborers as "voluntary militia." This allowed them to mobilize effectively against the party in opposition or the central government and to better control local insurrections from below.

Echoing well-known hypotheses on the relations between state and parties, Francisco Leal Buitrago (1984:28–53) reminds us that party and state strength in Colombia evolved in an inversely proportional manner. These are precisely the findings that require explanation. Malcolm Deas (1973, 1983) has questioned the weakness of the state in nineteenth-century Colombia, arguing that it does not make sense to think of the state as a hollow shell, and contending that nation building was not exclusively the realm of party activity. State makers did create a mild sense of integration as well as a notion of citizenship in the rural areas, where most of the Colombian population lived. As Deas (1983:156–57) writes, they also enforced regulations on slavery, determined the role of the church in the community, regulated elections, and, in Congress, provided for land legislation. I agree. Nevertheless, the state carried out these tasks with great difficulty and inefficiency, and as in Uruguay, unmediated party rule meant that state makers and party leaders were one and the same.

José Manuel Restrepo's (1827:vol. 1:173–249, and most of vol. 2) year-by-year account of the period conveys the image of a weak state. Bogotá failed to become a centralizing power, and the life of Gran Colombia was short.[9] Throughout the nineteenth century, some regions even found more commonalities with Venezuela or Ecuador than with Nueva Granada and tried to leave the union.[10] Nationhood, as Marco Palacios (1986:400–417) put it, was just an ideological project with a feeble structural base. In the late 1840s, even the pro-centralist administration of Tomás Cipriano de Mosquera yielded to the regions by endorsing provincial tax collection. David Bushnell (1993:36) argues that "no part of Spanish America had so many obstacles to unity, so many obstacles to transportation and communication per square kilometer."

As he suggests, Colombia became a nation "in spite of itself"; the state lacked the volunteers to fill even the basic governmental posts, and government bureaucrats did not have enough status to lure local elites in the provinces. Alfredo Vázquez Carrizosa (1986:95) has suggested that the state was weak because this type of institutional design remained the "ideal" political formula for the country, as expressed in the 1853, 1858, and 1863 constitutions. Indeed, taxation, a good indicator of state strength, showed a dismal record in Colombia.[11] Various taxes, including customs duties, brought scarce revenues to the state, frustrating the hopes of outstanding lawmakers during the mid-1840s.[12] Colombia's demographics contributed to poor tax revenues, making it, according to Deas (1980:147) one of the "less taxable economies of Latin America." By 1832, the *tributo de indios* (Indian tribute) had been eliminated, and by 1842 the *diezmo* (tithe) was in decline as well, finally disappearing in 1856. Numerous and confusing taxes with too many regulations characterized Colombia, according to Salvador Camacho Roldán.[13] Reflecting the strength of landowners and the larger business sectors, the direct tax was never implemented, despite the insistence on direct taxation in the 1821 constitution. In November 1857 Manuel Murillo Toro, formerly minister of finances in the Hilario López administration, still struggled in his native state to convince Congress of the advantages of a system of fixed, direct taxation on landowners.[14]

For good reasons, literature on state making in Colombia has concentrated on the last three decades of the century, the period under La Regeneración. This was no doubt a time of power centralization, and in May 1888, Congress granted extraordinary powers to the president.[15] In 1880, Ley 19 (Law 19) had already given the federal government the right to intervene in the internal disputes of the estados, but it was not until after the defeat of the Liberals in the war of 1885 that the estados were transformed into departamentos, and the president could appoint governors and political chiefs.[16] Similar to the literature about José Batlle y Ordoñez, authors such as James William Park (1985:1–3) have argued that Núñez's political skills laid the institutional basis of Colombia's state building, political stability, and economic development. Núñez "shaped" Colombia as important leaders do everywhere, but as in the case of Batlle, neither Núñez's leadership alone nor economic growth seems sufficient to explain the emergence of a polity in which the central army remained weak and parties supreme despite the three wars that marked the rise of La Regeneración. Under Núñez, prolonged war and opportunities in the international market convinced elites of the advantages of having a central army to impose order. Nonetheless, the military remained as weak as the state (see section 3.4).[17]

Throughout the nineteenth century, civilians made a concerted effort to weaken the military, which they rightly perceived as a potential competitor in the political scene. This applied to La Regeneración period as well. Although more active recruitment took place during the 1880s and 1890s, and the military academy was created, the military remained a partisan force.[18] State makers and the national army did collaborate in state building, but the army was still perceived as an extension of partisan power and a proxy for big business rather than an independent political actor. Therefore, with Jonathan Hartlyn (1988:13), one can summarize the Colombian polity as one in which two parties emerged and consolidated, the military and the state remained weak, strong regionalism persisted, and the incorporation of the popular sectors occurred through the parties rather than the state. This chapter measures these features against other Latin American cases. Section 3.1 offers a brief review of the somewhat lengthy literature on state making and democracy in Colombia. Sections 3.2 and 3.3 examine the influence of war and the mobilization of the rural poor on party building. Section 3.4 presents an analysis of civilian rule and the military and highlights some of the conclusions of the chapter.

3.1. Colombian State Making and Democracy: Interpretations and Comparisons

State Formation as Counterrevolution and the Rural Poor

State formation in Colombia can be interpreted as a long counterrevolutionary process. We usually think of counterrevolutions as rapid processes that attempt to undermine another juncture of fast and radical change, such as the revolution itself. Yet a counterrevolution can extend for a longer period, as it did in Colombia. Although state making did not start, as in Uruguay, with a revolution from below, republican rule did trigger some "revolutionary" measures, and the rural poor played a role in bringing them about.

After the failure of Gran Colombia, a group of state makers pushed for drastic reform, and during the late 1840s and the early 1850s, they were able to implement radical "progressive" changes in the context of weak central authority.[19] Indeed, Gerardo Molina (1987:102–3) interprets the 1850s as a time of anticolonial revolution that, triggering the collective action of the poor, especially the artisans, took the Liberals to power. A strong counterrevolution, however, progressively turned the tide of events in their favor. While Uruguay became liberal, the last wars of the nineteenth century in Colombia, especially the 1885 "revolution," marked a "transition" to the so-called República Conservadora (Conservative Republic) of 1886 to 1930.[20] Given the similarity of institutional arrangements in both countries, this suggests that the different degrees of inclusion of Colombia and Uruguay did not depend completely on the type of polity. By the time of the 1910 constitution, Colombia still had not made much progress with social and political reform, a situation that remained almost unchanged until 1936.[21] This tendency to exclude popular participation gained strength as the conservative counterrevolution consolidated. In the Colombian constitution of 1821, "the people" had no real role in selecting the heads of provincial governments. To take part in the primary elections, electors had to be more than twenty-five years old or be married, "know how to read or write, possess property to the value of 300 pesos or have 150 pesos in income from any activity other than manual, domestic servant, or day laborer and . . . not [be] . . . in relation of dependence to others."

Of course, this was customary in the nineteenth century, and this document did not differ much from the 1830 Uruguayan constitution or, for that matter, the constitutions of some European countries or the United States. Two developments, however, made the difference in Colombia. One was that the constitutions that followed did not advance the rights of citizens. Strong reform-minded leaders in the late 1840s and 1850s and revolts in small towns and the countryside generated windows of opportunity for radical reform unknown in Uruguay or Argentina. But what was won was almost all quickly lost; furthermore,

social/political reform v. slow.

at times the rights of citizens were severely curtailed. A second and related development, which makes an even more important difference in the comparison to Uruguay, is that the intense mobilization of the rural poor in Colombia did not have such a profound impact on the state. The poor often rose in revolt, and in some regions, their actions marked the pace and direction of state making. Their legendary struggle for land, resources, and political autonomy still goes on today, but these grassroots organizations confronted a sturdy conservative bloc in both parties that more often than not successfully obstructed reform.

In the 1843 constitution, citizenship still required the same qualifications, and citizens had to pay taxes. Bushnell (1954:19) notes that the extension of the franchise was debated but carried little weight, and that the clerical Conservatives, rather than the Liberals, looked at the vote of the "honorable poor" with some sympathy. Table 3.1 represents the evolution of citizenship qualifications in the Colombian constitutions from 1821 to 1936.

As table 3.1 shows, the 1832 and the 1853 constitutions represented a revolutionary leap forward; indeed, the 1853 constitution adopted unrestricted, universal, and direct suffrage. In other words, every male in an overwhelmingly rural population who was at least twenty-one years old could cast a ballot. However, an alliance of the most powerful Colombians against state power was in the making behind liberalism and federalism. The progressive empowerment of regional elites meant the reinforcement of clientele ties between political bosses, and the increasing dependence of the rural poor on local elites. In the "chaotic" 1858 constitution, top Liberals and Conservatives agreed on a further assault on the state by sanctioning the right to bear arms, which of course further empowered local party militia.[22] When in 1863 the country adopted yet another exemplary constitution, praised in the words of Victor Hugo as a "constitution for Angels," the regions gained further strength.[23] This document imposed a two-year presidential term and institutionalized further measures to limit the president's power vis-à-vis both Congress and the states. It departed from the "historical and legal fiction" that the United States of Colombia originated to form a "free, sovereign, and independent nation."[24]

Citizen rights did not improve under this federalism, since the system allowed the regions to legislate on their own terms; and in most

Table 3.1. Elections in Colombia, 1821–1936

Year	Type of Election	Reforms
1821	Restrictive	
	Married males over 21	
	Indirect	
1832	Restrictive	
	Married males over 21	
	Indirect	
1843	Restrictive	
	Married males over 21	
	Indirect	
1853	Universal	Universal
	Married males over 21	Direct
	Direct	
1863	Different in each state	
1886	Restrictive	
	Males over 21	
	Indirect	
1910	Restrictive	Direct
	Males over 21	
	Indirect	
1936	Universal	Universal
	Males over 21	
	Direct	

Sources: Cepeda 1945:20–21; constitutions of Colombia; W. Gibson 1948; Vázquez Carrizosa 1986.

states, the 1863 constitution meant a setback in the expansion of the franchise. Sharp differences over these issues emerged among the South and the Oriente, and among the regions and the central states. In 1885, reflecting back on the 1863 constitution, the Spanish consul reported that "the Liberal party gave birth to the Río Negro Constitution of 1863 without considering at all any possible counterbalance to its exaggerated political ideas about the unlimited sovereignty of the different states . . . leaving the National Government reduced to a simple delegate without effective authority. *No central despotism existed, but it was substituted by nine sectional autocracies.*"[25]

Most sources indicate that these "autocracies," whether Liberal or

Conservative, took advantage of federalism to increase their control over the lower classes. The Liberal regimes that extended from 1863 to 1885 progressively cut the liberties gained in the 1840s and 1850s, a trend that continued unabated until the first half of the twentieth century. In the 1886 constitution, the country returned to indirect elections and attempted to exclude the Liberal opposition.[26] Further, the more intense commercialization of agriculture in Colombia during La Regeneración did not reverse the trend. Rather, citizenship rights and the democratic reforms of the late 1840s and early 1850s further eroded as a result of the need for labor control under the pressure of an expanding export economy, coupled with the fear of rural insurrection.[27]

Colombia: Democracy and Land of Recent Settlement

In early 1822 a concerned citizen anticipated current arguments about Colombian democracy. He claimed that this democracy rested on solid foundations: "Among us, everything conspires toward the establishment of representative government; moderate wealth, a weak nobility, plenty of talent, a bit of illustration, a clergy that fanatically approves of the freedom of our motherland, and, what is more, a militia infused of liberal sentiment. Everything rejects the idea of usurpation of authority."[28] Most literature has focused on all the other factors mentioned in the quote, but the "militia infused of liberal sentiment" remained a powerful but less explored feature of the political system. Meanwhile, contrasting with that observer's optimism, the Colombian democracy has experienced persistent elitism and a poor record of inclusion.

limited democracy

In trying to explain this, scholars have customarily blamed the limitations of democracy on the machinations of unusually talented and manipulative elites who were able to create a polity that preserved their privileges through a sham of party competition. Similar to conspiracy theory, this approach has suggested that skillful politicians controlled party loyalties for their own benefit while preaching political freedom and democracy.[29] In the early twentieth century, these elites were able to conduct state business through "conversations among gentlemen."[30] When measured comparatively, however, this argument proves somewhat limiting. In Uruguay, smart leadership alone could not explain the

Batlle y Ordoñez reform period. And as we shall see in the next chapter, a similar argument can be made about the supposedly "extraordinary" skills of the Buenos Aires intelligentsia. What these arguments fail to explain is why, in other countries, similarly skillful elites with very similar worldviews did not achieve comparable goals.

Perhaps Colombia's restricted democracy can be explained by recent settlement characteristics. Although Colombia has not customarily been included in the list of "classic" cases of recent settlement, the country can claim to have had a "frontier" experience,[31] resulting from the struggle of entrepreneurs to "colonize" the Colombian highlands of Antioquia, Santander, and Cundinamarca.[32] Leal Buitrago (1984:17) argues that the Colombian frontier was unlimited, as in the United States, Australia, and Canada. William Paul McGreevey (1971:131) has also acknowledged the Antioquia region as a land of recent settlement and suggested, with other authors such as Charles Bergquist (1978), that coffee farming had a democratizing effect on the economy and society as a whole. Colombia also exhibited other features shared by lands of recent settlement, such as labor scarcity. It possessed a sizable peasantry; yet, scholars including Leal Buitrago (1984:61–64) argue that peasants contributed to preventing landowners from obtaining an adequate labor supply. Labor shortages hurt key export-oriented regions the most, which explains low productivity and output.[33]

Colombia had slavery, but the existence of slavery enclaves alone would not exclude the country from the recent-settlement group, since slavery was still more prominent in traditional members of the group, such as the United States. Indeed, in Colombia, slavery eroded relatively faster. Immediately after independence, gold mining in particular, and some "big" agriculture that traditionally depended on slave labor, remained prosperous and profitable enterprises; but the first constitution favored, instead, hacendados who viewed slaveholders as a "privileged" group.[34] This triggered the slaveholders' rebellion of 1851.[35] They claimed that "property without Negroes to cultivate it, was worthless."[36] Pro-slavery groups, however, could not stop a process that had begun during the early years of the Francisco de Paula Santander's administration (1819–1827), when both church and state accepted the advantages of free labor. It was not "rare" that slaves' complaints "very often found a favorable reception" in government. Indeed, slaveholders were advised by their representatives in Congress that their struggle was hopeless.[37] By the 1850s, the institution had been abolished altogether.[38]

These land-of-recent-settlement features, however, remain insufficient as an explanation for the party system and civilian control of the military, the two developments that made Colombia a democracy. Labor scarcity affected most American economies during the nineteenth century, but only a few developed into competitive party systems. Also, small rural entrepreneurs formed a large part of the populations of El Salvador and Guatemala, countries that evolved very differently. And other countries whose record of military intervention was higher also abolished slavery rather quickly. Rather, if anything, Colombia challenges the core of land-of-recent-settlement theory. Recent-settlement arguments strongly rely on culture, for the theory highlights the cultural influence of white Europeans in building democracy. In Colombia, that influence was lacking. Even in urban centers, to the dismay of government, Creole nationals constituted an overwhelming majority of the population. Echoing the government's concern, the British consul general in Cartagena complained in June 1840 that the lack of European immigrants in the land was "lamentable."[39] Even Liberals such as Camacho Roldán or José María Samper, sympathetic to European influence, recognized that it was native Colombians, rather than Europeans, who had greatly contributed to the formation of prosperous haciendas "that one can observe in the slopes towards the south and south west until reaching Alabema."[40]

Artisans, Farmers, and Democracy

Many scholars, including Molina (1987:112–13), argue that artisans were a democratizing force in Colombia and use the artisans' political defeat to explain why institutions tended to increasingly exclude the lower classes.[41] Artisans were active in the Liberal Party, counterbalanced the power of urban upper classes, and opposed the economic policies supported by large landowners.[42] Many scholars perceive the artisan organizations, the so-called *sociedades democraticas* (democratic societies), as democratic or "socialist."[43] Artisans attempted to "elevate the common man" to the status of active citizen.[44] One could even argue that the sociedades represented an alliance—of skilled laborers, the middle sectors, the working classes, and urban professionals—that led conservative-minded elements in both parties to fear the rise of socialism in New Granada.

Artisans no doubt offer an exemplary instance of collective action, and their mobilization did make a difference. In the 1850s, foretelling a situation that a century later would become almost stereotypical in Latin America, artisans who had been hurt by economic liberalism and the advent of steam navigation in the Magdalena River strongly demanded freedom in the political realm with protection in the economic sphere.[45] Ultimately the artisans' militancy divided the Liberal Party. Although they could not agree on economic policy and party strategy, most Liberals strongly promoted the political liberties of the individual and the adoption of universal suffrage and even advocated women's right to vote for the first time in the Americas.[46] Two factions surfaced: the more radical Golgotas, who, influenced by English radicalism, supported extreme free trade and absolute political liberties;[47] and the Draconianos, who, persuaded by Benjamin Constant, strongly contested free trade.

Conservatives had good reasons to be alarmed and, with the assistance of the church, reacted to the Draconianos' strategy of mass alliances by rallying the support of the lower classes and organizing their own artisan societies. Autonomous collective action was now challenged by the Conservative bloc and the church through more collective action under their tutelage. The strength of the artisans dwindled. Artisans had sought an alliance with the professional military and found receptive ears, but a divided military could not come to the rescue. In the final analysis, the democratic legacy of the sociedades democraticas remained ambiguous, and in terms of state formation, their push for a stronger state fell short owing to the weakness of their alliance with the army and divisions within the Liberal Party. Álvaro Tirado Mejía (1970:115) writes that free traders on the Liberal and Conservative sides emerged victorious, defeating populist tendencies within the army and weakening both the artisans and the state. The most important legacy of the artisan movement was to offer a strong precedent of collective action and popular protest; indeed, the defeated forces were feared long after they had disappeared from the political scene.

Scholarly literature on Colombia also identifies farmers and small rural producers as democratizing forces. Starting in the late 1860s, the scarcity of available land for market opportunities encouraged the expansion of the agricultural frontier through the colonization of unoccupied areas by landless peasants (especially in the Cauca and Magdalena River valleys). Catherine LeGrand (1984) has documented their contribution to development, but Salomón Kalmanovitz (1986: 111–14, 173) goes further. He claims that they provided the major force behind the modest expansion of Colombian capitalism, and that they also had a democratizing effect. For both Kalmanovitz (1986) and Leal Buitrago (1984:60–64), the peasant economy democratized the rural sector because it limited the expansion of large landowners. Bergquist (1986) indicates that the proliferation of coffee farms on the Colombian slopes contributed to fighting latifundia and encouraged entrepreneurship and individualism. As it did with artisans, the literature has found in the political defeat of small coffee producers an explanation for stagnation,[48] the oppressive character of democratic institutions, and even the absence of other parties that could compete with the Liberals and Conservatives. Indeed, unlike in Eastern Europe, a peasant or artisan-based party never emerged.

But not everyone has seen farmers as a major engine of democracy. Germán Colmenares (1968:56) argues that the farmer's political, cultural, and economic legacies were never great in the first place and could not have presented a real threat to landowners. With the exception of some regions such as Antioquia, which happened to be rather conservative, the small farmer's legacy remained minimal. Furthermore, evidence is ambiguous regarding whether small agricultural producers shared the same political platform or were able to overcome fundamental problems of collective action. My position is that these poor small producers did create a more egalitarian culture. Their efforts as *colonos,* or their struggle for property rights against large landholders, shaped party politics and regional institutions. The effect of their collective action on the central state, however, was more diffuse. Conservatives successfully blocked populist initiatives from developing into legislation, and when they did, the Conservatives quickly responded by organizing their own populist movements to undermine them.

The Commercialization of Agriculture and Coffee Cultivation

Among the many structural factors that shaped the state in Colombia, three seem to have had paramount influence: the geographic characteristics of a very diverse country, a complex pattern of urbanization and demographics, and the coffee "revolution," that is, the expansion of the coffee economy in the later part of the century. Whereas the two first factors slowed power centralization, scholars have assumed that the third had the opposite effect.

Geography, urbanization, and demographics in Colombia were definitely different from those in our other cases. Bogotá possessed no monopoly over the routes of overseas commerce, and the regions underwent different types of urban and rural development.[49] For most of the nineteenth century, small urban centers managed to remain more or less self-sufficient, and despite regional perceptions of Bogotá as a radical antirural stronghold, one finds no comparable situation to the River Plate republics. Topography and demography caused markets to evolve regionally and not nationally in most parts of New Granada, where "even the need for long distance commerce was not exactly urgent."[50] The relative limitations of these important structural variables, however, are apparent when one compares this case to Argentina and Uruguay. Argentine state makers also faced regional and ethnic diversity within a larger territory and yet succeeded at centralizing power faster. Uruguayan state makers operated in a smaller country with few geographic obstacles but nonetheless had enormous difficulty in centralizing power. And after all, federalism in the United States emerged on a large scale despite elite heterogeneity, cultural differences among regions, and adverse geographic conditions.[51]

To explain state making, the literature has concentrated more on the commercialization of agriculture under coffee cultivation than on geography and demography. The coffee boom has by far been the most studied subject in the development of the nation-state in Colombia. Many have argued that the cultivation and processing of coffee in the last decades of the nineteenth century contributed the most important economic and social transformation of Colombia.[52] Francie R. Chassen de López (1982:22–26) equates coffee with the main engine of progress and capitalist development.[53] Indeed, by the late 1870s, coffee provided 50 percent of the export economy (Jorge Orlando Melo 1991b:80), and the development of the coffee hacienda deeply transformed regions that played a central role in state making, such as Cundinamarca and Tolima.[54] At some time around the late 1860s, the so-called "colonization" process for coffee farming began to affect labor relations and land tenure, which was also true in Quindio and the Cauca Valley. In the well-researched case of Antioquia, traditionally rich in gold mining, colonization became a dominant form of land appropriation, transforming the region into a farmland.[55] Luis Eduardo Nieto Arteta (1970:vol. 2:253) suggests that coffee brought about the "formation of a national economy that had not before existed."

The enormous impact of coffee notwithstanding, the formation of the Colombian polity cannot be understood exclusively in these terms. Moreover, the very development of the coffee economy was shaped by frequent rebellions and even civil wars that had a deep impact on institutions. The impact of coffee on the economy was great, and the state profited from the industry, but closer analysis reveals that overall economic growth during the coffee boom was far from spectacular. And as indicated by the ratio of exports to imports, the growing coffee sector could not compensate for other sluggish sectors of the economy. Unpretentious growth characterized the initial phases of coffee cultivation from midcentury to approximately 1875 or 1876, and as a source of state revenue, the contribution of coffee remained moderate during the boom.[56] Jorge Orlando Melo (1991b:79) points out that contraband may at any point unbalance the equilibrium between exports and imports, yet his data show that during the boom, imports were consistently far greater. In fact, exports developed at a low rate, barely keeping pace with population growth. A significant increase in state revenues did take place in the period from 1865 to 1878, when the state budget grew by 86 percent, with import duties providing the bulk of the increase.[57] By the same token, however, the eradication of colonial taxes,[58] the abolition of the tobacco monopoly, and the transfer of some tax collection to the municipalities and the regions meant that after 1850, import duties plainly were insufficient to balance the state budget.[59] From 1865 to 1874, expenditures exceeded revenues every year except one.[60] Transportation remained a problem, and local elites were not able or willing to finance domestic trade.

Perhaps with the exceptions of the El Socorro and Antioquia regions, Colombian exporters—like their Uruguayan counterparts—could boast only modest incomes.[61] According to Tirado Mejía (1970:77), coffee cultivation reached its peak in the 1890s, but even then, the state boasted modest revenues. The pace of power centralization increased under the Regeneración, and Bergquist (1978:36) has argued that it is against the background of the expanding coffee industry (1886–1896) and its subsequent crisis (1896–1899) "that the political history of La Regeneración is best understood." Centralization, however, was moderate, and the institutional design of the polity remained virtually the same as it had been since the 1830s.

What were the democratizing effects of coffee cultivation? It surely benefited small producers, but only to a point. Its trickle-down effects depended on regional characteristics and the capacity of already established political institutions that could channel the demands of new coffee growers.[62] Overall, parties and the state remained unable to democratize their organizations in order to empower small coffee growers. Mariano Arango (1981:90–93, 96–98), among others, has argued that the coffee boom did not benefit the small producer. Rather, it enabled large hacendados to monopolize distribution, making the poor more dependent on the rich, especially in the prosperous coffee regions of Antioquia, Caldas, and Valle. By the 1880s, large property owners were responsible for most of the commercialization in these regions. Finally, La Regeneración directly benefited large agrarian exporters, merchants, and bankers, rather than the rural poor, while tightening political control over the urban and rural masses.[63]

My suggestion is that a more powerful explanation of Colombian democracy can be found in a much earlier period, in the late 1840s and 1850s, when cattle raising, rather than coffee, was the most important expanding sector of the economy.[64] Civilian rule, for instance, was strengthened during the Mosquera presidency (1845–1849), which—by consolidating a firm cross-party alliance—may serve as the first precedent of the mid-twentieth-century National Front. Mosquera also paved the way for the Liberal presidency of Hilario López (1849–1853) and its sweeping democratic reforms.[65] Once elected, López radically democratized the political system. He implemented policy that had been conceived even earlier, in the 1821 constitution.[66] If the separation of church and state can be seen as reformism, then the López regime radically reformed the state. He expelled the Jesuit order in May 1850, challenged the church's role in education (April, May, and June 1850), abolished ecclesiastic privileges (May 1851), and gave parish communities and town councils the right to elect their priests (May 1851). Democratization included freedom of speech, press, and religion; universal male suffrage and the secret ballot; the eradication of monopolies on land and crops; and the elimination of imprisonment for bankruptcy or debt. To an extent, his reforms were more pro-civilian than the Uruguayan *civilismo* of the 1880s.

As the coffee economy expanded, however, these daring reforms started to reverse as the state lost autonomy to the economic elites. As table 3.1 indicates, the evolution of the Colombian state after the 1860s reflected a strong tendency toward the decentralization of authority, but not necessarily toward democracy. A trend toward the curtailment of civil liberties remained dominant into the twentieth century, through the administration of General Rafael Reyes (1904–1910).[67]

Who did finally benefit from the late-nineteenth-century commercialization of agriculture? Coffee triggered changes in the upper and lower classes but ultimately favored the lot of the larger growers. Changes in the ruling coalition favored more entrepreneurial groups engaged in international trade. Some scholars disagree, but most of them focus first on the reforms of the 1850s, a time when the commercialization of coffee had not reached its peak, and then on the 1880s and 1890s, when it did. Some have seen in coffee cultivation a development that favored merchants, artisans, and even the masses (including slaves); meanwhile, Conservatives and the church were hurt.[68] Colmenares (1968:91) notes that the old elites endured these changes with "resignation and fatalism." For Molina (1988–1989), the experience of the new Colombian merchant classes is comparable to that of the European bourgeoisie. He sees a connection between the democratic reforms of the 1850s and the nascent "national bourgeoisie" composed of export agriculture, miners, merchants, and incipient manufacturers.

They made common cause against the "parasitic" oligarchy responsible for the 1851 anti-Liberal uprising: the southern states, which had much to lose on both economic and social grounds. I agree with these authors that a real step toward democracy took place in the 1850s. Yet they are still attempting to connect these democratic reforms of the 1850s with changes in agriculture, rather than explaining the conservative 1880s or 1890s, when the coffee boom really hit Colombia.

Literature on Colombia points to changes among the economic elites and in the structure of production but does not clearly tie the coffee boom to more open forms of political participation for the lower classes. Large landowners who sympathized with the Liberal Party embraced free trade and welcomed the expansion of the export market. They did not, however, necessarily oppose their Conservative counterparts on the issue of political reform. Differences between the older and more aristocratic "oligarchy" and the more entrepreneurial, newly landed elites made for interesting divisions, as Nieto Arteta argues, but we see no clear indication that this differentiation coincided with the cleavage separating reform and reaction. Indeed, labor relations and the situation of the rural poor did not improve substantially. Studying labor mobilization in the later part of the century, for instance, Miguel Urrutia Montoya and Mario Arrubla (1970) find an improvement in income during the 1860s, but also a sharp decline in wages starting in 1886 and continuing until the 1930s. And according to Kalmanovitz (1984:290–91), more advanced "capitalist forms of production" led to more exploitative forms of labor coercion, comparable to the second serfdom in Eastern Europe. Jorge Orlando Melo (1978:86) and others also identify this "new bourgeoisie" as a partner of the old oligarchy. Coffee prosperity provided the backbone for Conservative Party rule from 1880 to 1930,[69] while strong opposition to the expansion of the export economy came from nonelite groups such as the artisans.

In sum, the expansion of the export economy favored the top elites the most, and its trickle-down democratizing effect remained limited. In the final analysis, contrary to the expectations of many social science theories, one can argue that the expansion of the export sector consolidated ties between landed and commercial interests to constitute, in Barrington Moore's (1966) terms, a "reactionary configuration."

3.2. Wars and the State

The Wars of Independence as Revolutionary Wars

War making during independence changed class actors, coalitions, and institutions.[70] During the wars, state makers were unable to centralize power effectively, and the history of the Colombian state remained one of decentralization. From 1810 to 1816, during the patria boba, the state failed to impose its authority.[71] The regions fought among themselves instead of providing a united front against Spain; thus the strength of the Spanish reconquest (1816–1819). Each region followed its own constitution, and some states, like Cartagena, even had two. Simón Bolívar and his supporters favored a centralized form of government, but efforts to restructure centralist colonial institutions failed.[72] Conservatism remained strong, but institutionally Bolívar's initiative to merge the regions into a centralized unit did not materialize.[73] Some unity was gained during the Spanish reconquest, and Gran Colombia was born. But once the threat was over, Gran Colombia dissolved. Colonial control over tobacco, salt, and *aguardiente* (brandy) did survive for a while after the wars only because state makers were, by and large, republicans who had faith in liberal economics—but at the same time, they feared the political effects of drastically cutting off fiscal revenues. A pro-centralist coalition held the state responsible for these monopolies as much as it could. In the end, however, state control was eliminated.

One can argue that the wars of independence and the subsequent conflict did two things. First, the wars weakened state and army. The provinces that formed Colombia were united loosely under the threat of external war, and union remained loose for most of the century.[74] Restrepo's (1827:180) account of the 1812 Leyba Convention is telling. Of the twelve provinces that constituted Nueva Granada (later present-day Colombia), eleven joined the union only because they felt threatened by Spain.[75] Second, the wars created a state that bore faint resemblance to the colonial administration before independence. Both centralists and federalists, in their own ways, aimed to restructure the state.

Some scholars disagree, presenting republican rule as a mere continuation of the colony. Despite the "incongruities" caused by the adoption of institutions of representative democracy, Orlando Fals Borda (1969:72, 75–77) contends that the colonial order provided the foundation for the postindependence period. Conservative policies that aimed at restoring colonial institutions during the process of state making seem to support his point. For example, José María Samper wrote that from the Guerra de los Supremos (War of the Supremes; see table 3.2) to the early 1850s, Conservatives attempted, through the constitution of 1843, to revive the centralization of "old regime institutions."[76] Luis Ospina Vázquez (1979:169–73) agrees. My argument, however, is that before and after the wars, we find contrasting polities. Before, the colonial state operated with a considerable degree of autonomy and capacity, controlled the exploitation of important export industries, and successfully linked important sectors of the upper classes to its bureaucracy.[77] After the wars, the state was stripped of all these privileges. Pressure groups and cliques of notables were replaced by a system in which parties, not necessarily associated with the state, built national alliances. In addition to party building, two other important developments marked a departure from the colonial heritage. One was the weak role played by the military in state making, and the other was the different character taken by war and popular mobilization under the republic.

As in Uruguay, wars took the form of party wars. An impressive number of civil wars and rural rebellions shaped both the state and the parties. In addition to more than fifty local rebellions, the country was swept by eight civil wars. Table 3.2 shows, in chronological order, the wars and rebellions that marked the process of state formation.

During what I call the first phase of state making (from independence to the late 1850s), anticentralist forces rose in 1826 and in 1828 against Gran Colombia and Bolívar's centralizing project. In 1830 and 1831, two other rebellions rose in opposition to power centralization, the second of which culminated in the Pasto-based revolt, La Guerra de los Supremos (1839–1842), a watershed in party formation and state building.

What I see as a second phase of state building started with the Liberal reforms of the 1850s, immediately followed by the 1851 Conservative

Table 3.2. Wars in Nineteenth-Century Colombia

Year	War
1811	Revolutionary forces in Cartagena shed the first blood of civil combat against the patriots of New Granada.
1811–1822	The wars of independence.
1826	Uprising led by José Antonio Páez against the government of Gran Colombia.
1828	Rebellion launched by José Maria Obando and José Hilario López against the dictatorship of Simón Bolívar.
1828	José Maria Cordova leads rebellion against the dictatorship of Simón Bolívar.
1830	Florencio Jiménez leads rebellion against the government of Joaquin Mosquera.
1831	Obando and López, aided by others, lead rebellion against dictator Rafael Urdaneta.
1839–1842	In La Guerra de los Supremos (War of the Supremes), Obando leads Progresistas (Santanderists) against the government of José Ignacio Marquez; Marquez turns to Bolivarian factions to suppress the rebellion, but government forces prevail.
1851	Conservative uprising against Liberal government of José Hilario López is easily repressed by government.
1854	Coup led by Liberal general José María Melo replaces Liberal government of Obando, and Melo establishes a short-lived military dictatorship.
1859–1862	Successful Liberal revolution led by Tomás Cipriano de Mosquera dedicated to the overthrow of Conservative president Mariano Ospina Rodríguez.
1867	Successful coup by Radical Liberals against Tomás Cipriano de Mosquera; Liberal Santos Acosta assumes office.
1876–1877	Unsuccessful Conservative uprising against Liberal government of Aquileo Parra.
1885	Unsuccessful Radical Liberal uprising against government of Independent Liberal Rafael Núñez.
1895	Failed Liberal uprising against Conservative government of Miguel Antonio Caro.
1899–1902	La Guerra de los Mil Dias (War of the Thousand Days), an unsuccessful Liberal revolt against Conservative government of Manuel Antonio Sanclemente.
1900	Coup led by Historical Conservative José Manuel Marroquin against Nationalist Conservative Manuel Antonio Sanclemente, in which Historical Conservatives prevail and Marroquin assumes office.

insurrection and the revolt against General José Maria Obando. That revolt started a counterrevolution that shaped the design of state institutions until the early twentieth century. War shook the country once again from 1859 to 1862 with the very important Liberal revolution of Tomás Cipriano de Mosquera, who was ultimately deposed by a coup led by dissatisfied Liberals within his own party.

A third period of state formation started with La Regeneración, which brought about frequent strife and further Liberal rebellions. It took La Regeneración three wars to establish its supremacy, of which the most devastating and intense was La Guerra de los Mil Dias (Thousand Day War).[78] McGreevey (1971:167) writes that elites seemed "unable" to institutionalize power relations of domination. This is correct. By the same token, however, local bosses in the regions did profit from this loose system, which cemented party power.

Constitutional amendments reflect the influence of war on the design of government institutions, and overall, the clear intent was to keep the rural poor at bay. From the early 1800s to the end of the century, the country went through many constitutions that coincided with upheavals and rebellions on the part of one party or another, including the constitutions of 1821, 1830, 1832, 1843, 1853, 1858, 1863, and 1886. In comparison with other new nations, especially the other cases considered here, the number of constitutions was unusually large. If we look outside Bogotá itself and count developments in all nine states, forty-two different constitutions materialized.[79] These constitutions were supplemented by amendments, put into effect in 1830, 1843, 1853, 1858, 1863, and 1886—to which one should add the unsuccessful Ocana Convention of 1828.[80] The country, indeed, even adopted different names for itself.[81]

War and the Economy

A major, urgent, and new problem faced by republican state makers was the cost of war. Independence became an enterprise accomplished through a policy of "economic emergency," according to Javier Ocampo López (1984:82). The prolonged conflict and the following revoluciónes de partido brought production down to alarming levels and drained the already scarce labor force. As in Uruguay, constant conflict involving important areas of the country made it "almost impossible to obtain labourers for the sowing of the crops." Frequent financial crises triggered by this almost constant conflict, and the need to finance the wars, encouraged government to issue "great amounts of paper money," raise taxes on the opposition party, and demand "horses, mules, and tools" from the rural population.[82] Rural youths were often forced into partisan militias, and liberated slaves found themselves serving local political chiefs as forced labor and partisan militias as well.[83]

Citizens in both the city and the countryside were habitually required to assist a bankrupt state with "forced loans" to finance the war efforts of one party or another. As in Uruguay, importers, exporters, and small merchants became financiers of war activity. Bushnell (1954:97–99) notes that Bogotá merchants lent money to the state in times of crisis and shouldered the burden left by the wars of independence. Landed interests suffered with rural strife, and it seems that they did not amass big fortunes, at least in the early period of state making. In fact, contemporaries such as Camacho Roldán (1976:25–26) claimed that "in the New Granada all big fortunes have sprung from mining and commerce, and almost none from agriculture." Europeans (particularly the British and the French) and nationals often abandoned the country as a result of violence, loss of property, and threats to their lives. In 1841 "starving citizens" and foreigners "stood in line asking passports to flee the country for entire days and nights at the doors of Foreign Delegations."[84] In the same year, the British consul wrote to one revolutionary leader that not only the government but the Spanish, Italian, and British delegations badly wanted a reconciliation between the parties in order to terminate "happily and for ever this truly disastrous fratricidal war [which has brought] . . . calamities, injuries, and ruin to the inhabitants."[85] Foreign powers, however, had little influence as mediators between the warring parties.

Opportunities for the young shrank as frequent conflicts contributed to the lack of economic opportunities, thus encouraging the rise of a bulky political elite. Bergquist (1978:3–6) points out that at least in the view of those who lived in the country at the time, the lack of new opportunities and slow economic growth "made politics an inordinately important avenue for social mobility" and an end in itself for the middle sectors.[86] Therefore, the already mentioned modest economic performance of the Colombian economy owed much to the frequency of conflict. What were the cleavages that kept the warring parties so active?

Parties, Centralists, and Federalists

Most scholarly literature has pointed to the importance of a federalist-centralist cleavage to explain party building and the ups and downs of power centralization. These labels are, of course, country specific. In Argentina, Unitarios and Federales wanted different things, with liberals supporting stronger state integration and federalists opposing it. In Uruguay, the terms "federalist" or "centralist" were hardly used. This chapter suggests that conflict resolution and the types of wars fought during state building maintained party differentiation; centralists, in reality, remained in a minority during the process of state building because a loose federation best served the power of regional bosses. Wars reinforced regionalism and that power. Furthermore, as Misael Pastrana Borrero ([1984?]:24–35) points out, regional autonomy did not halt commerce and helped to keep political control over the rural poor in the localities.

In this context, the emerging parties provided the fundamental vehicles to exercise control. On paper, constitutions looked centralizing. For example, the 1830 constitution concentrated power in the presidency. In practice, however, the local caudillos made important decisions. Local warlords, a "kind of little kings supported by horsemen and some infantry quickly mustered and poorly disciplined," closely limited state power and benefited from the system.[87] Surely Bogotá's inability to form a central army contributed greatly to federalism as well. Colombian presidents were pressured to appoint provincial governors from a list of nominees submitted by the local assemblies, and to abide by constitutions that conferred power on the regions.

The 1832 constitution further limited presidential power and reduced senatorial terms from eight to four years. Representatives' terms were curtailed from four to two years. The constitution required representatives to be elected entirely in the provinces on the basis of proportional representation. In each, a provincial house limited the president's latitude to appoint governors and participated in the selection of important offices in all three branches of government.[88] In 1853, legislation gave the provinces control over their own taxes. Federalism grew stronger, as it fit the needs of regional elites and left the control of the rural workforce in their hands. The popular view that emphasizes the power of ideas to explain the federation (i.e., the clash between free-trader Liberals, or federalists, and conservative unitarios who promoted "national security" and "nation building") has some persuasive power. I find, however, that control of labor and a convenient distribution of regional power made federalism prevail. The danger of federalism was frequent war, and indeed, Colombia had plenty of that.

Another popular argument points to differences over the tariff to explain party cleavages and their position on the role of the state. When one digs deeper into the available data, however, it seems excessive to argue for a lasting cleavage over the tariff. For most of the nineteenth century, both parties accepted free trade.[89] Protection policies, promoted after 1810, were in steady decline by the early 1840s, partly due to a "fatalist" consensus among the elites that industrialization (and thus protection) was not a "natural" strategy for Colombia.[90] According to Colmenares (1968:34–36), free trade prevailed as an accepted policy by both parties, even during the deep split between Draconianos and Golgotas. And certainly the emerging "commercial bourgeoisie" described by Palacios (1980:26–27) championed free trade in both parties. Safford (1988:55–57) notes that when Colombia engaged, with some success, in tobacco and cinchona bark exports to England, this trade reinforced a prior faith in liberal economics shared by most members of the ruling coalition.

We mentioned that in the second half of the nineteenth century, increasing portfolio diversification in the export industry further favored free trade. This points to a common interest in trade policy among the elites.[91] Consensus on economic policy can be detected clearly in the 1858 (Conservative) and the 1863 (Liberal) constitutions, and the parties pretty much agreed on trade policy. By the last decades of the century, Palacios (1980:29) finds that partly as a result of the rise of coffee as a main export, "the list of pioneer coffee planters generally coincided with the lists of main urban property owners, merchants, cattlemen, recipients of public lands, and importers." Most of these groups were free traders and belonged to both parties.

A standard but cliché and faulty conclusion, therefore, is that Liberals were free traders and Conservatives were protectionists. But Liberals did not invariably subscribe to free trade, nor Conservatives to protection. Conservatives, in fact, often promoted formulas that combined liberal economics and federalism, while Liberals at times adopted mild protectionism and federalism as well. Probably the most apparent clashes over the tariff emerged in the 1840s, when artisans and an urban middle sector "who did not really live better than the members of the working class"[92] asked for protection and organized sociedades democraticas. As noted, however, for all their importance, the artisans' influence was short-lived.

Party policy on the tariff depended on context, political and structural. During the depression of the 1830s, the Liberal government kept tariffs high to secure revenues and to protect national manufacturing (which was basically in the hands of artisans). Among Liberals at the time, a sizable majority asked for a more centralized government. And during the late 1840s in Cartagena, a stronghold of federalism, the Liberals also promoted a movement toward centralism. In fact, "Both the great parties and the state [were] desirous to see a form of government . . . which would insure a permanency of the institutions . . . [and] a decided preference [has been] indicated for a Monarchy under the guardianship of Great Britain, or . . . [that] the Executive power be strengthened by British Protection."[93] In Antioquia, Park (1985:29–31) points out that prosperous Conservative administrations supported federalism because they feared that a strong state would interfere with local business.

War at times decided, more than anything else, whether coalitions of Liberals and Conservatives, or one or the other party, supported federalism or centralism. After the bloody events from 1839 to 1842 (see table 3.2), for example, Conservatives—allied with the church and fearing more rebellions—promoted a more centralized state through the 1843 constitution (see table 3.1). By the same token, however, the same groups that had favored a more centralized form of government in the 1858 constitution preferred federalism during the Conservative administration of Mariano Ospina Rodríguez (1857–1861). And a few years

Liberals ↑ Conservatives
supported federalism ↑ Free Trade
at various points of 19th Cent.

after the Mosquera revolution (see table 3.2), Conservatives supported federalism.[94] In the final analysis, federalists and unitarios clashed over a *looser* and a more centralized federalism rather than over centralism versus federalism. At this point, the impact of war and the mobilization of the rural poor on party building adds a valuable clue to explaining cleavages and party building.

3.3. War and Parties

The causes of party wars varied. Some were triggered by control over resources and labor. After independence, slaveholders identified with the old regime and Bolívar.[95] Santander (1819–1827), favoring non-slaveholders, counted the support of merchants. Twenty-one merchants voted for his project in the first assembly, and only four backed Bolívar. Bolívar gained more support among landowners, with the exception of agricultural exporters who did not use slave work, and who sided seventeen to seven with Santander. As mentioned earlier, after the first war, both the control of labor in the localities and militia organizing remained a constant reason for conflict until the early twentieth century.

Class differences seem to have triggered wars as well. Nieto Arteta (1970) has argued along class analysis lines; the same can be said of Fernando Guillén Martínez (1986:20), who nonetheless flatly denies Nieto Arteta's thesis. My claim is that party wars cannot sufficiently be explained by class alignments. Rather, I agree with Safford's (1972b:362–63) overall argument that the same classes can be found in both parties, and Bushnell's (1993:93) suggestion that "both parties were multiclass and nationwide." The same individuals were "often landowner, merchant, and lawyer." In fact, a cross-party merchant-hacendado alliance did develop, forming the so-called oligarchy. We have already examined the impact of portfolio diversification on the ruling elite and seen how, in the second and third phases of state making, some merchants lost power to other merchants who had progressively invested in land. This oligarchy found representation in both parties.

The traditional landed sector, represented in both the Conservative and Liberal parties, gradually lost some of its control. In the 1850s, reform was carried through in the name of all of agriculture, but it really favored "that branch of agriculture that merchants monopolized."[96] Although during the 1850s that "branch" was identified more with the Liberals, the Conservative landed sectors also participated in that sector of agriculture. In the following decades, traditional hacendados in both parties lost some of their grip on political power.[97] In a way, they developed a dependent relationship with urban *letrados* (lawyers), and to the extent that the landowners remained on their haciendas, they played a lesser role in directing national politics. This, again, can be argued of landlords in *both* parties. The great difference from Uruguay is that in relative terms, those who invested in land in Colombia, whether from the older or newer vintage, overcame serious problems of collective action that their Uruguayan counterparts did not.

Conflict and Party Building

The origin of Colombian parties, Michael Coppedge (1991:4) argues, is not a "mystery." Like their Uruguayan counterparts, they began as warring alliances of caudillos and peasant militias in a country in which the expectation of party rule was high. What remains to be explored, however, is why these expectations were higher in some countries, and why simple expectations can be sufficient for the construction of a party system.[98] Hopes about party competition, apparently associated with the American Revolution and accepted notions of republicanism, were widespread on the continent. Only a handful of countries, however, that developed similar war patterns and mobilized the rural populations in similar ways consolidated party systems. Safford (1972b:367) has suggested that "we are a long way from an adequate statement on the social basis of political alignments."[99] I agree but suggest that war provides an important clue. The foregoing discussion made clear that during the first half of the nineteenth century, some important differences separated the parties in terms of their position on the role of the state, the central army, and ideology. It was also suggested, however, that as portfolio diversification progressed, the differences in the composition of the party blurred, and a ruling bloc that crossed party lines and favored federalism emerged. Frequent war, necessary to keep the state weak and the regions supreme, strengthened parties and party factions, which were almost always able to embark on a "revolution." These revolutions became important collective action events, which ended up shaping party profiles and subcultures.

Contemporaries reported that "war always shaped the preferences of those who are in command of society."[100] Gonzalo Sanchez Gómez (1991:17) writes that war in Colombia "was not a . . . substitute for politics. Rather, war was the fastest and (most efficient) way of doing politics. . . [and] constituted . . . a means to access citizenship." Parties and coalitions changed in war after war, and war shaped party platforms and electoral competition.[101] One can argue that party differentiation started before independence, in the social protest known as the Insurrección de los Comuneros of 1781,[102] and in the different rebellions that agitated the region that was to become Colombia.[103] Nieto Arteta claims that the insurrection reflected rifts that would evolve into the centerpiece of party alignments.[104] Most authors, however, have identified the emergence of protoparties with the struggle for independence.[105]

In his memoirs, Camacho Roldán strongly argues that the differences between federalists and centralists were forged during the "revolution." He points to the destruction of the old federalist leadership in the war, and the reconquest of a part of the Colombian territory by Spain in 1816.[106] Conservative ideologue Mariano Ospina Rodríguez also suggests that early party divisions were tied to the wars of independence and the dissolution of Gran Colombia. The war triggered an important cleavage within the Liberal Party, that is, the Liberal Conservatives and Red Conservatives.[107] Another war in 1831 had further consequences for party differentiation. Groups that came to constitute the Conservative Party gained cohesiveness as a response to caudillo Rafael Urdaneta's insurrection. One can argue that the party was born in this war, which greatly contributed to the elimination of "the parties of the middle."[108] By 1845, when Tomás Cipriano de Mosquera gained power by election, the Ministeriales and those in the opposition (the Liberals) had already gained distinguishable followings, and much of their profiles had been forged during the prior wars.[109]

The Guerra de los Supremos was a watershed for party building, shaping party subcultures and organizations (see table 3.2). During the administration of José Ignacio Marquez (1837–1841), a decision to suppress smaller monasteries in Pasto triggered this revolt, which lasted from 1839 to 1842. Although the group of "offenders" could best be characterized as a movement rather than an organized party and army, Congress considered the admission of foreign troops to confront the revolutionaries and solicited the intervention of Great Britain.[110] The Conservative Party emerged a more consolidated coalition after the insurrection. This pushed the church into association with the inner circle of the Marquez government, the Partido Ministerial, supported by large hacendados and slave owners. Together, they became the backbone of the Conservative Party.[111] As Bushnell (1993:91–92) observes, the Ministeriales "constituted in embryo the party that in 1849 would formally adopt the title of Conservative." The Supremos sharpened the Liberal profile as well, for the Progresistas claimed for themselves the label of Liberal. The party system, therefore, finds grounds in this insurrection.

At the time, many believed that after the Supremos war, Colombia had entered a new era. José Eusebio Caro tells us that the war transformed the country into a much more authoritarian society, for "[while] in 1839 the people had started to understand liberty . . . and education was starting to be available to the lower classes. . . . The revolution came and everything went up in smoke . . . the country militarized, and became a huge military base."[112] To be sure, to an extent one can argue that the Liberal reforms of the 1850s were a reaction against these changes triggered by the war. It is in light of the Guerra de los Supremos that one can better understand Liberal fears about a Conservative reaction, which indeed materialized in the counterrevolution that started with the government of Conservative Mariano Ospina Rodríguez (1857–1861).

Liberals revolted against Conservative governments as well. In 1859, groups within the Liberals took up arms and reinforced party alignments that served as a prelude (a year later) to the uprising of Cauca leader Tomás Cipriano de Mosquera. He opposed the church, power centralization, and the building of a central army.[113] His revolt deeply split the Liberal Party and promoted cross-party alliances. It also involved the country in a civil war that only partially ended in 1861, when Mosquera took Bogotá and deposed Ospina. Fighting lingered on for another year. At the end, Mosquera gained control and, according to some, accomplished "the only successful revolution in Colombian history."[114] The church, which had collaborated closely with the Conservatives, found itself again under heavy attack, which further reinforced its association with the defeated Conservative Party. This war was one of the "longest and most devastating," according to Jaime Jaramillo Uribe (1985:45), and it deeply restructured institutions—by 1862, the "modernizer"[115] Mosquera and his "revolution" had "legitimated the right to wage war" and destroyed the state. The name of the country was changed to Estados Unidos de Colombia (the United States of Colombia), presidential terms were reduced to two years, and the Senate was called to approve all nominations of cabinet members and ambassadors.[116] Osterling (1989:68) notes that the 1863 constitution granted every estado the right to have its own army, but the central state still lacked one.

When Conservative Party factions gave birth to La Regeneración in the late 1860s, they did so in reaction to the outcome of prior wars. In 1867 a coup orchestrated by Conservative general Santos Acosta, and backed as well by some Liberals, deposed Mosquera. His anticlerical policy had provoked increasing rural unrest, which helped the coup. In the absence of a central army, a widespread feeling that order and central direction were needed gained momentum, and disputes over the church came to the forefront again in the war from 1876 to 1877, an uprising that caused the death of ten thousand and financial losses estimated at twenty million pesos.[117] The country was at war again in 1885 (see table 3.2). The consolidation of La Regeneración took place during this war, and Núñez undermined the "federal structure of the state," according to Vázquez Carrizosa (1986:186–87). When in 1884 Núñez was able to increase the number of battalions to "counteract sedition . . . and save the country from anarchy,"[118] the army started growing. Reminiscent of Uruguay, militias of both parties formed the central army that countered the uprisings of the late nineteenth century. Army recruitment was accelerated by the most devastating war of all, the Guerra de los Mil Días (1899–1902).

Lucas Caballero (1939:12–17) tells us that this war strengthened the state, reconstructed the central army, and definitely established the Conservative Party as the most powerful force in the polity. It affected portfolio diversification, triggering a somewhat reverse movement in terms of investment. Landowners now made inroads into urban businesses and displaced old merchant networks.[119] The rather conventional estimate of 100,000 casualties is extremely high, especially when one considers that the population of Colombia at the time amounted to about four million; in other words, the war exterminated about 2.5 percent of the country's population.[120] The war's brutality surprised even contemporaries who were used to living in a violent climate.[121] Regional collective action, as in prior conflicts, remained the war's engine. In terms of party organization, the war caused increasing tension between party leaders and their militias, particularly on the Liberal side. Unable to wage conventional warfare, the Liberal Party was forced to fight a guerrilla war that encouraged banditry and caused the feeling among the leadership that it had lost control of its party.[122] The struggle reinforced the power of midlevel caudillos[123] and set an important precedent in the use of guerrilla strategies in the Liberal Party, which can be compared to its experience in the mid–twentieth century. Reminiscent of the Blancos in Uruguay, Liberal guerrilla tactics epitomized the old way of doing things, whereas the Conservatives, like the Colorados, fought with the support of an emerging army.[124]

As abundant literature has shown, at the end of the struggle, a peace treaty offered protection to the Liberals and determined quotas of representation and the rights of the opposition to participate in policy making under a strictly Conservative regime.[125] A big difference from Uruguay was that the Colombian victors were in a position to delay political reform, whereas the victors in Uruguay wanted to implement it.

The Rural Poor, Collective Action, and Party Cultures

Organizationally, the parties resembled each other because they were based on a similar system of "voluntary" militias that were allowed to gain power in the regions and to access the state in Bogotá.[126] The political map of collective action included the hacienda as a supplier of militiamen, and the parties as vehicles of conflict settlement. This constituted a sort of service expected from local residents, as compensation for the use of their *parcelas*. The more land and protégés a landowner had, the larger his voluntary army. Jorge Villegas and José Yunis (1978:26) write that if two or three landowners joined efforts in a region, "the situation was ready for an uprising." As General Gaitan Obeso and other party commanders argued, their armies were "armies of citizens."[127] "Citizens" and militias were one and the same, and as in Uruguay, party organization served to both incorporate and keep the rural poor at bay.

During the Thousand Day War, local bosses imposed the so-called forced military service on renters and peasants living in their domains, so that the conflict expressed one of the most overreaching efforts at concerted party action on both sides. One can argue that the legacy of the Thousand Day War lasted well into the next century and reflected one of the most intense eras of party violence, La Violencia.[128] Hésper Eduardo Pérez (1989:14) has shown that the system rewarded regional leaders by "catapulting" them into political life. Given these similarities in the way parties acted collectively in Uruguay and Colombia, it should not be surprising that they looked alike.

Ideologically and organizationally, the parties maintained a similar structure, with a radical or leftist sector and a conservative sector.[129] Thus both parties could recruit militias with different ideologies. In fact, party leaders were not that different, and Safford (1972b:349, 351) has shown that in terms of class extraction, principal Colombian Conservatives were not of a particular aristocratic lineage; nor were the Liberals of a particular populist background. Guillén Martínez (1986) has adamantly claimed that given their similar class composition, the parties represented no real political choice. As in Uruguay, the political system at times looked more like a one-party-dominant system than a competitive party system.

With a weak central military and Bogotá unable to impose political control, leadership and skills in armed conflict strongly shaped the emerging political culture in the regions. Parties in Colombia, as elsewhere, were partially a product of the central legislature, but the fundamental organizational impulse went from the "periphery" toward the "center." Authors applying the Duvergerian model to Colombia tend to leave this important engine of party organization in the dark.[130] After independence, a critical organizational shift from the cabildos to the rural areas took place.[131] Independent juntas that sprang up in poor towns and parishes expressed the power of local notables, their clientele networks, and the regionalism of politics. Landowners, who commanded *concertados* (sharecroppers), followed *gamonales* (bosses of higher prestige), who, united under party labels, "were always ready for an uprising or a civil war."[132] Rene de la Pedraja Toman (1978) states that revolts and mutinies forced the elites to make concessions. Even in the twentieth century, when the state was more firmly placed, Sanchez Gómez (1991) notes that militiamen-turned-bandits caused serious problems in the rural areas. As late as January 1893, the Italian consul in Bogotá was concerned that no one was safe in the countryside and that "even Bogotá suffered from bloody low class riots." The revolt of 1893, sure enough, had a strong urban underclass component, when the "plebes" succeeded at seizing the city for almost a day.[133] In some regions such as the Cauca Valley, small-town *sociedades democraticas* also took up arms against the established order.[134]

War became both a political and cultural ritual. Usually, it did not take anybody by surprise. Tirado Mejía (1970:31) points out that insurrections with the consequent show of rural mobilization were planned in advance by the heads of one or the other party, or by a coalition of the two. The leaders gathered at prearranged points and proclaimed autonomy from the government in the so-called *pronunciamientos* (military revolts). This demonstration of the capacity of one party or another to mobilize the rural poor was often enough to obtain favors and deter the enemy. Tirado Mejía (ibid.) notes that leaders "came alone or with their workers; after that, the rank and file was added by force." Intense voluntarism also characterized the Guerra de los Supremos. When chiefs of the "seditious" faction summoned their following, "all the population of the districts" responded with extraordinary "celerity [and] . . . showed up in guerrilla fashion, coming from all over."[135] A similar description applies to the Thousand Day War. Party recruitment constituted a social and cultural event in which "the different roads that leave Bogotá . . . were invaded by long lines of revolutionaries [and] . . . the farewell given to these volunteers was almost happy and effusive, as if they were pilgrims departing for a carnival or a promise."[136]

Mobilization and war also contributed to geographic identification across party lines. Indeed, war splintered Colombia into four main political regions.[137] Safford's (1972b:345) finding that party networks depended on geographic location fits nicely with the emphasis I place on the effects of shared collective action on party building and regional identity. So do Helen V. Delpar's (1981) comparative data on the 1848 and 1856 elections, for they confirm that parties effectively controlled their constituencies regionally.

Owing to the provisions of the 1853 constitution, by 1856 basically every male over twenty-one years of age could vote. Usually, an abrupt expansion of the suffrage changes electoral returns and constituencies, and old systems of patronage weaken and new parties emerge.[138] In Colombia, however, Delpar (1981:19–20) notes that electoral results indicate a remarkable continuity. Despite considerable augmentation in the number of people who could vote, provinces that had been Liberal in the 1848 election voted Liberal in the 1856 election. This was also true for the Conservative Party.[139] Therefore both parties were able to increase their constituencies proportionally in accordance with the increased number of voters, indicating strong party identities. Bushnell's (1970:221–312) study on the votes of secondary electors from 1825 to 1856 at the canton and provincial levels also shows the existence of definite constituencies loyal to the two parties.[140]

As in Uruguay, the party in opposition never disappeared, and periods of one-party hegemony actually reinforced the two-party system. The period of Conservative rule that extended from 1885 or 1886 to the 1930s in reality favored the consolidation of the Liberal Party, because the Liberals were left free to increase their influence among the poor and working classes.[141] Finally, in the 1930s, Liberals reemerged as the representatives of the popular sectors. Unlike in Uruguay, the social and political role of the church was a reason for war, and it must be included as a factor to explain party subcultures and alliances.

During the colonial administration and through the *patronato* system (an agreement uniting church and state), the clergy played an important and complex mediating role between the localities and the central government.[142] It was one of the few institutional structures in place, and the clash between clerical and anticlerical forces remained alive for most of the period of state building. It reached intense levels, as in the Supremos war, when several bishops and diplomatic representatives from the Vatican were actually expelled from the country; meanwhile, the Jesuit order as a whole was dismissed twice.[143]

The Conservative-church alliance was built on common ideological and organizational grounds; Conservatives and Liberals knew that an association with a well-organized institution definitely favored party cohesiveness. To be sure, the Conservatives benefited from it greatly, especially in a context of weak institutionalization.[144] Local warlords courted the church as a resource for mobilization and social influence. Culturally and ideologically, the clergy contributed to the identity of leaders and followers and facilitated militia recruitment. Fernando Díaz Díaz (1984:esp. 442–61) states that the church shaped the capacity of party mobilization, depending on the region and on the ongoing process of the appropriation of church property set in motion after independence.

Liberals feared the church as a cartel that monopolized public opinion through the educational system and held great economic power capable of competing with the state. It was indeed Liberal anticlerical policy that pushed the church even closer to the Conservative Party, and the heritage of these clashes remained strong in the twentieth century. While it has been easier for Liberals to develop alliances with populists, socialists, and even communists, Conservatives continued a tradition that supported the church and clericalism. Fernan González (1985:4) states that it was not until 1957, during the National Front, that both parties accepted the church as a factor of national unity.

Internal dissidence, within both the church and the parties, left a lasting legacy as well. Within the church, divisions rose regarding the marriage of church and state. Some radical clerics joined the Masons and even supported government initiatives to increase European immigration from non-Catholic countries. Within pro-secular forces, according to Liberal Manuel Murillo Toro, the old Santanderista Liberals defended the same principles as the Conservatives during independence: the patronato system, centralism, authoritarianism, and a permanent army.[145] Indeed, some Liberals had no quarrel with keeping the ties between state and church.[146] Moreover, at one point, Liberals tried to attract the church to their side.[147]

3.4. Civilian Rule and the Military

In this polity at war, the officer corps never dominated the state. The evolution of the army in relation to the parties has provided a useful clue to understanding nation building, for while the parties won strength, the army lost it.[148] James L. Payne (1968) offers one of the best studies on the composition of the army and its demise. Lack of overall data may explain why studies on the army have lagged behind literature on the parties.[149] The comparisons with the other cases in this book allow us to draw some conclusions as to why the army remained a secondary player in state building.

Payne suggests that the Colombian army lost ground as a political force during independence. Along the lines of our overall argument, the army was reduced drastically as a consequence of the war pattern of independence, especially its geographic location. In the battle of Boyacá in 1819, the first region to be liberated was Colombia, but then the war moved south to Ecuador and Peru, and east to Venezuela. When the effort ended, the armed forces (approximately twenty-five thousand men) were therefore not in Colombia but in Venezuela and the southern regions.[150] As we shall see, the army split into several factions following different generals, but these "armies" did not possess the cohesiveness of the Venezuelan guerrillas discussed in a later chapter. Mercenary troops could not find available employment on the payroll of the central government, and large numbers of soldiers in the localities were absorbed by landlord party militias. Meanwhile others found jobs in the rural economy, benefiting landowners seeking laborers.[151]

By the 1830s, the central army was already smaller than that of Ecuador or Peru, and by 1842, Tirado Mejía (1970:22) notes that it comprised less than five thousand men. Soldiers often revolted because they were unable to cash in their wages or obtain clothing and other basic needs. Desertion contributed to unemployment and banditry, which added to the army's bad reputation.[152] These radical changes contributed to the decline of the military as a professional career. Although Anthony P. Maingot (1969:303) described the bulk of the officer corps of the first Colombian army as composed of "Creole military hidalgos, some Spaniards, and enthusiastic civilians of the upper status group," the requirements of the war led by Bolívar transformed this army into an institution that recruited from the lowest strata of society. Plenty of testimonies show how the need for new recruits changed the organizational structure, the class extraction, and the sense of self-identity of the institution, making the military unpopular and an undesirable career choice.[153]

Racial tension also was an important factor that hurt collective action within the military. As in many other countries, the army in Colombia provided career opportunities for men of mestizo origin. However, the racial tension in the Colombian army between the high command and middle-ranking officers, and between the institution as a whole and the white and Creole elites, reached unusually higher levels.[154] Although the wars of independence had forced the republican government to assemble an army and to train military officers, the subsequent character of the struggle worked against the construction of a central army. Divisions among the founders triggered the establishment of private armies, and the only stable institution at the onset of state formation remained the church. It was at this point that a small group of patriots[155] quickly filled the vacuum left by the military to consolidate the republic.[156]

The penetration of the professional army by civilian politicians is reminiscent of Uruguay. Generals aligned with one or the other party, and in control of their own militias, also formed part of the army during the state-making process. During the early 1830s, even before the dissolution of Gran Colombia, public posts that had traditionally been held by army officers were abolished for the benefit of civilian caudillos loyal to the party in power. Maingot (1969:329) also notes that the decree converted the regional leader into an "instrument of the national leadership." The 1821 constitution excluded professional military men from voting.[157] The measurement was reinforced in the 1930s by Law 72, and again in 1945. Officers sought support among political leaders, and in times of revolt, the rank and file enrolled as militia for one or the other party. Several "generations" of partisan generals, who were both party and army men, secured party penetration of the central army.[158] Under the banners of Liberal or Conservative, regional political bosses often mustered militias that surpassed the strength of the army. As late as 1876, Antioquia was able to quickly put together an army of fourteen thousand that was much better equipped than the central military.[159]

Antimilitarism was not only pervasive but successful. Influential Golgotas, high-status city youth, some large landowners—especially those with urban residence—and merchants all expressed strong antimilitarism. Influential Conservatives also argued for the total abolition of the standard army, which they perceived as a low-class institution that should not be allowed to compete for power.[160] Surely some centralists did support army building, including some Conservatives and the Draconianos, or General José Maria Obando, who in 1853, however, was quickly deposed despite the support of artisans and large sectors of the rural poor.[161] The 1854 coup d'etat was led by another pro-army man, José María Melo, who was not devoid of popular support.[162] According to Fernan González (1985:36), when in 1854 Conservative Melo overthrew Obando, his backers took to the streets chanting, "Vive religion, General Melo, and the permanent army." Melo, however, was defeated as well, centralism under the tutelage of a central army remained a minority position, and the army in Colombia was never able to forge a solid alliance with the powerful houses of the upper classes.

Unlike in Argentina, the draft scarcely affected the rural poor. Federalism, also unlike the Argentine case, meant the weakening of the army. In its name, the Liberal constitutions of 1853 and 1863 formally eliminated reserve troops and granted citizens the right to bear arms.[163] In the wars represented in table 3.3, the army played a minor role, for most of the fighting was done by party militias. The high command of the confederate army lacked cohesiveness and "vigor" and was continuously supervised by the president or his ministers, even when in action on the battlefield.[164] Partisan and penetrated by the parties, the central army never gained autonomy. Table 3.3 shows that regardless of state revenues and the general balance of payments, army growth was not a priority. Until the 1880s, the army remained small, and the military budget low and irregular.

The birth of a more organized central army that took a more coordinated offensive in the Thousand Day War showed the powerful patronage of the Conservative Party during La Regeneración. Tirado Mejía (1970:177–78) and Vázquez Carrizosa (1986:187–88) note that for a long time, the army remained Conservative. Still, Bergquist's (1978) findings suggest that during this war, commanders on both sides were civilian politicians. At the end, the strengthening of the army during La Regeneración did not grant the military political power, for it remained strongly dependent on the parties.[165] The standing army hardly held a monopoly over violence and arms, and its size was kept remarkably small.

Table 3.3. Growth of the Colombian Army, 1831–1921

Year	Dominant Political Philosophy	Balance or Deficit in National Revenue[a]		Approximate Actual Size of the Military[b]
1831			—	2,370
1832		(+)	Col$244,707	3,880
1834	Moderate	(+)	175,342	3,230
1835	Liberal	(+)	1,421,013	3,230
1837		(+)	76,156	3,330
1853		(−)	940,168	1,220
1855		(+)	286,515	—
1856		(+)	77,432	109
1857		(+)	98,312	400
1858	Liberal	(−)	167,858	1,000
1867		(−)	519,439	2,000
1868		(−)	1,043,172	1,700
1870		(+)	264,778	1,000
1872	Radical-Liberal	(−)	1,202,969	1,246
1874		(−)	572,375	1,200
1881			—	3,500
1883			—	3,264
1888	Núñez		—	6,231
1890	Conservative		—	6,230
1892			—	5,500
1910			None	5,300
1912	Conservative		None	5,585
1921		(−)	8,829,725	6,000

Source: Maingot 1969:328.
[a] Memorias or Informes from the Ministro de Hacienda of the respective dates. Currency is Colombian pesos.
[b] Memorias or Informes from the Ministro de Guerra of the respective dates. Figures include officer corps.

The big upswing in army growth in 1888 under Núñez followed the unification of the nine Colombian states on 4 August 1886. But in 1892 the number of men was again reduced. It did not reach a figure close to that of 1888 until 1921. Most of Núñez's supporters saw the military as a necessary evil and opposed further army growth. By the 1890s, like its Uruguayan counterpart, the Colombian military was top-heavy. Military pensions furnished an effective mechanism to keep the army dependent on the political parties. Land grants and honorable pensions to caudillo heroes of the many party wars reflected on a military that, in 1893, had too many generals and too few soldiers.[166]

Therefore, a pattern of conflict in which party militias took the lead and the army experienced an important erosion during the first and second phases of state building provided the building blocks for the consolidation of the state and the party system under the Conservative Party. This polity resolved the problem of elite renovation and alternation through party rivalry but remained conservative. Party competition among officers within the military institution, not to mention severe budget cuts in a context in which the army did not control coercion, precluded the military from acting as a bloc. On the few occasions that military coups were orchestrated, the army plainly failed. Payne (1968:123) notes that in 1830, "Colombia . . . began its life with the suppression of a military coup." After this first frustrated attempt to gain control of the political process at the time of independence, when the military tried again behind José María Melo in the so-called populist coup of 1854, it failed once more. The main leaders of both parties fled to the regions, organized militias of their own, and defeated Melo and his supporters a few months later. Still a third coup presented the same characteristics: the 1867 "auto golpe" of General Mosquera. Repeating the same pattern, regional gamonales were able to organize their militias to depose Mosquera and arranged his quick removal. These three coups totaled all the instances of military intervention the country experienced during the process of state making. As we shall see, this picture contrasts sharply with Argentina, which also adopted federalism, but under an almost inverse pattern of conflict.

4

A Stronger State and Urban Military:

Argentina, 1810–1890

This chapter argues that the period between Argentina's independence in 1816 and its first constitution in 1853 marked a fundamental juncture of state building and regime formation. A popular thesis portrays state building as the struggle between Federales (Federalists) and Unitarios (Unitarists), groups that Marcela Ternavasio (1996:3) argues can be traced back to the elections of 1827, and that built the state during the 1860s and 1870s. This chapter suggests some correctives to that thesis.

Gino Germani (1955), following the dominant consensus about the different phases of nation building in Argentina, distinguishes between six stages of state formation. The wars of independence formed the first phase (1810–1820), and the following civil wars (1820–1830) the second. Germani identifies a third phase in the period of Juan Manuel de Rosas (1830–1852), calling it the *dictadura unificadora* (unifying dictatorship). A fourth phase of "limited representative democracy" extended from 1852 to 1916, and a fifth, with more extended participation, spanned from 1916 to 1943. The sixth and final phase started in 1946. Comparisons with the other cases in this book stress the importance of Germani's first three periods and especially point to Rosas's terms as governor of Buenos Aires (1829–1832, and 1835–1852) as a crucial phase of state building. Along the lines of the argument submitted here, John Lynch (1981, 1993) has suggested that the Rosas administrations go a long way toward explaining Argentina's political development.[1]

Most literature, however, agrees with Germani's (1971:267) emphasis on the "four crucial decades" roughly from 1870 to 1910.[2] Some have also noted the importance of the 1860s,[3] but most authors have favored the economic growth of the 1870s and 1880s as the crucial variable in explanations of state building.[4] Among other things, these two decades are appealing to social scientists and historians because they offer supportive evidence for good social science theory, like world system and dependency theory, or even neoclassical economic theory with its emphasis on rational choice and markets. During this time of economic prosperity in Argentina, the legendary military figure Julio A. Roca (1880–1886) succeeded Nicholás Avellaneda as president of the new federation and consolidated the Orden Conservador (Conservative Order). The new regime "fully integrated Argentina into the circle of modern nations" by reforming the educational system, separating church and state, and clearing the frontier.[5]

David Rock (1987:153) suggests that the expansion of the 1880s "dwarfed those of any preceding decade," and Natalio R. Botana (1979:71–72) describes the 1880s as a period in which, more than ever before, wealth became the dominant prerequisite to access governmental posts. Economic prosperity formed the backbone of the Orden Conservador, for it persuaded economic elites in the province of Buenos Aires, who had already greatly diversified their portfolio investments, to strengthen their ties with landed and commercial sectors in the other provinces. Be that as it may, comparisons with Uruguay and Colombia highlight the importance of earlier periods as critical junctures in institutional design and state making. During these earlier phases of nation building, alliances between the upper classes, the military, and the rural populations paved the way for the faster pace of power centralization that characterized the last decades of the nineteenth century.

I see the period that spanned from the May Revolution to the fall of Rosas (1810–1852) as a first and crucial phase of polity formation. From the fall of Rosas to the Orden Conservador (circa 1860–1880), I find a second phase of state formation, which I call "state building through coercion." In this phase, the basic style of power centralization favored by Rosas in the province of Buenos Aires further developed and consolidated at the national level. A strong army, weak party competition, centralization of authority in the executive, and weak mediating institutions between the state and the lower classes remained features of state building until the 1880s, albeit within the parameters of liberalism. I see the 1880s as a third phase, in which an already prevalent institutional design was aided by favorable transformations in the structure of trade and agriculture.

As in Uruguay, state making in Argentina was marked by tensions between city and countryside. Conflict between Buenos Aires and the provinces over the character of the federal system was reflected in a delayed constitution. Whereas most countries after the struggle for independence experienced an obsession with the writing of a founding document, Argentina did not have a constitution until the 1850s. The 1810 May Revolution did not produce one, and the declaration of independence in 1816 merely bred the abortive constitution of 1819. The same thing happened again in 1826, and the federal pact that embraced some of the provinces in 1831 cannot be considered a constitution. Thus the first national constitution dates from 1853, and the first constitutional government for all the provinces was ratified only in 1862 and continued in force until the so-called federalization of Buenos Aires in 1880. Although this "federalization" represented a move toward power centralization, however, the centralizing trend in Argentina started long before full-fledged modernization and Argentina's total integration into the world economy.

Intense conflict over self-rule and the final victory of a conservative coalition places Argentina closer to Colombia than Uruguay. After the Guerra Grande in Uruguay, the centrality of Montevideo as the locus of state formation was never really an issue, whereas in Argentina local caudillos challenged the centrality of Buenos Aires under the banner of self-rule, *cabildos abiertos* (open councils for general deliberation of public matters), and federalism. The army in Argentina played a major role as a state maker and became a major vehicle for the incorporation of the rural poor, unlike in both Colombia and Uruguay. This helped the army to become a more prominent player in twentieth-century Argentine politics than in our other two cases.

Under Hipólito Yrigoyen (1916–1922, 1928–1930), the country experienced its first period of liberal and popular democracy. Yrigoyen, a democratic reformer who took the Radical Party to power, opened the political system to wider political participation and focused on the construction of grassroots organizations.[6] Yet his last term in office was ended prematurely by a military coup, the so-called Revolution of 1930. Given the conservative corporatist-Catholic persuasion of General José F. Uriburu (one of the coup's leaders, who then became president of the provisional government), one can view this as a return to corporatist practices. The major goal of the coup was to keep Yrigoyenism and popular liberalism out of power, and to exclude the lower classes. Argentina thus started one of the saddest phases of its political history, the *decada infame* (infamous decade) of the 1930s. From that point, most of the history of twentieth-century Argentina reflects the gradual victory of the army over the political leadership. There is also much to the suggestion that at some point, the army replaced the oligarchy as an institution maker.[7]

This chapter shows how a pattern of conflict that began in the first decade of the nineteenth century, when British invasions triggered the development of an urban militia, greatly aided army growth. By the onset of the twentieth century, the army had evolved into a professional body backed by the obligatory military service of all Argentine males at the age of twenty. Unlike in Uruguay and Colombia, officers participated in government without altering their status as members of the army, and after the army's reorganization in 1910, merit counted as much as seniority for promotions.[8]

The different involvement of the rural poor in militias corresponds with the faster pace of army building. Although the recruitment of the rural poor during wartime appears similar in all three cases, starting with Rosas, a central army served as an important mechanism of incorporation and mobilization of the rural poor.[9] Unlike in Uruguay and Colombia, early-twentieth-century Argentine elites clearly viewed the army as an instrument of social integration of the lower classes. In 1895, when one-fourth of the total population was foreign-born, contemporaries argued that compulsory conscription would help nation building by "nationalizing" the first generation of Argentineans, "sons of the immigrants who have flooded the country with their 'cosmopolitanism.' "[10] The different role played by the army made a difference in the type of organization that fought the nation-building wars. In Colombia and Uruguay, parties fought each other with nearly equal intensity. Only at the end of the process of state building did the opposition party confront a central army representing the state. In Argentina, that occurred much earlier.

Not surprisingly, the pace of power centralization in Argentina was faster, and the state was stronger. Provincial caudillos were defeated rather swiftly.[11] In the early 1880s, President Avellaneda quashed the last rebellion that struck at the heart of the central bureaucracy in Buenos Aires. This established the city as the national capital of the Argentine Republic, a name officially sanctioned in 1826; and in the 1870s, one can already visualize an Argentine state backed by a central army, struggling to attract European capital and immigrants.[12]

This faster pace of state making and the prevalence of a centralizing federalism has been attributed to two basic sets of variables: ideological and economic. In the "history of ideas" category, evidence suggests that the system that consolidated the state in the 1880s, the Orden Conservador, had its roots in a prior tradition that favored centralization and exclusivism.[13] The regime was indeed elitist. Botana (1979:69) tells us that it centralized power in the executive and the Senate and built strong barriers to entry. Nonetheless, as we shall see in section 4.1, Argentina possessed a strong tradition of democratic liberalism as well, achieving early and significant democratization. The most cited example is the expansion of the franchise by President Bernardino Rivadavia in 1821, when the province of Buenos Aires adopted universal male suffrage for "every male in the city and countryside."[14] The 1853 extension of these reforms to the whole country is also well known.

These two strong intellectual traditions are not necessarily contradictory, and which one prevailed depended on other factors, mainly conflict resolution. The emphasis on the agricultural boom experienced by the province of Buenos Aires has already been mentioned. While both Uruguayans and Colombians ended the nineteenth century with humble growth rates and an acknowledgment that their economic future remained uncertain, the porteños (people of the port) and inhabitants of the province of Buenos Aires (or even Entre Ríos and Santa Fe) perceived their country as prosperous and competitive. Both ideological and economic development approaches consider war patterns and collective action only tangentially. This comparison tells us that while the spoils of war were similar to Uruguay and Colombia, the ways of acting collectively and the character of the conflict differed.

During the struggle for independence, Buenos Aires was the generator of revolutionary war. The city displayed intense and organized military initiative,[15] but the battles took place outside the perimeters of its hinterland. Subsequent civil wars were also fought in the regions or in the periphery of Buenos Aires, and unlike in Uruguay or Colombia, the wars did not drain the center economically or politically. Most of the war effort, therefore, moved from the city to the countryside. This is not to say that the opposite did not ever happen. Despite serious problems of collective action, the provinces, either united or on an individual basis, put together battalions and successfully campaigned against Buenos Aires. The overall pattern, however, shows a much more aggressive and organized military initiative on the city's part.

In Montevideo, the city defended the king and Spain, but the countryside took up arms in the name of independence and rural populism. In Bogotá, the revolutionary effort gained momentum as the movement advanced from Venezuela into Nueva Granada. Neither Montevideo or Bogotá gained control of the revolution, and both labored hard and unsuccessfully to keep their hinterlands under control—as shown by the frequent Blanco revolts in Uruguay, or the dissolution of Gran Colombia and the strong separatist movement that followed. Buenos Aires did lose Upper Peru, Paraguay, and Uruguay but was ultimately able to retain a much larger territory and keep its northern, western (from Santa Fe to Tucumán and Cuyo), and southern hinterlands.[16] In other words, as we learned from lessons in Europe, the role of the city in the war effort and its capacity to retain its hinterland did shape the state. The stronger role played by the city in state formation, however, did not favor a more democratic outcome.

Section 4.1 offers a review of the major thesis of nation building in Argentina. Section 4.2 emphasizes the role of wars in state making. Section 4.3 analyzes what I argue is a crucial period of polity formation, focusing on parties and state makers in the province of Buenos Aires. Section 4.4 offers an overview of the evolution of the military and the incorporation of the rural poor in the early phase of state building, and section 4.5 closes the chapter with a discussion of civil-military relations after the fall of Juan Manuel de Rosas in the later part of the nineteenth century.

4.1. Argentina, the Exception

Land of Plenty

The economic decline of Argentina in the second half of the twentieth century has generated very different explanations, from Carlos Escudé's (1988) discussion of an international conspiracy, to Carlos H. Waisman's (1987) focus on the economic and social policies of *perónismo*. The very notion of "decline" has of course assumed that at some point Argentina enjoyed high levels of economic development, which it did. By the early twentieth century, Roberto Cortés Conde (1979) tells us, *el progreso argentino* (the Argentine progress) was apparent. Higher salaries and new windows of economic opportunity made the country attractive for both foreign investment (particularly British and later American) and European immigration. Argentina, according to some contemporaries the "*El dorado* of today,"[17] gained a reputation as a land of opportunity comparable only to the United States, Australia, and Canada.

The story is well known. After midcentury, the elites' plan of development featured four goals: to attract massive immigration in order to "substantially change the composition of the population,"[18] to impose universal and obligatory education, to develop a modern agriculture and livestock sector aided by foreign capital investment, and to construct an adequate transportation network. Today's accepted wisdom— that Argentina somewhat escaped the fate of most Latin American countries—goes back to the relative success of this development plan. At the beginning of the 1870s, the second elected president of the republic, Domingo Faustino Sarmiento (1868), expressed this belief loudly and clearly: "The revolution that will make North Americans of us, that will dethrone the *Estanciero* who in turn has given rise to the gaucho and the *montonera* [irregular army], is already underway. Here, in this area of the *pampa* that stretches to Córdoba, a new society will arise, a new nation, leaving the dead to bury the dead."[19]

Sarmiento was right that by the 1870s, the provinces of Buenos Aires and the Littoral had boomed as the most rapidly growing agricultural export regions. Yet not everyone agrees on the impact this growth had

(above) 9. *Battle of Suipacha, November 7, 1810*, and (below)
10. *The Morning of May 25, 1810, Buenos Aires*. From *Ilustracion Historia Argentina bajo la Direccion de Adolfo P. Carranza*, vol. 2 (Buenos Aires: Weiss y Treusche Editores, 1909).

11. *Map of Buenos Aires, 1856.*
From *Ilustracion Historia Argentina bajo la Direccion
de Adolfo P. Carranza,* vol. 2 (Buenos Aires:
Weiss y Treusche Editores, 1909).

(above) 12. *The Slaughterhouse,* and (below) 13. *Sea Battle off the Coast of Monte-video, 1826.* From *Ilustracion Historia Argentina bajo la Direccion de Adolfo P. Carranza,* vol. 2 (Buenos Aires: Weiss y Treusche Editores, 1909).

(above) 14. *Argentinean
Founding Fathers,* and
15. *Portrait of Belgrano,
Buenos Aires.* From
*Ilustracion Historia Argentina
bajo la Direccion de Adolfo P.
Carranza,* vol. 2 (Buenos
Aires: Weiss y Treusche
Editores, 1909).

on development and institutions. Can we really talk about sustained development in the case of Argentina when, also according to most literature, the country never escaped the status of a "dependent" agrarian economy?

Many have pointed to the limitations of this pastoral mode of development, its dependent status,[20] and its colonial roots, which favored latifundia and concentration of land property.[21] Indeed, Hilda Sábato (1990:3) calls our attention to what she calls "pessimistic" versions of Argentine development. This pessimism rests on strong foundations. Inflationary policies first adopted in the 1820s continued with few variations throughout the rest of the century. In fact, María Alejandra Irigoin (1995:10) reports that they provided the foundation for what has been called a *cultura inflacionaria* (inflationary culture). The failure to repay loans to European lenders has been well documented by Henry Stanley Ferns (1960), among others. We also know of the government's recurrent artificial emissions of paper money to cover war expenses and fiscal crises.[22]

In this light, the Argentine economic success looks rather questionable. It is only against the background of other agrarian economies that shared a similar colonial past and dependence that one can assess accurately the Argentine model's success. Comparatively, elites enjoyed an affluence unknown to most of their Uruguayan and Colombian analogues, while the urban lower classes' share of the country's prosperity remained, for most of the late nineteenth and early twentieth centuries, larger than in the rest of Latin America. And although the Venezuelan cocoa and coffee elites achieved great wealth in the early nineteenth century, the pampean elites of the later nineteenth century far surpassed it. The success of the development plan is also reflected in higher state revenues. One can argue that by the time the country unified in 1862, the state, based in Buenos Aires, possessed a reasonable financial stability.[23] By the mid-1880s, the province of Buenos Aires held wealth estimated to be three times that of all of Uruguay, and a population of approximately 900,000 (compared to 500,000 in Uruguay). Argentina proved that a pastoralist economy could experience sustained growth and high rates of urbanization. Relatively, then, the record is one of prosperity and capital accumulation.

Scarce farming shows the more advantageous alternatives of investment in livestock production.[24] The failure of the farm sector to progress in the provinces of Buenos Aires and the Littoral, which Juan Bautista Alberdi had envisioned as the solution to Argentina's problems, resulted more from market and investment opportunities than from a cultural propensity against farming. When more land became available, large landowners purchased it and established monopolies that prevented farming. The 1876 Colonization Law reflected the preferences of large landowners, for it favored the immigration of peons rather than families and prevented farming altogether.[25]

Cattle raising, more than anything else, dominated this economy from the onset. In the 1820s, it expanded into the pampa region while other agricultural enterprises remained stagnant. Halperín Donghi (1975) considers estanciero influence great enough to argue that livestock production, more than Rivadavia's leadership, changed the province. The landowners' influence was economic, social, and cultural; hence we see what has been called the "ruralization of social life," and closer contact between estancieros and intellectuals.[26] By the late 1840s, cattle had become "the main resource of the province," and the number grew steadily.[27] It rose from approximately 26 million head in the decade from 1856 to 1866, to more than 60 million from 1866 to 1876; that is, the industry's annual growth rate was 7.6 percent.[28] In the period from 1880 to 1914, the value of exports increased from 50 million to 500 million gold pesos. James R. Scobie (1971:97) notes that the volume of hides and salted meat tripled between 1837 and 1851 as well, with wool exports increasing five times and tallow six times. Foreign portfolio investment was remarkable. Growth in capital stock in British direct and portfolio investments from 1865 to 1913 is telling, for an upward trend prevailed until the crisis of 1912.[29] Growth in the livestock sector, particularly in the province of Buenos Aires, far surpassed that of Uruguay. A commentary from 1899 claimed that "looking back [on] the past thirty years, it is impossible to avoid being struck with the enormous difference between the progress of Argentina as compared with that of Uruguay, which can hardly be said to have advanced at all."[30]

While the country's grain sector showed slow growth during its early period of expansion—according to Cortés Conde (1979:69), because of a labor scarcity and the pampa's lack of navigable rivers for transportation—by the later part of the century, this sector was doing quite well.[31] Rock (1987:136) points out that grain became a major component of economic prosperity. A forecast from the United States predicted that "the Argentine Republic promises soon to become the greatest wheat-producing country in the world."[32]

Such projections did not seem unreasonable. From 1872 to 1895, cultivated acreage in the pampa region increased fifteen times (by almost 10 million acres), and exports (cereals and wheat) rose from 30 million gold pesos in 1870, to 60 million in 1880 and 100 million in 1890, ultimately to reach 150 million by the early twentieth century. By 1900, this agricultural sector produced 50 percent of the value exports. From the 1840s to the late 1880s, wool contributed greatly to the country's exports, although by the end of the century, Herbert Gibson (1893) reported that wool had declined vis-à-vis cattle and agriculture. This is similar to what happened in Uruguay during the "wool revolution."

In summary, Argentina's growth was uneven,[33] sometimes even counterproductive.[34] Yet it was altogether impressive. In the forty years from 1840 to 1880, the country increased its population fivefold and its volume of trade sevenfold. Immigration, the "second component" of the development plan,[35] was no doubt a remarkable achievement in comparison to other Latin American countries. By midcentury, the country had reached almost three million inhabitants, and by 1914 it had grown to nearly eight million, with 52 percent of the total living in urban areas. Urbanization reached European proportions, revealing the importance of Buenos Aires as a center of development and international trade and creating tensions with the other provinces.

One of the features of state making sometimes missed by this record is that many times, the growth of the state bureaucracy responded to military and political motivations rather than to the needs of development. The same applies to the expansion of the frontier. The large land annexation during the presidencies of Rodríguez (1821–1824) and Rosas, for instance, did not respond solely to development pressures. Indeed, cattle raisers did not immediately occupy the land. Cortés Conde (1979:40) states that the pampa remained "practically empty" in the first half of the nineteenth century. Also, the ascendancy of cattle raisers to power in the 1820s was not exclusively caused by the thrust of development. It also owed much to the May Revolution, which, as much as development, triggered a growing consensus on free trade in the province of Buenos Aires and took the rural upper class to power.[36] And in terms of institutional design, there is no necessary correlation between higher rates of development and the type of polity that emerged in Argentina. Strong armies and centralizing institutions also emerged in poor societies that hardly experienced a comparable level of development, such as Paraguay.

Democracy and the Commercialization of Agriculture

Like Uruguay and Colombia, Argentina presents ambiguous evidence regarding the connection between the commercialization of agriculture, the use of labor, and the rise of more inclusive regimes. As in Colombia, the switch to commercial agriculture coincided with a move toward a more elitist and centralized regime and occurred rather late to explain one of the most significant reforms of the Argentine political system: the adoption of universal male suffrage in 1821. Sergio Bagú (1966) states that Rivadavia, the first president of independence, implemented bold political and economic reforms that—as David Bushnell (1983:4) points out—were "carried further, at least on paper, than anywhere else in Latin America at that time." In light of the argument presented in this book, the strong urban component of these reforms is important. As Halperín Donghi (1975:360–61) writes, the reforms owed much to the "urban popular agitation and its allies in the regular army." He goes on to say that the revolutionary government in 1812 had already called for universal suffrage, although only within the Hall of the Cabildo, and that the election for deputies to the Cabildo in 1815 closely resembled the electoral reform of 1821. All these changes took place at a time of modest agricultural development, for example during the "progressive" administration of Rodríguez (1821–1824), who tried to reconstruct the province of Buenos Aires in the "image of the most advanced Western economic institutions."[37] And at the time of the 1853 constitutional reform, which granted universal suffrage, Argentina had not yet been affected by the expansion of agriculture. Rather, one can argue that the fall of Rosas and the strong reaction against his regime motivated Congress to extend the franchise bill.

Moreover, none of the daring reforms imposed by Rivadavia in 1821 or the bills passed in 1853 influenced the political climax of the 1870s and 1880s. In the prosperous 1870s, the political system centralized power in the president, the minister of the interior, and the Senate. The government relied heavily on the army, indirect elections, and the loyalty of the provincial governors, and a tight system of succession was devised to secure power in a few hands. Ranchers were strong in the ruling coalition. Reminiscent of Barrington Moore's (1966) theory, and contrary to the expectations of modernization theory, development failed to favor the political rights of the lower classes. The composition of the most important government body, the Senate, changed for the worse during the expansion of agricultural development. The newspaper *La Prensa* noticed the influence of the army, commenting that senators no longer represented the popular will: "[They] became governors in the first place by presidential influence or under the auspices of the bayonet. . . . Offsprings of the army, they have to operate as the army's agents in their roles as the leaders of the province."[38]

In the Orden Conservador, the national government could name its own successors and control the appointment of governors in the provinces as well.[39] Therefore, the centralizing structure of the 1880s owed much to coercion and the defeat of separatist forces during earlier periods. Once in place, it facilitated the emergence of an exclusive regime with weak opposition parties, or as Botana (1979:78) has written, "moderate opposition." Such strong elite consensus was surely reinforced by prosperity, but at the same time, prior institutionalization contributed to hold the system together when prosperity was seriously threatened, as in 1889 when Baring Brothers of London denied a loan that would reorganize the water supply in Buenos Aires. The failure of the loan provoked panic because, as Rock (1987:158) writes, "new British investment ceased abruptly"; indeed, in 1890 the government was already defaulting on its foreign debt.[40]

Rock (1987:70) points out that the polity was centralized enough to allow senators and governors to choose their own successors. Competitive elections did not seem to have much meaning. In 1902, former president Carlos Pellegrini, addressing Congress, described elections as times of struggle "centered around taking possession of this or that precinct. [This was] . . . the preliminary political action of every election, and once a party dominated a particular precinct, then . . . the election was finished. We all knew that this particular party would win . . . because fraud was sanctioned and admitted as a regular phenomena."[41]

Argentina:
Feeble Democracy in a White Land of Recent Settlement

Within Latin America, Argentina has been regarded as "the" case of recent settlement and has often been included in comparative work inspired by the theory.[42] Some have likened the country to Australia, Canada, and New Zealand, and those who subscribe to staple theory have argued that in the late nineteenth and early twentieth centuries, Australian wool, Canadian wheat, and Argentine beef served as "super staples" that led to similar transformations.[43] Others, however, have questioned the value of these comparisons.

Staple theory turned out to be disappointing, since it demonstrated no recognizable pattern of development in these societies, with much depending on local circumstances and markets. Carlos Diaz Alejandro (1985) rejects the idea that Australia and Argentina were similar during the 1880s. Australia was "born rich" with much more solid mineral endowments and a well-organized working class. Land distribution policies, mineral resources, the timing and character of immigration, and the different development of the working classes and union organization separated Argentina from Australia or Canada. Moreover, comparisons show great differences in the pattern of capital accumulation, fiscal policy, taxation, and industrial development, not only between Argentina and the rest but also between Canada, Australia, and New Zealand.

Only a strong European culture seems to link Argentina with other lands of recent settlement. Nineteenth-century state makers such as Alberdi and Sarmiento regarded European culture and immigration as crucial components of development and democracy.[44] As in Uruguay and Colombia, state makers repeatedly expressed disappointment that their countries did not attract larger numbers of Anglo-Saxons, but reports showed that Italians "went nowhere else to settle."[45] Gastón Gori (1964) reports that the state was assigned the huge task of securing a steady flow of immigration from Europe. In 1876, Congress passed a bill to encourage farming and land ownership for foreigners.[46] As is well known, war and shrinking economic opportunities in Europe contributed to spectacular emigration. Rock (1987:132) notes that Argentina's population increased from 1.1 million in 1857 to 3.3 million by 1890, while the population of the city of Buenos Aires sextupled between the census of 1854 and the second national census in 1895. Smith (1969:14) tells us that whereas Argentina had only 1.7 million residents in 1869 (among whom foreigners already constituted a high percentage), forty years later, new arrivals had added 2.6 million to the population. During the 1880s alone, 1 million immigrants arrived, of whom 850,000 remained in the country.[47]

In relation to the total population, these figures are comparable only to the United States.[48] In terms of the absorption of this immigrant labor force, a major difference from neighboring pastoral Uruguay was that a group of immigrants (particularly Italians) became tenant farmers. They provided the engine for the sensational growth of the grain economy, particularly in the province of Buenos Aires, while their participation in cattle raising—as Germani (1971:259) points out—remained much more modest.

As in Uruguay, war to some extent contributed to the fortune of many immigrants, who were exempted from serving in the army and therefore free to concentrate on lucrative activities. Like many Argentines, they prospered during the Paraguayan War. As an American reporter observed, "While the Argentinean goes to war, the foreigner steps into his place in the estancia, behind the counter, in the teacher's desk, everywhere, in fact, where money can be made, until the business of the country seems likely to be carried on by strangers."[49] The 1895 census indicates that 80 percent of industry and commerce was in the hands of immigrants. They constituted nearly 75 percent of the growing middle sector, particularly in urban areas and in Buenos Aires, whereas the landed elites remained Creole.[50]

This is no doubt an impressive record of European immigration, and it stands as a strong statement of the influence of European culture in Argentina. But the country developed a centralized and less competitive political system than the European states. Argentina somewhat stubbornly followed a more militaristic path, despite its white European population and the advanced liberal thinking of its founding fathers.

The Founding Fathers and Nation Building

The strong heritage of the writings of founder Domingo Faustino Sarmiento remains one of the most striking features of the literature on

Argentina, both for the criticism it has provoked and for its captivating distinction between "civilized" and "barbaric" forces in the making of the Argentine state. Federales and Unitarios ended up incarnating these dichotomous forces. Unitarios, one can argue, adopted a modernizing standpoint and sought to re-create Argentina on the basis of European models. In contrast, the Federales, particularly the version represented by Rosas and his coalition, attempted to shape the institutions of the newly created republic to the image of Spanish Catholicism and paternalism, mixed with caudillism and populism. Despite some disagreements, the Rosas administrations definitely fall on the "barbaric" side of Sarmiento's equation.[51]

Sarmiento was a modernizer, but not necessarily a liberal democrat. Other founding fathers, however, were more liberal. Their writings and thinking have captivated many authors who, from Ricardo Rojas in 1922 to Nicholas Shumway in the 1990s, believe that the "creation" of Argentina owes much to the leading role played by a distinguished and praised group of intellectuals. Crucial debates among them regarding the type of state that was to be built seem to have shaped the polity.[52] To this, others have added the uniqueness of Argentine liberalism. This made the Buenos Aires "experience" both "original" and "superior" in the framework of Spanish America.[53]

Similar to literature on the United States that focuses on the liberalism of the founders, these arguments point to the strength of the Argentine founders' liberal ideas in the 1810 junta and the following triumvirate, in the 1814 Congress,[54] and in the May Revolution.[55] Hilda Sábato points out that the changes underway in the province of Buenos Aires in this early period were quite advanced, not only within the context of Latin America but in comparison to North America and Europe, where the process of enfranchisement took place gradually. She contends that if we add that elections for the Argentine Sala de Representantes (House of Representatives) were direct, "we have a unique case in all of Latin America" (1991:6). Perhaps the strongest claim of exceptionalism in terms of nation building comes from Halperín Donghi (1980:xii), who writes that the "exceptionality of Argentina" is that only there did a "common and frustrated aspiration in the rest of Latin America" materialize. The "progress" of Argentina "incarnated" the writings of the founding fathers, Argentines "whose only political weapon was their clairvoyance."

Beyond the early period of state making, however, the influence of this liberalism becomes somewhat difficult to assess. A key question that remains to be fully answered involves the dissonance (as Halperín Donghi himself acknowledges) between the original project(s) and the actual process of institution building that Argentina experienced.[56] In fact, the reversal of democracy in Argentina poses an important problem to this approach, for contrary to what the founding fathers seemed to have intended, the country had to wait until the so-called Radical era under Hipólito Yrigoyen (1916–1930) for the only extended period of party competition in the nation's history. And after that, military intervention resumed.

Perhaps one could solve this problem from the same history-of-ideas standpoint by changing the focus to the strong conservative and reactionary thinking that paralleled nation building. Given the outcome of the 1880s, this seems safer. Deep-rooted antiliberal thinking,[57] well into the twentieth century, would explain the failure to bring the May Revolution to full completion. Moreover, some have claimed that antiliberal ideology forged back in the colonial era shaped all twentieth-century politics.[58] For example, Shumway (1991:40) connects the "Dirty War" waged by the military government of 1976 to 1983 to the founder Mariano Moreno's ideology. Shumway also maintains that Bartolomé Mitre and Sarmiento have surfaced in the conservative views and elitism lurking behind the military's antipopulist policies and its vision of the populace as barbaric.

This explanation, however, faces a simple but important criticism from within the same approach: one cannot actually be sure that these more recent military leaders acted on Moreno's ideas or Mitre's rejection of populism when they argued for an elitist political system. It is at least as probable that they acted on the training they received in the military academy or were expressing a new ideological subculture that happened to resemble Moreno's, Mitre's, or Sarmiento's. Perhaps more important, this explanation, as any other, also needs to account for the unintended consequences of state making.

4.2. War Making and State Making

Table 4.1 indicates the character of the wars of independence, the civil wars that followed, and the international conflicts that shaped the

Table 4.1. International and Domestic Conflict in Argentina, 1810–1880

WARS OF INDEPENDENCE

1810	May Revolution. Military expedition against Paraguay.
1810–1820	Friction between Federalists and Unitarists, and wars with Spain.
1811–1813	War against Artigas and the Liga Federal.
1812–1813	Final liberation of Tucumán from the Spaniards and the second expedition to Upper Peru led by Belgrano, who tries (and fails) again to take Potosi and Upper Peru.
1814	Intensification of the war with Spain.
1817	War on Chile. San Martín crosses the Andes with an army of 5,000 to liberate Chile from Spain, supported financially and logistically by Buenos Aires under Juan Martín de Pueyrredón, appointed "director of Congress" after the 1816 declaration of independence.

CIVIL WARS BEFORE ROSAS

1819–1820	Conquest of Buenos Aires by Federalist caudillos Ramírez and López, and defeat of the central Unitarist government at the field of Cepeda.
1821	Rivalry between provincial caudillos Ramírez and López. Ramírez begins a campaign similar to Artigas's and is defeated, captured, and killed. López loses military power, and Buenos Aires imposes Rodríguez as new president.
1825	Blockade of Buenos Aires by Brazilian forces.
1827	Four provinces (Córdoba, La Rioja, Catamarca, and Santiago del Estero) form a military alliance led by Bustos, Juan "Facundo" Quiroga and Ibarra, to resist the constitution.
1828	General Juan Lavalle, returning from the war against Uruguay, deposes Dorrego by military coup.
1829	General José María Paz, returning from the war against Uruguay, takes Córdoba under his control, defeats Quiroga in 1830, and establishes League of the Interior.
1829	Rural militias under the command of Juan Manuel de Rosas defeat Lavalle.

WARS DURING THE ROSAS PERIOD

1838–1840	French blockade of the city of Buenos Aires.
1839	Uruguay declares war on Rosas.
1839–1841	Juan Lavalle invades Entre Ríos from Montevideo, and Bolivians invade Argentina from the northwest. Rosas's forces defeat both.
1839–1841	As a result of French blockade, cattle raisers revolt south of Buenos Aires, in Chascomus. The revolt is put down by an army led by Rosas's brother.
1845–1848	Military confrontations between Rosas, France, and Britain over control of trade routes in the Paraná River, in which Rosas prevails.

(continued)

(*Table 4.1. continued*)

1851–1852	Battle of Caseros. Urquiza, Rosas's provincial military commander, allies with Uruguay and Brazil against Rosas. With an army of 28,000, he takes Buenos Aires.
	CIVIL WARS AFTER THE ROSAS PERIOD
1859	War in Cepeda. Confederation led by Urquiza invades Buenos Aires.
1860–1861	Small revolts in support of Bartolomé Mitre.
1861	Battle of Pavón. Mitre defeats Uzquiza's gaucho calvary.
1863	Caudillo revolt in La Rioja led by Vicente Peñaloza, "El Chaco."
1865–1870	Paraguayan War.
1866	Revolt by Felipe Varela, successor of "El Chacho" Peñaloza in La Rioja.
1867	Taboada brothers from the province of Santiago del Estero (in alliance with Mitre and his supporters) defeat Felipe Varela.
1874	Mitre (Unitarist) rises up against president Nicholás Avellaneda but is defeated by a coalition led by Avellaneda in Buenos Aires that includes Domingo Faustino Sarmiento, governor of Entre Ríos. Mitre's military forces under General Aguerrondo are defeated by Julio A. Roca in Mendoza.
1880	Carlos Tejedor revolts against President Roca in Buenos Aires but is quickly defeated.

Argentine state. Note the high frequency of conflict and the types of war that characterized the first years of state formation. As Buenos Aires sought to retain the territories of the old viceroyalty, the wars took an urban-led character, which characterized Argentine conflicts from the beginning. This contributed to the creation of an urban political elite that did not depend much on rural caudillos for its survival. As Lynch (1992:84) observes, in Buenos Aires, the "war against Spain did not create caudillos. The war leaders were civilian politicians aided . . . by professional soldiers, and the war was fought on distant frontiers. In the process, they happened to produce caudillos in the interior, but not in Buenos Aires itself." So despite some loss of territory, the province of Buenos Aires managed to retain a large domain.

In table 4.1, one can see the importance of the Rosas administrations in state building. During his tenure, the frequency of civil war decreased, and the governor was able to unify the province of Buenos Aires against its European and regional enemies. This was a first important step toward power centralization, by which provincial caudillos were absorbed or co-opted into the central government. Table 4.1 also shows that unlike Uruguay, Argentina avoided serious invasions, and the province of Buenos Aires, in particular, survived almost intact despite foreign blockades. Progress owed much to the relative "peace in the countryside" enjoyed by the province.[59] Further and faster power centralization, as table 4.1 shows, was linked to a greater number of wars and a different type of conflict. From 1816 to the 1880s, excluding José de San Martín's campaign against Chile, Argentina went through twenty-four wars, civil and international. Most of these involved larger numbers of soldiers and combatants than the civil wars in Colombia and Uruguay. Despite the comparatively larger geographic size of Argentina, the state penetrated its territory more rapidly and effectively. After the wars of independence, which took the form of military expeditions to distant frontiers under the command of patriot generals (see table 4.2), the army became a major component of the ruling coalition.

Rock (1996a:12) tells us that battalions reinforced the power of the so-called justices of the peace in the hinterland and converted them into representatives of the central government. Despite Benito Diaz's (1967) study that shows the inefficiencies in the *organización de la justicia de campaña* (countryside organization of justice), one cannot help being struck by serious differences from Uruguay and Colombia, or from Venezuela. From the onset of state formation, at least in the province of Buenos Aires, the governor's influence reached into rural small towns,[60] establishing a system in which state makers and justices depended on and supported one another. A very similar system that also relied on justices of the peace existed in Uruguay and Colombia but proved much less effective, since it relied too greatly on the ill-equipped local police rather than the army.

The civil wars displayed in table 4.1 show the fierce reaction of the other provinces against the advances of Buenos Aires. At different times, these thirteen provinces organized large militias, with both the Littoral and the Interior building up forces that defeated the central army (see tables 4.1 and 4.2). During the early 1820s, for example, the provinces of Santa Fe and Entre Ríos were able to put together a cavalry of sixteen hundred men to invade Buenos Aires,[61] and finally caudillos Estanislao López of Santa Fe and Francisco "Pancho" Ramírez of Entre Ríos briefly took Buenos Aires (see table 4.1). It was at that time that Buenos Aires called to the rescue the southern land-

Table 4.2. Military Campaigns and Conflict in Argentina from
Independence to State Consolidation, 1810–1880

1810	First expedition to Alto Peru.
1811	Second expedition to Alto Peru.
1810–1811	Military expedition to Paraguay.
1811	Military expedition to Uruguay (first phase).
1812–1813	Expedition to Uruguay (second phase).
1811–1814	Expedition to Uruguay (third phase).
1812	Spanish invasion from the north (first phase).
1813	Spanish invasion from the north (second phase).
1813	Second expedition to Alto Peru.
1814–1815	Third expedition to Alto Peru.
1816–1817	Second Spanish invasion from the north.
1814–1815	Expeditions against Artigas in Uruguayan territory.
1816–1819	Expeditions against Artigas in Argentine territory.
1814–1817	Expedition to Chile (first phase).
1817–1818	Expedition to Chile (second phase).
1820	Campaigns against the caudillos in the Littoral.
1821	The central army confronts caudillos in the province of Buenos Aires and in Cuyo.
1820–1822	First expedition to Lima, and third, fourth, fifth, and sixth phases of the expedition to liberate Peru.
1823–1824	Expedition to Colombia as part of the Peruvian campaign.
1825–1826	Expedition against the Brazilian empire (first phase in Uruguayan territory).
1827–1829	Expedition against the Brazilian empire (second and third phases in Rio Grande do Sul).
1828–1829	General Lavalle's campaign against the Confederation.
1829–1830	General Paz's campaign against the Confederation.
1837–1838	War against the alliance of Peru and Bolivia.
1838–1847	Unitarios' campaign against Rosas (General Paz in Entre Ríos and Corrientes; General Oribe against President Rivera in Uruguay; General Lavalle in Buenos Aires and Santa Fe; General Paz against General Urquiza; General Madariaga against Eugenio Garzon).
1845–1849	Defense of Buenos Aires against the British and the French.
1847	Campaign of General Urquiza against General Madariaga.
1851–1852	Battle of Caseros.
1859	Battle of Cepeda.
1861	Battle of Pavón.
1865–1870	Paraguayan War.
1870–1873	Expedition against López Jordan in Entre Ríos.
1874	Expedition against Mitre.
1880	Repression of the Tejedor's rebellion in Buenos Aires.

Source: Colegio Militar de la Nación 1942:i–iv.
Note: Table includes only military campaigns led by the central army and conflict in which the army played a central role.

owners who feared the loss of their prosperous estancias. One of them was Juan Manuel de Rosas, and the Unitarios of Buenos Aires prevailed. Their opposition, however, did not really oppose unification. The issue was *control* over that union.

Unlike in Colombia, most Federales showed as much eagerness to centralize power as the Unitarios. Victories on both sides strengthened the union of army and state and the role of the central government. After Rosas, centralization continued under leaders from both sides. In 1852 the dissident general Justo José de Urquiza finally defeated Rosas (in the battle of Caseros), and in 1859 Buenos Aires was invaded by Federales after Urquiza won at Cepeda. The Federales then continued the process of power centralization started by Rosas. Shortly afterward, in 1861, the Unitarios and dissident Federales under the command of General Bartolomé Mitre defeated Urquiza in the battle of Pavón.[62] Mitre then subdued the other provinces, establishing a Unitarist state (see table 4.1) that also was centralizing.[63] With the help of the Paraguayan War, which facilitated the further expansion of the army, Mitre was able to dominate militarily the remnants of provincial self-rule.[64] From that point on, state expansion found very little resistance.

War led to a phase of negotiation and incorporation that, in a sense, meant a gain for the thirteen provinces outside Buenos Aires. The province of Buenos Aires ultimately lost its monopoly over its maritime trade in the election of 1874, when provincial interests won control of the legislature and made Buenos Aires the capital of the Argentine state. The Unitarios contested the electoral results and launched a revolt that left approximately three thousand dead, but an accord that included the provinces was finally reached. Although Buenos Aires militarily defeated the other thirteen provinces, Botana (1979:141–47) describes how the regime that emerged in the 1880s included an important coalition of political and military forces from the conquered territories.

What role did political parties play in this coalition? Comparatively speaking, a minor one. During the early years of independence, and certainly by the 1820s when the struggle against the royalists ended, parties were a definite presence in the Argentine political landscape. Indeed, one can argue that the Unitarios (later called the Liberals) and the Federales represented the emerging political parties. However, in contrast to Uruguay and Colombia, party competition did not dominate state making. In the 1880s, one party (the reorganized Partido Autonomista Nacional [PAN] under Nicholás Avellaneda and later Julio A. Roca) dominated the political system, galvanizing the alliance of Buenos Aires and provincial interests.[65] At the time of the party's foundation (1868), and under the influence of Valentín Alsina and Domingo Faustino Sarmiento, the Autonomistas based in Buenos Aires rejected a coalition with the provinces because they saw it as a costly enterprise that would drain the wealth of Buenos Aires. In the 1880s, however, both provincial and Buenos Aires interests joined the PAN, establishing what has been called the federalization of Buenos Aires. The PAN chose Avellaneda, a native of the remote Tucumán province, as president.[66] The resulting agreement was reflected in the composition of the Senate; in 1902, a commentary observed that "it is enough to have reached governorship in the provinces to secure an appointment in the Senate; and if you are a Senator you can run successfully for provincial governor. . . . It is a game . . . a simple change in seats."[67]

Botana (1979:110) observes that the Senate welcomed provincial governors and also that the Senate, conceived as a conservative institution, embodied the overall consensus of the political and economic elites. Indeed, most former presidents formed part of the Senate. Under this system, provincial governors represented by the PAN were able to strengthen their power in the localities and acquired more influence than their counterparts in the other two cases. Governors influenced the provincial juntas through the electors and exercised great leverage in the nomination of presidential candidates.

The PAN's emergence spoke of the weak level of institutionalization in party politics, for the PAN actually represented an alternative to party competition. A powerful reason for this outcome was that the wars of state making had not been fought by parties—and the few parties that did emerge featured weak or nonexistent armed wings. Those who rose against Buenos Aires did so not through revolucióries de partido but through armies with regional (rather than partisan) identification. Although parties organized on the basis of patronage and electoral campaigns, they developed as loose organizations—similar to movements. In the provinces, they competed for public posts through elections and acted as pressure groups, but at the national level, and even at the provincial level, they did not last long. Often they merged with other groups after an election or two. In part because they were relegated to a secondary role as state makers, parties eroded and proliferated into multiple, overlapping organizations with reduced mobilization capacity, particularly among the lower classes.

4.3. Parties and State Makers in the Province of Buenos Aires

Why Not a Party System? Theses on Argentine Parties

A party system requires competitive and regular elections, the existence of at least one party in opposition, and agreements on quotas of representation in Congress. Argentina ranked low in the first two criteria and achieved the third only under the PAN at the end of the century. Although the scope of popular political participation can be broader in a situation where a party system has not yet been established,[68] a party system usually lessens the chances of military intervention and encourages competitive politics. In Uruguay and Colombia, each party received no less than 40 percent and, for most of the twentieth century, no more than 60 percent of the total seats. Other types of party systems also exist,[69] but Argentina does not fit any of them.

Weak party activity characterized even the most democratic Argentine regime, that of Yrigoyen (1916–1922, 1928–1930). Tellingly, he and other founders of the Unión Cívica Radical characterized their party not as a competitive political force but as representing "the nation" itself.[70] In Uruguay and in Colombia, the prevailing patterns of armed struggle meant that divided power remained an accepted notion; in Argentina, party competition was perceived as a sign of weakness.

During the process of state formation, parties found it difficult to compete for public posts even in provinces that experienced more party activity. At times, elections featured only one party; at others, so few voters cast ballots that elections were not meaningful or even symbolic. Elected political authorities rarely represented citizens' preferences. As late as 1878, the British consul in Rosario reported that in that province (we can assume this was true elsewhere), the gubernatorial election took place without incident, mainly "because only one party voted."[71] Rock (1996b:40) found that as late as 1869 in some small towns, only "three persons voted, one of whom was the justice . . . [of the Peace]." To be sure, scholars have long noted voter apathy as a salient feature of Argentine politics.[72] Although most males had the franchise by midcentury, President Sarmiento still argued in the 1880s that a president in Argentina could do "and will do what he wants because this is a republic without citizens."[73] Germani (1955:225) points out that as late as 1910, only 20 percent of the native male population voted; and if one counts immigrants, the figure drops to about 9 percent. The point is telling, since nearly the whole population was enfranchised.

Many foreigners refused to participate in politics. While political parties and pressure groups became more efficiently organized as a result of the modernization process, the number of foreigners also increased, making recruitment difficult among a fast-growing sector of the population. By 1869, foreigners in Buenos Aires represented 47 percent of the population, and in urban centers with more than 100,000 inhabitants, 9 percent. By 1895, half of the population in the capital city was foreign-born, and in centers with more than 100,000 residents, 34 percent was. By 1914, Germani (1971:271) notes that the percentages were 49 and 35 respectively. Could this explain the low profile of political parties? Although it is a critical variable, we must remember that although foreigners also constituted a large part of the Uruguayan population, parties there were much more successful at recruitment—especially in Montevideo.

A different pattern of conflict provides a more important explanation for party development than the foreign component of constituencies. In Argentina, for the most part, the core of party organization remained urban based,[74] with rural constituencies in the minority, or participating only slightly in party activity and maintenance. One can conclude the existence of a low level of rural mobilization through parties from most work on Argentina's rural politics.[75] Rather than parties, the compulsory draft and the army became a major force of rural recruitment—as Ricardo D. Salvatore (1992:19) writes, the "activity that snatched more labor power." Although the Duvergerian model hardly applies to party formation in Uruguay or Colombia, it goes a long way toward explaining party development in Argentina.

Conflict in Argentina took the form of the provinces' struggles to maintain self-rule and Buenos Aires' determination to achieve hegemony. Cleavages started with the struggle between the revolutionary Primer Triunvirato (First Triumvirate) and the Conservative junta in 1811, which divided Unitarios and Federales.[76] During the first (1810–1852) and second (1852–1880) phases of state formation, these divisions remained strong but did not result in regular party competition. Modern parties did not emerge in other regions of Latin America either, but in the 1830s and 1840s, parties elsewhere developed definite profiles and became major state makers. Indeed, Karen Remmer's (1984:25) comparison of party organization in Argentina and Chile during the later part of the century concludes that the existence of political groups rather than parties in Argentina "owed little to the general principles of diffuse partisan feeling." Most of the political groupings that occurred in the first phase of state formation did not survive the second phase, and although the issue of federalism remained divisive, even the labels of "Federale" and "Unitario" after the Rosas era came to mean different things. By the late 1870s, self-rule as a motivation for party activity had declined steadily as a result of the aggressive power centralization that Buenos Aires' military strength allowed it to impose on the dissident provinces.

The literature disagrees on the characteristics, composition, and cleavages of the Federales and Unitarios. Gabriel del Mazo (1971:xi), introducing Leandro Alem's (1933) main opus on the issue of *autonomismo* versus *centralismo,* follows Alem's portrayal of the centralists (Unitarios) as a powerful (and evil) organization formed by "eminent men" able to bring about political change and control the state during the first phase of state formation in the abortive constitution of 1819. The Autonomists are also described as strong, both in the aftermath of the May Revolution and in the Assembly of 1813, perhaps the most significant event in state building in the pre-Rosas period. Shumway (1991:113–14) agrees in a way, based on the telling testimony of a contemporary, General Tómas de Iriarte. Shumway quotes Iriarte's argument that the Unitarios were considered aristocratic, whereas the Federales represented a more popular tendency. In an argument reminiscent of Weberian views on party formation, Halperín Donghi (1975:345) stresses ideology and disagreements about the role of the

state in society and the design of institutions: the Unitarios were believed "by gross oversimplification" to inherit the "novel" political
experience represented by the revolution and the regimes of the 1820s.
Meanwhile the Federales, having given Rosas the title of "Restorer
of the Laws," somewhat attempted to bring back the colonial institutional design.

What we do know is that party subcultures and differences in class
and ethnicity between Federales and Unitarios, however, became more
diffused as the process of state formation advanced; the distinctions
between old and new elites weakened, as did ideological differences.
Rather than class origins, the insightful Miron Burgin (1946) stresses
differences in strategies of development. He writes that the Unitarios
favored modernization and development and perceived the road to
progress in the strengthening of a central authority and the sacrifice
of provincial autonomy. They believed that commerce, not agriculture,
provided the engine of economic development. Burgin (1946:80) reports that the Federales, although they did not question the need for
central planning, stood for the "widest economic, fiscal, and political
autonomy" of the provinces. In the final analysis, Burgin adopts a
familiar position: Unitarios and Federales reproduced the familiar free
trade–protection cleavage.

Divisions over the tariff, however, were not so sharp, and free traders
became a majority within both groups as state making advanced.[77] In
addition, Burgin himself discusses complexities of party politics that
cannot be captured by the free trade–protection split. He leaves out
much of what this chapter emphasizes; that is, the effects of conflict and
the growth of the military and the state on the emerging parties. This is
reflected in his final argument, which conveys some important disunity
in both parties over the tariff. For example, he points out that opposition
to the Unitarios' program was especially strong in rural districts among
cattle breeders and farmers.[78] We can assume, then, that estancieros
identified with those Federales who did not have a coherent economic
program but opposed the Unitarios and, as Burgin (1946:101) notes,
left "the solution of economic problems to the Constituent Congress."
But Burgin himself concluded that the Federales looked more like several parties than one, and that different economic interests clashed
within the group itself. This would undoubtedly tend to undermine the

cohesiveness of the party precisely on the issue of protection, with the same holding true for the Unitarios. Shifting market opportunities divided the Unitarios, and not all sectors of the Unitarios' commercial elite were internationally oriented and free traders. Rather, many depended on trade with the provinces, so that the merchants' preferences on the issue of the tariff varied according to their engagement in the domestic market. Burgin (1946:81) himself suggests that neither Federales nor Unitarios elaborated a consistent body of economic doctrine.

Lynch (1993:7) offers a different argument but stresses the importance of the tariff as much as Burgin. Lynch contends that after the wars of independence, the provinces (particularly the Littoral, Santa Fe, Entre Ríos, and Corrientes) found themselves in a poor economic position and at the same time discovered that Buenos Aires dominated trade, monopolized custom duties, and attacked protection. Thus a strong protectionist movement led by the provinces—with Corrientes heading the effort—gained momentum and strengthened the Federales. Both Burgin's and Lynch's arguments seem to concentrate more on explaining party formation than on explaining party decline or the absence of lasting agreements between competing parties. The advantage of stressing the tariff is that it seems to explain why competition between Federales and Unitarios eroded during the 1870s, just when elites were favoring free trade. Jorge Sábato (1988:39) has shown that the tariff issue eroded as the agricultural boom hit Argentina.[79] The disadvantage is that the tariff does not account for the lack of a party system, or even party weakness during the period that the tariff was still a hot issue.

Speaking comparatively, my suggestion is that wars affected when and how free trade and protectionist interests lobbied, the success they had, and the kind of institutions they forged.[80] In the three main cases in this book, free traders formed the stronger coalition, but for other reasons, they operated in different institutional frameworks that responded to different war patterns. In response to conflict and perceived levels of threat, very much like protectionists in all the main cases, free traders demanded a ruthless use of state power to enforce property rights, especially in the countryside. In Argentina, the agricultural boom alone did not dissolve the parties; rather, it accentuated a tendency of weak party competition that was already in the making during the first phase of state formation.

*Parties and the Rural Poor in the First Phase
of State Formation*

During the first phase of state formation, from the May Revolution to Rosas, organized parties did not exist in Argentina, including in the province of Buenos Aires. One cannot talk about party organization and competition until the constitution of 1853, or more precisely, the electoral law of 1857.[81] Parties did not take the lead in the wars of independence, and their armed wings were no match for the professional army; in light of the examples of Uruguay and Colombia, one can argue that this weakened party organizing. Neither Federales nor Unitarios represented homogeneous blocs; nor were their organizations necessarily designed for electoral competition. There were frequent attempts to create *listas unicas,* a system with a fixed ballot that left no option for alternative candidates.[82] Candidates running for office in the province of Buenos Aires and in the hinterlands did not necessarily champion the Unitarist or Federalist cause. Rather, the *listas* (ballots) on which they ran listed candidates in terms of their local social influence, which meant that it was common to find the same candidates running on both sides.[83] So while listas proliferated, they proposed the same names. In fact, electoral competition during the first decade after the revolution reveals a regime of notables who rotated in public posts,[84] rather than a real competitive system. Before Rosas's ascension to power, one can argue that no more than one hundred notables were, in fact, elected to the two most important government bodies, the Sala de Representantes and the Poder Ejecutivo (Executive Office).[85]

Some incorporation of the lower classes through protoparties during this first phase did of course take place. Halperín Donghi (1975:361) tells us that by the 1823 election, the Ministerial list, then victorious, owed its triumph in part to the "honorable class of craftsmen" who supported the party. Yet we can assume that incorporation remained minimal. Rock (1996a:30) reports that registered voters in the city usually "numbered less than 200 men in each parish, or around 2,000 in all 11 parishes." The number of actual voters depended on the mobilization of army battalions on election day, and thus on government sponsorship and control of the electoral process. For instance, in 1824 the number of voters dropped to 1,700, but when the next year the government mobilized the army to vote for the Ministerial party, the number rose to more than 3,000.[86]

Army intervention in politics offers a very good explanation for voter apathy. In a prologue to Enrique Barba's 1974 book on Unitarios and Federales, Julio Godio notes that before the Rosas period, the two alternated in power, mainly through urban uprisings and coups. These coups were staged by the central militia, which shifted alliances from one party to the other. When Unitario Rivadavia became president of the United Provinces of the River Plate (1826–1827), his reforms triggered a reaction from the Federales, who rejected the "Europeanization" of Buenos Aires promoted by the Rivadavians, the extension of the franchise, and the centralization of power in Buenos Aires. Therefore, in 1828, federal battalions deposed Rivadavia and named Manuel Dorrego the governor of the province. Later, Dorrego was assassinated. Shumway (1991:116) states that the Unitarios were persuaded that the assassination of a few leaders would bring about the definite destruction of the Federales and saw no possible accommodation with them. Although the Unitarios seemed to gain a firmer grip on the government under General Lavalle, he proved unable to forge a supportive coalition and was shortly deposed. Military coups, rather than revolucións de partido, created what Andres M. Carretero (1971a) calls "institutional anarchy."

This pattern of urban insurrection was different from the Uruguayan and Colombian patterns. It involved military figures returning from distant wars of independence, who continued to undermine the state and created alarm in the ruling groups.[87] Another pattern emerged with Rosas, a leader who represented the best of *caudillismo* and rural interests in Buenos Aires, and who did not have a distinguished service in foreign frontiers. Although he did not come to power through open elections, his tenure as governor of the province of Buenos Aires was the longest, lasting from 1829 to 1852 (minus a short voluntary retirement from 1832 to 1835).

In the provinces, party activity and elections were as problematic. Basically uncontested elections chose the "eleven representatives from the rural areas" who, out of a legislature of twenty-three, ruled the campaña. Majority rule seemed to carry little weight as well. In 1815 in Tucumán, one precinct agreed to alter the electoral results because "the quality of the voters widely differed."[88] José Carlos Chiaramonte and Marcela Ternavasio (1995:33–34) note that voters were preponderantly from the middle sectors, and the irregularities in the electoral process meant that elections often did not even take place, either because "no one was present to set up the voting tables" or because the people were too lazy.

Universal male suffrage represented no major threat to elites who could mobilize the army to vote on their behalf.[89] As in Uruguay or Colombia, complaints about corrupt electoral practices abounded, but in contrast to these other two countries, the opposition party in Argentina had little ability to contest an election on the battlefield. Still, in 1864, during the second phase of state formation, it was clear that "he who has the power, takes over the precinct, and wins the election."[90] Elections in all three cases spoke of a ritual associated with the republican character of the new regimes, tangible proof that monarchy was over, and the promise that a better future lay ahead. Yet in Argentina, electoral activity suffered more serious discontinuities than in the other two cases.

Until the 1850s, the scarce electoral activity in the province of Buenos Aires eroded further under the Rosas administrations, deviating Argentina onto a different path of state building. The governor did not eliminate or modify the early extension of the franchise but abolished competitive elections and substituted a system of *unanimidad* (unanimity).[91] The implementation of the lista unica went hand in hand with increasing power centralization. The Unitarios basically disappeared from the political scene, and some of the divisions that one usually associates with party competition emerged instead within the Federales. The Federales Doctrinarios defended competitive politics, and the Federales Netos supported Rosas. This emerging cleavage, however, failed to provide a solid enough foundation for party building in a society that had experienced little party competition. We should also note that just as the enfranchisement law was not entirely Rivadavia's creation, so the lista unica was not completely Rosas's. It had a long-standing precedent in most of the provinces and in prior agreements between Rosas and Lavalle (the Pacto de Canuelas), which reestablished elections to encourage peace but also imposed the so-called *lista unificadora*.[92]

By the mid-1830s, the preeminence of the executive was secured, and the system succeeded at something that both Uruguay and Colombia failed to do: it centralized power, reduced party competition, and gained control of the militias. By the 1838 elections, the governor and his advisers were in charge of elaborating the listas for the representatives of the city of Buenos Aires, listas that were chosen almost unanimously in that election and in the following ones. These listas were then elaborated by Buenos Aires and imposed in the provinces. This electoral system succeeded at creating a stable political elite. Members were more often than not reelected as soon as they finished their terms, and the system, similar in many ways to the Orden Conservador of the 1880s, created a privileged group of almost permanent legislators.[93] Ternavasio (1996:20) writes that Rosas himself made up the *listas electorales* and supervised the process of printing and distribution. Thus while the system that Rivadavia established could have encouraged competition among members of the elite and thus might have promoted party organization, Rosas did just the opposite.

The legacy of this polity did not die with Rosas. After his fall, the Liberals, heirs of the Unitarios, became the major political force and absorbed some of the old Federales through alliance and military defeat. Similar to Rosas, the Liberals supported a stronger state, now within the framework of a federal system embracing the whole nation. Despite the Liberal resurgence, one crucial factor remained absent in the polity that emerged after Rosas: a strong opposition party and organized party competition.

Parties and Wars during the Second Phase
of State Formation

Urquiza's defeat of Rosas at the battle of Caseros in 1852 established the Argentine Confederation, which sought to impose an equitable sharing of revenues among the provinces (see table 4.1). Urquiza, in turn, was deposed by the *mitristas,* followers of General Bartolomé Mitre, who served as the first president of Argentina (1862–1868). In what Ricardo H. Levene (1963:13) calls this "stormy time," Mitre—regarded in most of the literature as the ultimate state maker—imposed unity, placing Buenos Aires at the center of political and economic power. During the 1860s, Mitre's party, the National Liberals, argued that Buenos Aires would benefit from giving up its political independence to form a union with the other provinces.[94] The Autonomistas argued that the wealthiest of all provinces had no reason to join the union, a union they believed would result in a constant drain of resources for Buenos Aires. Within Buenos Aires, Mitre was opposed by Autonomista Adolfo Alsina, also a porteño; in the provinces, he was resisted first by Vicente Peñaloza ("El Chaco"), caudillo of La Rioja, and later by Peñaloza's lieutenant, Felipe Varela. Rock (1996a:11–25) argues that these parties followed the major guidelines associated with the Federales and Unitarios in the years after independence, and that they had a strong network in the provinces.[95] Nonetheless, neither resistance in La Rioja nor the Autonomistas created parties. And the parties did not equal the power of the central army.

In the mid-1870s, remnants of Rosas's noncompetitive system were strong. At a time when modern parties competing for office were the norm in Europe and other parts of Latin America, the state in Argentina again took an active role in organizing a unifying party, the League of Governors. This was a coalition of already elected governors. The League played a crucial role in the elections of 1874 and 1880. For the most part, it and other similar movements remained exactly what they were called, leagues or movements. The erosion of one party (the Federales) and the transfer of political competition to factions of the surviving party (the Liberals) does not invariably mean that party activity ceases. A similar process occurred in Uruguay and Colombia; in the latter, the Golgotas and Draconianos stemmed from the Liberal Party—a party that, unlike the Argentine Liberals, supported a looser version of federalism. Yet Remmer (1984:10) contends that in Argentina, splits within the Liberals did not ultimately develop into competitive organizations. Indeed, until the "cleansing of corruption" effected by the 1912 Sáenz Peña Law, elections meant little, and party alignments were weak.

In the regions, once resistance against the central power abated, political movements focused their energy on local issues and problems of representation in the federal government. The intense wars that characterized the period from 1860 to 1880 and the limited role parties played in them constrained the interaction among movements and the scope of their competition. Not until the 1890s did two organizations emerge that were comparable to modern political parties. One was the Unión Cívica. In 1890, Luis V. Sommi (1972) reports, this group rose in rebellion against the government and suffered a quick defeat. Afterward the movement divided in two factions. One of them was the Radicales, who rejected any kind of negotiation with the government they had failed to undermine. They formed the Radical Party and, as Rock (1975:75) notes, became the first group to demand an end to electoral fraud and adopt a strategy of "abstention." In 1896 a second modern party, the Socialist Party, emerged. The Socialistas organized on a more permanent basis, not just during elections. These two parties and other movements, however, remained unable to interact in the form of a party system. Again, as in the first phase of state making, a very important difference between Argentina and the other two main cases in this book was that the "armed wing" of the Argentine parties remained rather weak. Under Rosas, the context of party formation resembled, to an extent, the Paraguayan situation, where external threats to the state facilitated power centralization while weakening the parties. And the second phase of state formation more closely resembled the situation in Venezuela, where rural armies fought for control of the government while parties took a secondary role.

4.4. Civil-Military Relations:
The Rural Poor and the Military as Nation Builders

In comparison to Europe or Asia, most nineteenth-century military forces in the Americas were untrained, ill equipped, and amateur. Yet Salvatore (1992:3–8) argues that the Argentine rural poor became familiar with conscription from the onset of state formation. The army comprised a heterogeneous mix of small producers, gauchos, and "vagrants"; the unemployed, in particular, were a favorite target of forced recruitment. Resources were rather scarce. Limited rationing and long marches weakened and even killed recruits, and harsh, cruel conditions of discipline made desertion endemic.[96] Yet this army was still an army. The wars of independence were fought by groups that looked more like armies than anything else.[97] Unlike in Uruguay or Colombia, in Argentina the Buenos Aires government retained control of an army that, although weak in the eyes of European observers, developed into a more robust force that enabled the Argentine state makers to secure power centralization through coercion. Unlike the other cases, the character and development of the urban militia and the military in the revolutionary period in Argentina, so painstakingly documented by Halperín Donghi (1975, 1982, 1989a), started the process.

The Military in the First Phase of State Making: The Urban Militia

The 1807 British invasions and the wars that followed strengthened the Buenos Aires urban military force. Still under colonial authorities, the recruitment of "one thousand eight hundred officers" paid by the government in a society where commerce and administrative posts had traditionally provided the only means of social betterment meant a "revolutionary deed."[98] The urban militia played a major role in the 1810 May Revolution. The struggle was short and geographically did not directly involve the capital.[99] The struggle for independence did not hamper economic development in the city and its hinterland; if one looks at the activity of the port of Buenos Aires and the value of exports over imports, one can argue that during almost ten years of struggle, the economy of the province remained mildly prosperous.[100] Moreover, war generated employment and some profitable ventures and transformed the urban environment in a way that differed from the other cases. The struggle against the British in the city produced a "profoundly transformed military establishment" that would "push aside the last vestiges of the colonial political order in two nearly bloodless military confrontations."[101] Compared with its isolation during the colonial period, the army experienced a much more direct integration into state and society.

As Lyman L. Johnson (1994:38) put it, both Creole and peninsular members of the local elite "quickly moved to create a larger, better trained, more disciplined military establishment." Distinguished public figures, merchants, and small store owners served as volunteers. Intellectuals, Shumway (1991:47) observes, "justified the wars" according to "fresh mythologies of a new people and a new nation" and also participated in the military. The militarization of the urban environment triggered some concern, as the militia was described as a heterogeneous body operating under the command of "a group of adventurers, self-designated officers who were able to command the rabble of Buenos Aires."[102] These comments, however, only testify to the visible changes brought about by military growth. Johnson (1994:39) and Halperín Donghi[103] give impressive figures as to its magnitude. Between the first and second British invasions, more than 800 militiamen were activated, most of them from the working-class immigrant ranks and the Creole lower classes, increasing the paid military to about 4,000. Halperín Donghi (1982:83–89) studies how the military involvement of about 30 percent of the city's population affected its social fiber and its economy. He writes that during the period before the May Revolution, the budget devoted to wages to the soldiers surpassed the value of exports, with the exception of mining. Johnson (1994:40–43) argues that the expanded military budget resulted from the imposition of taxes on imports and exports in addition to voluntary contributions and shows that new taxes hurt the same urban elites who had supported the expansion of the military wage bill. After the invader was expelled, however, the military budget kept expanding, and the urban military continued to augment under a compulsory draft. Those who did not want to serve, or could afford not to, hired others to replace them.

One can argue that the urban militia came to represent a development associated with a new order. Both Creoles and Spaniards, for instance, sought leadership positions in the militia, making this military force different from the army created through the Bourbon reforms. It differed from the royal army not only in terms of class composition but also in terms of discipline and the degree of identification with the city and the revolutionary junta. It expressed the autonomous militarization of the city of Buenos Aires and marked a shift in the relationship between the state and the military. Halperín Donghi (1975:191) reports that the military was elevated as a "first pillar" of the state, and "military leaders enjoyed a popularity which few civilian leaders could rival." This affected the composition of the political elite. Those who desired power needed to court the militia; thus the defeat of some of the most radical members of the revolutionary junta who failed to gain its support, such as revolutionary lawyer Mariano Moreno.[104]

As the central military grew under Rosas and later during the second phase of state making, the urban militia merged with provincial battalions. Yet the urban officer corps only slowly gave way to officers coming from the regions.[105] Not surprisingly, unlike in Uruguay or Colombia, the political elites promoted a military culture, best expressed in the objectives of the 1811 junta: "Military virtues will be the path to distinctions, honors, and dignities. . . . All citizens will be born as soldiers and will receive from their infancy an education appropriate to their destiny. . . . In short, every citizen will look on . . . war as his natural condition."[106] These virtues continued to be encouraged under Rosas.[107]

"Permanent War," Rosas, the Rural Poor, and the Army

Rock (1987:119–20) describes the period from the fall of Rosas to the 1880s as one in which the Federales made a final bid against Buenos Aires, but he notes that "in the early 1860s they were overcome. Buenos Aires then led the way in consolidating the new national state, which by the 1880s had achieved complete supremacy."[108] My suggestion is that this supremacy was, to a great extent, made possible by the prior strengthening of the state and the military during the Rosas era.[109] In fact, Rosas's efforts at centralization had illustrious precedents. The May Revolution openly favored a strong state. In the National Assembly of Tucumán (1816), Belgrano put forward *una monarquia temperada*, a monarchical project favoring a king native to the Americas—probably a monarch of Inca descent rather than of European lineage—as a necessary alternative to chaos and instability, and as a prerequisite to obtaining European approval. San Martín also favored a monarchical solution to the problems of Argentina in particular, and of Latin America in general. The directory, which survived the Tucumán meeting, placed at its head the military hero Juan Martín de Pueyrredón, who lasted from 1816 to 1819 and proved to be as centralizing as a monarch.[110] A federal system granting self-rule to the provinces was out of the question during the Pueyrredón administration,[111] and in Buenos Aires, political activity remained tightly controlled.

Furthermore, the constitution of 1819 clearly strengthened the centralism and conservatism of the directory. It was this, among other things, that triggered the revolts of the legendary caudillos López in

Santa Fe and Ramírez in Entre Ríos. In 1819 they finally joined forces and defeated the centralist porteño forces at the battle of Cepeda (see table 4.1), imposing on Buenos Aires the treaty of San Nicolás. Yet their victory was brief. During the tenure of another military leader, Rodríguez, and later under the presidency of his chief minister, Rivadavia, the centralizing trend continued. In this light, one can argue that Rosas incarnated a trend already present in the revolutionary movement. One can perceive even Rivadavia as representing a liberal variety within a centralizing tradition, for as Aldolfo Saldias (1977:83) tells us, Rivadavia's government fostered centralization in the context of liberal democracy or "social revolution."

Tables 4.1 and 4.2 show that external aggression and a high level of perceived threat strongly marked the first period of state making, thus leading to militarization.[112] Rosas used wars against invaders and the expansionist ambitions of the elite of Buenos Aires to strengthen his power and acquire popularity, not only among the middle and lower strata of the population of Buenos Aires but also among legendary figures of the independence period. The 1826 war with Brazil favored power centralization within the province, since it contributed to the fall of Rivadavia and the rise of Rosas. Indeed, fear of Brazil and of domestic turmoil triggered the Assembly's 1829 decision to grant Rosas *facultades extraordinarias* (extraordinary faculties) for a period of five years.[113] To a great extent, prior conflicts also had similar effects. In 1811, 1812, and 1815, the Assembly had granted similar facultades to the executive, and in 1820, similar powers were bestowed on De Sarratea and Balcarce.[114] Likewise, governors in the provinces had also enjoyed similar prerogatives, such as Bustos in Córdoba, López in Santa Fe, and Ferre in Corrientes. In 1830 the same facultades were granted to General Paz in his role of supreme commander of the provinces of the Interior. In Rosas's case, however, the facultades were even more ample, and he ruled almost unchallenged as the grantor of social order.[115] At this time, European aggression (see tables 4.1 and 4.2) and regional conflict favored militarization, further centralization, and national unity.[116] Similar to the situation in Paraguay, Argentina under Rosas fought its enemies by militarizing society and strengthening border controls under the command of a recognizable officer corps that responded directly to the executive. Foreigners were not welcomed in either country, and in the case of Argentina, the regime basically re-established colonial immigration policies.

The campaigns against Rosas by the Unitarios from 1838 to 1847 are also included in table 4.2, although the forces under Rosas retained control. Table 4.2 makes apparent the high level of military activity during the first phase of state formation, particularly from 1810 to 1830. During the first years after the May Revolution, the revolutionaries were able to send expeditions against the realists and counter-revolutionaries in Córdona, Peru, Paraguay, and Uruguay. These expeditions stood as prior steps to more ambitious political and military objectives that included annexation and permanent military occupation of the involved territories.[117] In this first phase of state expansion, Buenos Aires also sent expeditions to contain Brazil and to dispute its territorial hegemony.

During these campaigns and afterward, intense recruitment in the countryside provided the bulk of the army.[118] Burgin (1946:111, 149) writes that when Rosas gained power, he already controlled an important rural militia, and during his government, the army grew into a rather organized body. Since the 1830s, the military wing of the Unitario Party had been almost totally annihilated, thus making it easier for Rosas to build the army under his tutelage. This army came from the loyal rural poor. We find that the participation of the rural poor in this first phase of state building was very different from in Uruguay or Colombia. While the governor did not attempt to create a party, his movement did achieve something that parties before and after him remained unable to accomplish: it secured constituencies among the rural population, at least in the province of Buenos Aires. Unitarios and Federales had campaigned among rural laborers, but unlike in the other cases, rifts among the Buenos Aires political elites and intellectual partisan circles dominated party organization. It was under the lista unica that the participation of the rural population rapidly increased, especially in the areas where the government made progress in confronting the Indians.

Saldias (1977:267) explains how the administration of the campaña became a priority for the government. The state was present in the creation of rural schools and new roads, and in the *reglamentos*, which regulated the attributes of the justices of the peace, in addition to other measures concerning rural justice. Even before Rosas gained office,

Lord Ponsonby reported that Rosas, the head of all the provincial militias, was also a "sort of idol among the country people."[119] Most evidence supports this impression.[120] Some of the incorporation of the rural poor was done by force, some by persuasion, and some through the intermediation of local business and craftsmen. Eduardo B. Astesano (1960:50–51) contends that labor control and army recruitment clearly remained top priorities for the government. The important point is that unlike in the other two cases, the state directly reached into the rural population without the mediation of political parties. Not surprisingly, under Rosas, the state promoted an increasing ruralization of political life.[121] Indeed, Lynch (1993:7) contends that Rosas's first government "was designed to primarily serve the cattle industry of Buenos Aires," a group that strongly defended free trade,[122] and that Rosas finally succeeded in attracting to his side.[123] The rural poor were also on Rosas's side, either through the patronage of loyal landholders or through a direct link with the Rosas movement.

At the same time, tighter control of the rural areas and the attempt to reduce rural mobility restricted the legendary gauchos' freedom and well-being. In a way almost reminiscent of South Africa under apartheid, and systems of labor control in conditions of labor scarcity in Eastern Europe under absolutism, the regime tried to tie labor to specific workplaces and secure a ready reservoir for the militia.[124] Therefore Rosas used the 1821 reforms (the extension of universal suffrage to all males) and what Chiaramonte and Ternavasio (1995:22) call established "electoral rituals" to incorporate the lower classes into a political system that banned competition and encouraged consensus.

Rosas represented, as Lynch (1992:88) argues, a "new elite, the estancieros," who increased their political weight and military power under his tenure. Waldo Ansaldi (1988:529–29) reports that in 1797, the Junta de Hacendados had managed to gain half of the seats in the Real Consulado (Royal Consulate), but landowners really acquired prominence over merchants after independence. During the 1820s they achieved a stronger position, but under Rosas they consolidated their grip on the state, a situation that distinguished Argentina from Uruguay and Colombia. Landowners found that their power increased substantially with the lista unica, in light of the regime's belief that the wealthiest were the most able to manage political affairs. The popularity of those with an education or a university degree declined. In the elections of 1823, the winning list was labeled the list of "proprietors," while the list that lost was identified with the "doctores."[125] Although many landowners resigned from public posts and others ruled in absentia, their social and political influence grew enormously.[126]

The regime, however, secured power through strong security measures and the establishment of a "state of terror" in which popular participation, according to many, was a farce.[127] The elimination of competing caudillos in the province, in addition to the weakening of caudillo activity in the Littoral and the rest of the thirteen provinces, marked a great contrast to Uruguay and Colombia. Minister of finance Manuel José García argued that by the 1820s, the caudillos "did not possess the talents or the means . . . [and] the purely personal authority of these chieftains is rapidly becoming a thing of the past."[128] With the defeat of the Northern League, Manuel Galvez (1949:129–48) describes how Rosas quickly established the predominance of Buenos Aires through the Pacto Federal (Federal Pact). This secured his influence in the Interior and would have made the dictator supreme in the whole country had it not been for the resistance of General José María Paz.[129] Unification meant accepting the premises of a centralizing federalism established in Buenos Aires.[130] The fluid commercial connection with the Littoral, the erosion of party rivalry, the consolidation of property rights, and the role of the army as protector of landed interests are features of state formation that emerged during the Rosas period and remained the critical building blocks of the following phases. Burgin (1946:153) states that army growth was facilitated by the scarce resistance of the provinces, which were in no condition to defy the state.

Therefore, Rosas became a pivotal state maker in a number of important senses. First, he institutionalized new political practices with the implantation of the lista unica. Second, although he did not create a set of totally new institutions, he considerably advanced state making by negotiating with provincial caudillos and keeping peace in the province of Buenos Aires. Third, and very importantly, during his administrations the rural poor in the hinterland of Buenos Aires were integrated into the state's sphere of influence.[131] While ranching interests had a firm grip on the regime, the state exercised some autonomy. For example, its 1835 decision to annex Indian territory was not a reaction to pressures from landowners; rather, it reflected the state's policy of rural incorporation. The "conquest" of Indian lands triggered the foundation of new pueblos, which were quickly integrated into the political system and greatly contributed to the creation of a popular culture in support of Rosas.[132]

The army expanded and reorganized. Lynch (1981:27) notes that already during the turbulent 1820s, before Rosas's tenure as governor, he had organized his peonage as a militia force ready to spring into action. Reminiscent of Paraguay under José Gaspár de Francia, the militia members under his direct command formed the Colorados del Monte, which began with five hundred men and became the first disciplined rural-based troops of the province.[133] As in the rest of Latin America, the militia was often deployed to serve political rather than military purposes or was called on as a domestic police force. However, unlike in Uruguay or Colombia, both the rural militia and the urban military remained fairly autonomous bodies. Halperín Donghi (1975:129) states that parties had a frail voice in the selection of officers, who were elected by the officer corps themselves.

The militia force intensively recruited among Indians, mestizos, and blacks as well.[134] Lynch (1981:54) reminds us that in 1833, Charles Darwin, stunned by the racial and class composition of Rosas's cavalry, described it as "a villainous, bandit-like army" that, in his opinion, was unprecedented. Conscription became an important mechanism of army growth and state formation. Despite the creation of the provincial police and difficulties in enforcing conscription, Salvatore (1992:38–39) argues persuasively that under Rosas the draft became a feared reality among gauchos and the lower rural strata, as well as the middle rural strata, including renters (somewhat similar to sharecroppers) who were dedicated to wool production and cattle raising. The Colorados del Monte, sponsored by landowners who wanted peace in the province, became more and more like a centralized army. It grew even further with the conquest of the so-called Indian frontier and the creation of special battalions and border patrols.

4.5. Conflict and the Army in the Second Phase of State Building

Oszlak (1985:25), in one of the best analyses of state formation in Argentina, has argued that Colombia presents a very similar case, but these two cases of state formation actually remained quite different. Army building and the type of wars fought in the two countries allowed Argentine state makers to centralize power at a much faster pace, although the Argentine territory was characterized—similar to Colombia—by strong local resistance. Oszlak (1985:50–52), who stresses economic factors and international market forces, nonetheless acknowledges that military actions during the 1860s fundamentally contributed to the construction of the nation; indeed, the consolidation of Buenos Aires elites after 1861 stemmed from a "military episode" that allowed them to "organize the state" and "nationalize" the Liberal revolution.[135]

Perhaps the best-known thesis about the formation of the state in Argentina in this second phase, particularly the period that starts after the battle of Pavón (see table 4.1), is that the economic disadvantage of the provinces vis-à-vis Buenos Aires, with its control of maritime trade and general wealth, explains the failure of alternative state projects.[136] What Rock (1987:131) calls the "economic revolution" that extended from the late 1850s to the end of the century featured a "trinity": foreign trade, immigration, and foreign investment. During the second half of the nineteenth century, the expansion of markets for beef and wool, plus the prosperous performance of agriculture, made it possible for the new, expanded state to modernize Argentina at a much faster pace.

My argument is that despite the apparent importance of these factors, a radical institutional break with the past did not take place. The most powerful heritage of the first phase was the prevailing notions of centralization and weak party competition. After the battle of Caseros, Oszlak (1985:51) points out, everyone was aware that "only the state had the power to construct the pillars of the new social order." Despite the federalization of the province of Buenos Aires in 1880 after Carlos Tejedor's failed revolt on behalf of the provincial government, the new state mirrored prior institutional and social arrangements that emerged in Buenos Aires during the first phase. True, the League of Governors represented a much more sophisticated system of centralized control, but it still functioned through patronage and coercion, discouraged political competition, and stimulated consensus. The provincial cliques sought representation in the state though their governors, but once in Congress, these governors highly depended on the president's support.

Modernization did not always foster power centralization. It did so in

Argentina and provided the backbone of the Orden Conservador because of a prior institutional history designed for low levels of political
competition. The ruling coalitions under Rosas and the Orden Conservador differed, of course, but one can argue that the differences are only
of degree, since a similar alliance supported both, and the "society of
the 1880 respected and worshipped the estanciero even more than in the
times of Rosas."[137] Although the mechanisms for the selection of the
political elite through the PAN were quite different from the lista unica of
Rosas, in the Orden Conservador, the national government could also—
as Rosas did through rougher means—name its own successors. Moreover, in a manner somewhat similar to the system used by Rosas to
appoint his loyal estancieros in the hinterland of Buenos Aires, the
Orden Conservador controlled the appointment of governors in the
provinces by patronage and clientele networks.[138] Reminiscent of
Rosas, the Orden Conservador functioned in the context of what could
be called a system of one-party rule, or better, one-movement rule. In
short, the regime of the 1880s, as in the first phase, was based on strong
clientele ties controlled by the state and consensus, along with exclu-
sionary policies and "weak parties in the opposition."[139]

This is not to say that *rosismo* and the second phase of state formation
were identical. After the battle of Caseros (see table 4.1), the reaction
against Rosas and his traditionally minded regime, coupled with the
now dominant liberal ideology in the ruling group, led to important
innovations. The government sought to attract foreign investment, dramatically reduced under Rosas, as new markets opened and the export
economy begged for deep reconstruction—from railroads, to industry,
to the elimination of the tight control of river navigation and the abolition of trade taxes among the provinces. The alliance of Buenos Aires
and the Littoral—favored by Rosas—had been broken, so that state
makers faced the daunting task of forging new alliances. Skilled labor
was scarce after the antiimmigration policy of Rosas, and despite the
expansion of the southern frontier under rosismo, vast and valuable
lands were still in the hands of the indigenous populations. Hence, *la
conquista del desierto* (the wilderness campaign). In a nutshell, Urquiza's
victory over Rosas meant the victory of state makers who did not follow
the regional approach taken by Rosas and his coalition.[140] Nonetheless,
the institutional design that was adopted resembled the administrations
of the "caudillo of caudillos." Indeed, in many ways, the wars of the sec-

ond phase of state formation helped extend to the whole country the institutional arrangements that had hitherto characterized Buenos Aires.

After Buenos Aires governor Mitre finally defeated Urquiza's alternate state project (the Argentine Confederation) at Pavón in 1861, Mitre followed a strategy of centralization and modernization that, overall, did not differ substantially from the establishment of the "proto State" under Rosas.[141] Mitre's Liberal regime and the first phase of state building shared a vertical character, mechanisms of control that relied on justices of the peace and military commanders responding to the central state, and an obsession with power centralization and limited political competition. To that, one can add the Mitre regime's clear awareness that the army should form an integral part of the ruling coalition, that the state should increase its capacity, that the ganadero sector was a key player in politics, and that the proliferation of parties and factions was a danger to be avoided. The goals were different, but the means similar. The modernizing side of Mitre's project included faith in progress, elimination of the gaucho, abolition of trade barriers, urbanization, immigration, and the improvement of international commerce. These daring goals blended gracefully with the centralizing structure inherited from the first phase.

The pattern of conflict in the second phase varied only slightly. Geographically, the province of Buenos Aires found itself more involved in armed struggle, although most wars were still fought outside the wealthy province. Urban battalions involved in military campaigns (see table 4.2) continued to play an essential role in the professionalization of the military and in gaining a political reputation for military leaders. For example, one year before his election in 1880, General Roca was in the South leading a military expedition that claimed Patagonia through the conquista del desierto—a campaign that enormously contributed to his electoral victory, closed the southern passages to Chile, eliminated the indigenous populations of the South, and established military garrisons at the borders.[142]

The Draft, Army Growth, and the Unification of the Provinces

The movement against the hegemony of Buenos Aires was led by great caudillos, some of whom, like Martín Güemes in Salta, were able to establish a populist system of governance somewhat reminiscent of Artigas's Liga Federal.[143] Yet as Beatriz Bosch (1971) reports, Güemes and other caudillos (e.g., Ricardo López Jordán, the Taboada brothers, and Urquiza of Entre Ríos) lost their wars against Buenos Aires, and a coalition of caudillos never materialized. When after the battle of Caseros in 1852, Urquiza became the first president of the Argentine Confederation, the backbone of his administration was a pact among caudillos. Unlike similar pacts in Uruguay and Colombia, this coalition regarded the construction of a "national army" under the command of the confederate president as a top priority. The San Nicolás Pact of 1852 resolved that the military forces of each province were to form a part of the national army under Urquiza's orders. Yet provincial forces were loosely organized and did not respond to a central command, and the president found it very hard to impose his authority over the tighter provincial government of Buenos Aires. As Oszlak (1985:65) put it, the confederation "never really counted with a national army." According to León Pomer (1985:284), Urquiza could neither break the influence of his own caudillo allies nor effectively challenge the power of Buenos Aires. This fatally weakened his government, for the president could not impose a coordinated plan for his associates or persuade them to contribute materially to the well-being of the confederation. Rock (1987: 123) tells us that Urquiza retreated from the battle at Pavón where he faced Mitre, leading Buenos Aires forces and the "city militia."

After that, the last caudillos—including Peñaloza, Juan Saa, Varela, and in the early 1870s, López Jordán—were utterly defeated in wars that became wars of annihilation in order to impose centralization and the "expansion of the bureaucracy centered in Buenos Aires."[144] The major and enduring cleavage after the 1870s remained between two powers based in Buenos Aires—the provincial government and the national administration—rather than between the city and the provinces. An example of this is the 1874 Tejedor rebellion (see table 4.1); this last insurrection against the federal government came from within the central bureaucracy. As caudillos weakened, federalist kinship networks and political bosses searched for new alliances with Liberals in Buenos Aires, and this practice stimulated commerce and facilitated the agricultural bonanza of the 1870s. In tandem with the eradication of provincial resistance, the central government became highly visible and was able to extend services to faraway provinces. Indeed, Rock (1996b:3) tells us that a British resident of Buenos Aires on a trip to Córdoba and San Luis found that the national college built by the state was "equal to those in many provincial towns in France."

The fall of caudillismo facilitated the emergence of the "Liberal Progressives" and strengthened power centralization; under the Revolución Liberal, federalist dissidence and caudillo uprisings became "illegal activities" against the nation and were repressed as such.[145] With the destruction of "traditional" federalism, bandits-for-hire emerged. A well-known example of the 1870s was Santos Guayama of La Rioja, who sold his services to Liberals after fighting for them under the banner of federalism.[146] But unlike the situation one finds in Venezuela, the presence of a more forceful central army (since the creation of the urban militia) made banditry a brief transitional phase in the formation of the Argentine state. Although one cannot take the enthusiastic Buenos Aires press at its word—particularly under the influence of Mitristas who thought of the city as the hub of all progress—reporters compared the preparation for Pavón with the beginning of the Civil War in the United States. Society should "unite in the struggle, women should volunteer as nurses, [and] physicians should attend the wounded without compensation."[147]

Oszlak (1985:92) suggests that in terms of the organization of the army, Buenos Aires and the provinces shared a similar situation. Yet he also acknowledges that after Pavón, Buenos Aires could rely on an army that responded to a minister of war and maritime affairs, and to the general armed command of the province of Buenos Aires. Although somewhat poorly equipped, its battalions mobilized at the order of governors and the justices of the peace, followed a direct line of command stemming from the governor, and counted among their urban core the best-trained battalions in the country. Indeed, when the Argentine Confederation dissolved, the national guard of Buenos Aires became the core of the new national army.

Army growth did not exclusively depend on the heritage of the first phase of state formation. Crucial differences, say, between the army in Buenos Aires and the confederate troops who were called the national army during the 1850s and 1860s resulted from the more abundant resources that Buenos Aires was able to allocate to army building. War

activity and institution building in the first phase of state making, however, contributed enormously to its influence, and war making con-
clusively strengthened the army once again during the Paraguayan
War, which according to Alberdi (as quoted by Elias S. Giménez Vega
1961:30), was fought in the name of civilization to "redeem" Paraguay.

Mitre's intense political campaigning before the war helped to consolidate a tarnished national identity and accomplished three important
goals. First, state makers and the military were able to expand the army
further. Second, it helped the economy of Buenos Aires and Santa Fe;
the business sector benefited from the war, and the city did not jeopar-
dize all its resources in fighting it. Despite some military setbacks, and
comments that the war was a waste of men and money, the war definitely stimulated these economies. Third, the war greatly helped consolidate the power of Buenos Aires nationwide. War had a number of
other social consequences as well.

Military building and its impact on the national budget and labor
supply created an antimilitary coalition. A major problem was the already scarce rural labor. With the support of large ranchers, Congress
passed a bill that, in theory, exempted workers in good standing from
serving in the army. Immigration emerged as a prompt solution, and
during the 1860s, the province sought to attract European immigrants
into the rural areas. Yet the military increased its power enough to
survive the attacks of dissatisfied ranchers and critics and to quash
Varela's rebellion in Mendoza (1866–1867), which was fueled, to an
extent, by discontent with the Paraguayan War of 1865 to 1870. In a
letter to a friend at the beginning of the hostilities, Mitre described
some of the early and impressive army mobilization provoked by the
Paraguayan War: "in 15 days I will be at the border with Paraguay with
an army of 25,000 Argentineans, 30,000 Brazilians . . . and 5,000 Uruguayans . . . in addition, Brazil will contribute 25 warships."[148] This
militarization transformed the rural areas. Even before the war, the
national guard went through considerable growth that affected the
provinces. The Argentines created seventeen new regiments to watch
over the countryside and established a marine corps that was autho-
rized to hire foreign legionaries.[149] In Mendoza, a local notable won-
dered about the purpose of "having the province militarize all year
round"; citizens had to attend special duties on Sundays, fill in forms,

and bear the "absolutism of the military commander."[150] During the struggle, Rock (1996b:56) notes that the army almost doubled, with army units rising to about fifty thousand.

The army bestowed abundant promotions on fresh officers and created battalions of veterans, and the rural draft continued unabashed. Gauchos, sharecroppers, and tenants were incorporated into organizations that appeared similar to the Uruguayan Blancos and Colorados or the Colombian Conservatives and Liberals, because mobilization for war acquired a mixture of banditry and almost patriotic regionalism. But unlike the rural mobilization that characterized Uruguay or Colombia, the Argentines incorporated the largest part of the rural militia into a professional military reporting to the central state.

Rural recruitment reached a peak during the effort. As *malvivientes*, gauchos, and seasonal laborers remained the target of the draft—and these groups proved to be a highly mobile population able to escape service, according to Salvatore (1992)—the state resorted to recruitment among small producers, peasants, and peons. It drafted both foreigners and nationals able to bear arms; the 1869 census in Mendoza showed that of 8,000 peons (including 2,500 Chileans), the 3,500 who were capable of bearing arms were compulsorily drafted.[151] Indeed, peons constantly fled their native provinces in fear of the draft, and although the war further opened the army to African Argentines and Indians, Bushnell (1983:13) points out that "colored people" were not allowed to become officers—unlike in the looser Venezuelan battalions. Similar to what happened in the United States, whites and blacks in Argentina formed separate regiments and divisions, but even in the black regiments, officers were invariably white.[152] Armed guards escorted recruits to Buenos Aires or other cities in chains, and Rock (1996b:41) notes that mutinies and resistance to the draft were common. The rural middle strata became what Halperín Donghi (1989a: 111) labeled the "main targets" of the draft. In the final analysis, however, the draft contributed to modernization by abolishing prior labor relations and favoring the use of money wages and higher salaries.

As expected, the consolidation of the central army did face obstacles. As in most of Latin America, both the groups in power and the lower classes feared that the military would grow into a political and social powerhouse, and already in the years between 1822 and 1824, the military suffered some serious reductions in its budget.[153] Immediately after the revolution, Halperín Donghi (1975:209) writes, the Buenos Aires militia found opposition from "the same revolutionary elite" that had placed it in power. From the 1840s to the 1860s, the military was again challenged both in the city and in the regions. In the 1850s, it looked as if the military had lost influence, and at times during the 1860s and 1870s, it appeared as if civil-military relations had followed a path reminiscent of Uruguay and Colombia, where the army grew somewhat dependent on the political elites. Comparatively, however, the Argentine military remained a state maker with a secure position in the ruling coalition, strongly contributing to shaping the polity that emerged at the onset of the twentieth century.

5

Two Alternative Paths of State Making:

Venezuela and Paraguay

Venezuela and Paraguay furnish two additional types of conflict and paths of nation building that put to a different test the argument submitted in the previous chapters. First, these countries allow us to examine further the impact of conflict on civil-military relations in a context in which the army emerged, in two different ways, as a central state maker. The comparison between Argentina and Paraguay, in particular, sheds light on the alternatives open to state makers in societies with a strong military. Second, the analysis of Venezuela and Paraguay shows different ways of incorporating the rural poor, and the construction of a different relationship between the rural poor and the state. Third, Venezuela and Paraguay point to the importance of other factors in state making, factors that played a more peripheral role in the prior cases. Last but not least, these two cases confirm that the thesis formulated in chapter 1 also holds true for these very different contexts of state formation.

In terms of the intensity of the wars of independence, one can place Venezuela at the highest end of the spectrum and Paraguay at the lowest end, with our other three cases somewhere in the middle. In terms of the switch toward commercial agriculture, these two cases offer a sharp contrast to the other three, for in Venezuela and Paraguay, the switch took place much earlier. This difference in timing notwithstanding, the ambiguous correlation between democracy and the more intense commercialization of agriculture is confirmed. In neither Venezuela nor

Paraguay did the expansion of the export economy improve the social and political status of the lower classes. Rather, similar to the second serfdom in Eastern Europe, the more intense commercialization of agriculture encouraged landowners to tie peasants to the land, and even to adopt slavery. Paraguay is a clear case of the state creating monopolies and stronger systems of labor control. The switch reinforced authoritarian (or "absolutist")[1] power structures that had long preceded it. In Venezuela, we also find the adoption of more intense systems of labor control, although in the hands of private landowners. The embrace of free trade during the cacao boom and the ensuing commercialization of coffee encouraged slavery or debt peonage, reinforcing oppressive systems of labor relations.

Going back briefly to the rural poor, we find that peasants, sharecroppers, and cowboys were incorporated in a way that somewhat mixed the strategies examined in the previous cases. In Venezuela, the rural poor were mobilized through armies not necessarily affiliated to parties. The tight labor control of cocoa and coffee did not erode with its more intense commercialization; rather, labor relations changed when the chief tenants of the wars of independence mobilized the rural poor into their armies, and when banditry began to provide an avenue of social betterment. Rural employers were forced to resort to wage labor when labor scarcity, due to the large death toll of war, made other types of labor relations obsolete. In Paraguay, the major agent of recruitment was an army tied to the central state. Rural laborers established, in a manner somewhat reminiscent of Argentina under Rosas, a more direct linkage with the central power. Army building progressed through the century but stopped in the Paraguayan War (1865–1870). In this sense, the War of the Triple Alliance had the reverse effect that we observed among other participants, such as Uruguay and Argentina. Here, rather than encouraging army growth, the war destroyed the army.

The core argument of this chapter is that the major differences in state building and regime outcomes that separate Venezuela and Paraguay can best be explained by examining the different patterns of war and conflict that encouraged the formation of loose guerrilla groups in Venezuela and a centralized army in Paraguay. The incorporation of the rural poor varied only slightly, but enough to make a great difference. In both, peasants, sharecroppers, cowboys, and seasonal laborers were recruited actively by armies rather than parties. But whereas in Venezuela linkages between these armies and the central state remained loose, in Paraguay they did not. These cases strongly confirm lessons from both Europe and the other three Latin American cases, which point to a strong correlation between the pace of state making and army building. In Venezuela, a central army emerged only in the late nineteenth century, and the country centralized power at a slower pace. In Paraguay, the state built a central army from the beginning of the state-making period and centralized power much faster.

Party building in these cases reflected differences in army building. By the close of the nineteenth century, Venezuelan parties remained weak, resembling the situation in Argentina. The military in Venezuela had neither the unity nor the capacity of the Argentine army, but the characteristics of conflict after independence contributed to a situation in which armies substituted for parties. In Paraguay, political parties became stronger only as the military weakened during the Paraguayan War. A heritage of military domination from earlier phases of state building, however, meant that during the period of party rule, the military retained a role as an active member of the ruling coalition. By the early twentieth century, the army had regained predominance.

Venezuelan Wars and State Making

Venezuela represents a path of state making in which neither parties nor a central army took the lead. Rather, armed groups under the leadership of war veterans did, and the period of independence evolved into the most intense war-making situation of all the cases considered here. From 1810 to 1821, Venezuela had three different constitutions and lost one-quarter of its population.[2] Widespread conflict generated heterogeneous and military-like groups of rural militias. Similar to a point to Argentina, military expeditions under the command of the liberators— particularly El Libertador, Simón Bolívar—were sent to neighboring regions to help the cause of independence for Gran Colombia, and during these military campaigns, Venezuelan-led armies established a strong presence in the region. Unlike in Argentina, however, the chief tenants acted much more independently from their central command, a command that was not necessarily stationed in Caracas.

The fight against the Spaniards, the creation of Gran Colombia, Bolívar's military campaigns, and the final separation of Venezuela from Gran Colombia created deep divisions among the generals who fought the wars and no single group could claim hegemony.[3] War veterans became one of the only sources of authority. *Jefes regionales* (regional bosses) kept control of their battalions and local resources during most of the process of state formation, and after independence in 1830, bandits and "heterogeneous groups" continued to plunder the countryside.[4]

During the First (1811–1812), Second (1813–1814), and Third Republics (1816–1819), and even under the stronger influence of General José Antonio Páez (1830–1848), war decided who ruled. In Caracas, civilians and the old, strong exporting elites depended on caudillos and militias they hardly controlled. This resulted in a state mainly run by chief tenants who had no necessary connection with the ruling elites, and for that reason, the state achieved a relatively large degree of autonomy. Such autonomy was apparent during the administration of Antonio Guzmán Blanco,[5] or during the Juan Vicente Gómez era, when the state, although dependent on foreign capital,[6] acted rather independently from local pressure groups. State autonomy emerged for different reasons than in Uruguay but still connected to a pattern of war that strengthened caudillos not necessarily allied with the economic elites. Urban businessmen and landowners did try to raise an urban militia but could not effectively oppose the rural-based regional armies.

In part, the rise of caudillo power remained the unintended consequence of the "elegant"[7] intellectual rebellion that characterized the establishment of the First Republic. The newly founded republic wanted to abandon the Spanish empire and venture into free trade but avoid the social consequences of independence. War changed this plan. The switch to an independent republic was intended to preserve the prevailing social structure and at the same time change market opportunities to the advantage of planters who wished to retain political control.[8] Instead, the wars shifted power into the hands of caudillos and their allies.[9] In this system, a great majority of the strongest players relied on armed struggle to secure and obtain power, which had a decentralizing effect on state authority. Thus, although relatively autonomous, the Venezuelan state possessed little capacity—reminiscent of Uruguay.

The Venezuelan Parties

Rivalry among army caudillos and civilian politicians during independence and thereafter weakened party organization. Politicians and officers did form alliances; from 1830 to 1848, for instance, *llanero* (plainsman) José Antonio Páez controlled politics through an alliance with "foreign and local merchants and bankers."[10] They even formed a Conservative protoparty, hence the term "Conservative Oligarchy."[11] Analogous coalitions characterized most administrations during the nineteenth and early twentieth centuries.[12] But party building did not prosper, and civilians remained the weaker partner in ruling coalitions.

One can argue that compared to Colombia, the feeble role played by prominent civilians in dismantling the Venezuelan armies of independence resulted in weaker parties. And one can argue that compared to Uruguay, in the absence of foreign invasions and alliances with foreign powers, Venezuelan parties could not prosper. Three more aspects of party building found in Uruguay and Colombia were absent as well. First, unlike Uruguayan and Colombian caudillos, Venezuelan party leaders did not act in coordination with neighboring party commanders. In light of the lessons learned from the other cases, one can argue that one strong reason Venezuelan lieutenants saw little need of forming interregional alliances was because they felt much more in control of their own regions, and chances of local insurrection against the caudillos were low. Second, whereas Uruguayan and Colombian party bosses devoted much time to the organization of cliques of local notables, Venezuelan army lieutenants did not. Notables and the local caudillos did interact, but not as part of a broader partisan organization. And third, the Venezuelan Church was weak and thus could not become the organizational backbone for a Conservative party, as it was in Colombia.[13] Therefore, party labels meant much less than in Uruguay or Colombia, and national elections were not as decisive a forum to decide power sharing.

With very few exceptions, when indirect elections took place, Venezuela elected generals rather than civilians. Only in 1835, after twenty-four years of independence, did the first civilian president, José María Vargas, achieve office—and then only for one year. After that, the country went through a series of authoritarian military governments led by caudillo-generals. It was not until 1888 that the second civilian president, Juan Pablo Rojas Paúl, was elected for a brief period. In 1890 a third civilian, Raimundo Andueza Palacio, gained the presidency, but in 1892 General Joaquín Crespo ousted Andueza Palacio, and another cycle of military-caudillo presidencies began that lasted until 1936.

This speaks of the usual low level of role differentiation between caudillos, line officers, and party politicians. Yet in Venezuela this situation survived longer, and the caudillo-military chief persisted as a political figure well into the twentieth century. Caudillos came to represent regional interests, and so did their governments. For instance, the Monagas brothers' administrations (1847–1858) represented the rule of the Oriente Provinces,[14] and the Cipriano Castro period, starting in 1899, represented the dominance of the Andean region. Until the 1930s, authoritarian regimes weakened party competition. Some underground party organizing did take place during the first decades of the twentieth century, but parties never achieved the level of cohesiveness exhibited by their Uruguayan and Colombian counterparts.

The accepted view that during the nineteenth century, two "historical parties" forged the Venezuelan nation seems to disregard all of the foregoing. According to this view, the Conservador party represented the "mercantile bourgeoisie, the large slave owners, and bankers," and the Liberal party was formed by landholders who did not use slavery.[15] These coalitions were very different from the ones found in Colombia or Uruguay. In comparison with the lessons learned from the other cases, however, parties were far from being major state makers. When in 1870 Antonio Guzmán Blanco seized power, party activity had scarcely progressed, and during his long tenure (1870–1888), parties were shattered. As we shall see, Guzmán Blanco did start an important phase of power centralization that halted rebellions by empowering caudillos, who in return refrained from waging war on the central state. But unlike in Uruguay or Colombia, his regime did not consolidate agreements among parties, and a party system did not develop. One must add that pacts among competing forces did not resemble the situation in Argentina, either. Rather than a system of provincial representation centered in a capital city controlled by civilians and military figures such as the Orden Conservador, state making in Venezuela retained the blueprint of a second and even third generation of military caudillos who did not identify with the central army.

Ottoman Lessons, Banditry, and the Rural Poor

In terms of the incorporation of the rural poor, the defining feature in Venezuela was incorporation through caudillo armies rather than through parties or a central military. These armies provided one of very few ways to climb the social ladder, as shown by the emergence of *pardo* (dark) officers and caudillos who became most of the celebrated leaders of the postindependence period. Most of the labor force, and therefore the bulk of the armies, comprised a mixture of slaves brought from Africa, African Venezuelans, indigenous groups, and mestizos. Whites constituted a minority of the Creole population.

Fear of an insurrection from below in this racially tense society ranked high, particularly after the Haitian Revolution in 1804, which encouraged the elites in Caracas to issue strong preventive measures.[16] As a consequence, elites tried to deprive the bulk of the armies of independence of voting rights, which was done in the 1811 constitution. Other groups among the elite, however, feared that this would provoke precisely the measure they intended to prevent in the first place, and thus they aborted the plan.[17] According to John V. Lombardi (1982:99), fear of racial insurrection went back to the eighteenth century, and in the nineteenth century, the discontent of the "poor, the dispossessed, and the angry" (165) materialized in endemic banditry. Somewhat reminiscent of Colombia, slavery was abolished in the constitution of 1858, and the direct and secret ballot was adopted. Yet these reforms lacked the adequate institutional structure for implementation, and according to Germán Carrera Damas (1983b:24–25), they reinforced the domination of the "Conservative Oligarchy."

The relationship of the rural poor with the army and the central state in Venezuela somewhat reminds us of the strategies of Ottoman state makers. During the nineteenth century, with a disorganized army and scarce party networks, the central state faced serious obstacles when it tried to reach into the rural areas. Thus the government started hiring mercenary troops to do the job. To a large degree, the government became dependent on the hiring of bandits and "generals," who were necessary to keep its enemies at bay. And there were many enemies, especially the regional-based lieutenants, who often expressed their opposition through guerrilla wars against the state. These local leaders had also developed steady ties to local elites, who both dreaded and supported their war activity. In a mixture of banditry and political leadership, regional bosses provided "protection" to the rural populations within their domain and offered the rural poor a place in their "armies." Therefore, the state attempted to impose a presence in the rural areas by employing the rural dwellers for short periods of time. Domingo G. Irwin (1990:16) has called these leaders and their armies "entrepreneurs of violence." From the standpoint of the state, however, this strategy backfired.

While some caudillos and their militias became regular mercenaries in this system, very few remained attached to the central government long enough to become a sort of regular battalion in a central military. And most of the time, the state could not afford to retain them, even if these armies wished to remain at its service. Unlike in the Ottoman case, all this further contributed to decentralization, because the caudillos and militias, who often were on the government payroll,[18] saw no incentive in undermining a system that best served their interests. In the first seven years of Guzmán Blanco's rule (1870–1876), for instance, the country experienced relative peace. During that period, it became apparent that the interests of caudillos, militias, and mercenaries were better served by prolonging conflict. During those seven years, it became harder for caudillos and militia members to sell their services, and the government took advantage of peace to block caudillos from obtaining their usual *partidas de guerra* (war grants).[19]

Banditry and the Central Army

In a situation in which small armies and bandits came to operate almost unchallenged in most of the national territory, the central army and the state in Venezuela developed quite slowly. The same, as we have noted, happened to the parties. The military was indeed far from constituting what Alain Rouquié (1987:42) has called the state's "military branch." Although most of the scholarly literature has indicated that weak states usually coexist with stronger parties, in Venezuela both state and party were weak until the 1890s, when the state gained centrality. Robert Louis Gilmore (1964) has argued for a long time that the intensity of the wars, the increasing militarization of social and political life, and the weak enforcement of property rights produced a fragmented polity in which all political organization encountered great obstacles. One is compelled to look at the complex and slow construction of the Venezuelan central army for answers.

Slow army building places Venezuela closer to Uruguay and Colombia than to Argentina. Despite feeble civilian opposition to the rise of a central army, until the 1890s, state makers remained unable to monopolize coercion. The painful development of a central army in this militarized society takes us back to our suggestion that the geographic deployment of military forces during the process of state building provides a variable of central importance to explain outcomes. In this case, this allocation did not favor Caracas and contributed much to state weakness. Geographically, militias were scattered throughout most of the Venezuelan territory, strengthening regionalism. Gilmore (1964:10–11) studied what he called the "era of the *caudillos*" from 1830 to 1935, arguing that these militias, more than anything else, were responsible for the construction of the Venezuelan state, a state that had been assembled "from the barracks." The analysis of nation building submitted by Lombardi (1982) does not differ much from Gilmore's. Militia commanders from different regions became the most important state makers, ruling for lengthy periods of time. Yet this pattern did not necessarily strengthen the army or the state.

When in 1830 General Páez and the Conservative oligarchy attempted centralization and army building, most of the military was still composed of a loose coalition of caudillo clientele and mercenary troops hired for the occasion. The next strong regime, the Monagas brothers' administrations, or Liberal oligarchy (approximately 1847–1858), tried again to build a central army. The Federal Wars (1859–1863), however, limited their efforts. The federalists won the wars, and the constitution of 1864 weakened party activity but made little progress toward power centralization or army building.[20] In the final analysis, the wars started a new era of strong caudillism and regionalism.[21] The loose organizations that fought these wars under the labels of "Conservative" and "Liberal" apparently clashed over the issue of federalism but demonstrated an inverse image of their Argentine counterparts. Whereas Argentine parties developed weak rural wings, their Venezuelan counterparts developed strong ones. And whereas in Argentina the parties' urban and intellectual components were strong, these components remained weak in Venezuela.

As many before him, Guzmán Blanco was unable either to integrate bandits and military chief tenants into the central army or to eliminate them completely. The state grew stronger in terms of the administration of services and tax collection, but it remained unable to monopolize coercion. During the period from 1865 to 1870, Liberal governments were shaken by uprisings and ultimately succumbed to Guzmán Blanco, who dismantled party activity and ruled from approximately 1870 to 1888. Contrary to some expectations, Guzmán Blanco did not build a central army, either. Ines Mercedes Quintero Montiel (1990:42) tells us that the Guzmán Blanco victory marked the emergence of an important coalition of caudillos that could not—or did not wish to— form a state army. He did centralize authority but did so by relying heavily on caudillo support.[22] Guzmán Blanco's stronger state resembled earlier stages of state making in Argentina under Rosas; as much as in the Rosas era, military caudillos could voice their interests and enjoy political representation, but the government simultaneously tried to undermine their sources of financial and military support.[23]

Expectations of army building arose again by 1899, when General Cipriano Castro gained power (which he retained until 1908) through the so-called Revolución Liberal Restauradora. As we shall see shortly, this revolution had lasting consequences for state making. Under Castro, however, the state still found strong obstacles that limited its monopoly on coercion. And although it started the process, it did not succeed at forming a loyal central army. Instead, at the end of the Castro period, a "reversion to anarchy" began.[24] In 1902 the American consul in Maracaibo voiced the opinion that Venezuela provided the perfect example of a "praetorian" society commanded by generals.[25] He was right. An identifiable and organized central army, however, still had not emerged by the time he wrote this report. One can argue that important steps toward its creation started under Castro, but the army consolidated during the authoritarian rule of Juan Vicente Gómez, from 1909 to 1935.

One can comfortably say that it was not until the government of Cipriano Castro that the caudillos lost significant influence as independent war machines. What weakened caudillo power was war (i.e., Castro's Revolución Restauradora), which created the Partido Liberal Restaurador (Restored Liberal Party) and changed the pattern of war making that had characterized the prior period. This revolution against Guzmán Blanco succeeded precisely because his administration could not count on an efficient army. The victory of the insurgents was rapid and overwhelming. The most important new development of this revolution lay in the superior military might of the invaders, for after taking power, Castro did not necessarily need to negotiate a pact with other caudillos.[26] It was under Castro and "after the last battle" was won[27] that the national army acquired a definite profile and the modernization of the armed forces began. In 1908 Gómez, the "caudillo of all caudillos," took power. He ruled Venezuela until 1935.

War Threats and a Praetorian State in Paraguay

During the nineteenth century, state making in Paraguay responded to two very different war patterns. During the first period, low levels of domestic conflict, high levels of external threat, weak regional bosses, and a short struggle for independence contributed to power centralization, army building, and the low profile of political parties. A second pattern of conflict resolution started with the traumatic experience of Paraguay's defeat in the War of the Triple Alliance (1864–1870) and the six years of foreign occupation that followed. This war placed Paraguay near Uruguay, since both countries, at different times, underwent foreign military intervention, and in both, the army was weakened as a result. Indeed, with its weak state and its military destroyed, after 1870 Paraguay moved closer to Uruguay or even Colombia and shared with the small River Plate republic a government dominated by parties and led by civilians.

In this second period of state formation, the state adopted more relaxed economic policies, foreigners found a place in Paraguayan society, and competition for political office moved the country closer to republican rule.[28] Paraguay, however, did not follow the Uruguayan path. The military buildup during the first phase of polity building meant that the country still differed from the Banda Oriental or Colombia, and the military remained a major actor in Paraguayan politics. One can argue that a third stage in the development of the Paraguayan state was triggered by another war, the February Revolution of 1936, which ended the dominance of the Liberal Party.[29] This was just what the 1904 Saravia revolution attempted to do with the Colorados in Uruguay; however, by that time, the polities of the two countries differed widely. In Paraguay the 1936 insurrection brought the military back to center stage as a policy maker. In Uruguay, there was no organized military to bring back in; thus the Blanco guerrilla war that ended in 1904 consolidated Colorado rule and helped to construct a mild military establishment under Colorado tutelage.

In other words, Paraguay offers a different type of conflict and path of state building. This difference finds an explanation in the variations of our main independent variables. A different war pattern started in the juncture marked by the conflict over independence—which involved confrontation with revolutionary Buenos Aires rather than with the Spanish monarchists. The fight for independence was short. It happened when Paraguayan troops, after declaring independence from both Argentina and Spain, defeated the porteños in 1811 in a low-intensity battle. Brazil, the other neighboring giant, had also threatened Paraguay, but no serious armed confrontation took place between Paraguayans and Brazilians during the early phase of state building. In essence, Paraguay was at war for a very short time. Whereas in Venezuela the high intensity of the wars triggered the rise of powerful military caudillos and fostered a polity with a weak state, parties, and army, the low intensity of the wars in Paraguay provided a window of opportunity for the centralization of the military. Therefore, Asunción was almost untouched by independence. More centralized forms of power inherited from the colony survived, and parties became important actors in the political scene only after the Paraguayan War.

Asunción, unlike Montevideo and Buenos Aires, was not favored by geographic location. Nonetheless, a high level of perceived threat associated with the imminence of foreign invasions, the quick assembling of the militia in the city, and a prior history of militarization compensated for structural disadvantages and made Asunción a centerpiece of state making. In terms of its quick militarization, the city resembled Buenos Aires. Located close to the Portuguese border and the Indian frontier, Asunción was already highly militarized during colonial times.[30] In the early 1780s, the most prominent landholding groups formed a semiprofessional officer corps, and by the time of independence, the military had been reorganized to closely resemble a standing army.[31] Like Montevideo, during independence the city fought against Buenos Aires. The great difference from Uruguay was that Asunción did not face rural resistance in its hinterland. Thus a centralizing, conservative, populist-paternalistic regime emerged as the first government of independence.[32]

In Paraguay, the inverse of the strength between parties and army suggested by the Uruguayan and Colombian cases finds further corroboration. Parties started weak and remained weak until the War of the Triple Alliance decimated the Paraguayan army. By the same token, Paraguay also confirms my argument about the strong influence of the early phases of institution building during the wars of independence and the first half of the nineteenth century. Despite the tremendous shock of the War of the Triple Alliance, the defeated army remained an integral part of the ruling coalition under the party system that emerged after the war, and the army finally regained center stage in the later part of the nineteenth century.

In terms of the commercialization of agriculture, one can argue that Paraguayan rural development went hand in hand with army building and power centralization, rather than democracy. This is so, unless one takes the paternalistic and "socialist" aspects[33] of the agrarian and economic policy from 1852 to 1865 as a sign of democracy, and I do not. The early commercialization of agriculture was in the hands of immigrants who cultivated and traded the *yerba mate* leaf (a type of tea leaf that grows in abundance in Paraguay), and in the hands of Creole landowners who engaged in cattle raising. The yerba mate trade prospered despite widespread labor scarcity. Among other things, this was true because a strong military contributed to securing property rights in the countryside and took an active role in supervising production. Moreover, feeble resistance from regional caudillos facilitated the state's control of resources and labor. Indeed, the state adopted a system of slavery controlled by the central government to guarantee timely output and to secure state patronage of both landowners and laborers.

The Rural Poor, the Army, and Lessons from Asia and Eastern Europe

Since the colonial period, a keen awareness of isolation and the knowledge that Paraguay was at the mercy of its powerful neighbors created a strong military culture. Reminiscent of some analyses of the eighteenth-century United States, John Hoyt Williams (1979:15) has called Paraguay a "nation of farmer warriors," where a scarcity of labor, plus constant alertness to foreign invasions, transformed the small farmer into a *filiado*, someone who served in the national militia when needed.[34] The country's strategic position as a buffer state between Brazil and other nations[35] was a constant concern of the Spanish crown, which kept the province on constant military alert. When neighboring states declared independence, the military alert became even stronger in royalist Paraguay, and the rural poor were drawn into a compulsory draft that, as early as 1813, triggered bitter complaints among planters. Border patrols were badly needed, but their laborers were essential to production in the hacienda as well. The rising awareness of external threats encouraged the Conservatives to raise a central army to defend the country in the context of a weak opposition.[36]

    Indeed, in 1816 an atmosphere of imminent war motivated the royalist cabildo to nominate José Gaspar Rodríguez de Francia to the presidency. Francia, the first state maker of independent Paraguay, remained in power until 1840, and he and his coalition strengthened the militia and integrated officers into the ruling group.[37] El Dictador successfully assembled militia units and continued to operate under the assumption of imminent external war; the militia was later transformed into the regular national army under his personal command. Similar to army building in Argentina, yet at a much faster pace, this militia was integrated into urban battalions concentrated in Asunción.[38] In part because he commanded the army and secured the loyalty of its first officers, Francia successfully discredited his competitors and remained mainly unchallenged. Not surprisingly, mutinies and coups were somewhat frequent during the first decades of state building, but no major challenge to the state and its army materialized. At the end, the Francia era not only accomplished a considerable degree of power centralization but also achieved considerable popularity.

It was under Francia that Paraguay embarked on a system of incorporation of the rural poor that sets it apart from the other cases and allows us to refine our argument. As in Argentina or Venezuela, the army became a major vehicle of incorporation of pardos, mestizos, and Indians. Unlike Venezuela and more like Argentina, however, Asunción was able to control this army and construct a strong sense of national identity among soldiers and the rural poor. Very much unlike Uruguay and Colombia, the state did not have to rely on parties to incorporate the rural populations into the polity. The distinguishing feature of Paraguay was that the state accomplished a direct and lasting linkage with the rural poor. A different pattern of conflict and early army building explains why, unlike Colombia, Uruguay, and most of the European cases considered in the first chapter, the Paraguayan state was able to penetrate the hinterland and reach the rural poor directly. The only comparable examples in the other cases were the Rosas administrations, tellingly, another case in which the government pursued an early militarization of social and political life and created a central army.

After 1816 a high level of perceived threat and increasing militarism rendered landlords unable to act collectively in the regions and to create parties or regional guerrilla organizations. In this aspect of polity formation, Paraguay falls more into the category of Asian and Middle Eastern cases described in chapter 1, cases that experienced a more direct connection between the rural population and the central state than the Latin American countries studied so far in this book. Alliances between the regional gentry and peasants and laborers remained frail and separated Paraguay from countries such as Uruguay, Colombia, and even Argentina, if one bears in mind the great insurrections of the provinces against Buenos Aires. All of this facilitated a paternal incorporation of rural laborers into the national guard, which responded directly to El Dictador. To many, Francia resembled more a liberal reformer than a real dictator.[39] Indeed, his government was able to capture important popular support, particularly from the peasantry.[40] The government became a presence among the rural poor, and a sense of nationality that tied the state to its rural population developed faster and stronger in Paraguay.

The policies of the government resembled mild forms of rural populism also found in Eastern Europe. To tie labor to the land was a top priority in the development policies of the Paraguayan state, and as we shall see, the state took a definite and active role in that policy. Indeed, it created a system of state-sponsored slavery to avoid labor flight from haciendas and plantations. The great difference from Eastern Europe, however, was the key role played by the central army in the incorporation of rural labor. This, along with weak local leadership, prevented the emergence of peasant parties.

Enjoying a situation in which the opposition was feeble and his popularity respectable, Francia found a window of opportunity to build a constituency among—as Guillermo Cabanellas (1946:123) put it— "peons, [and] shabby characters of the underworld." At the same time, Francia successfully courted the officers of the emerging central army in Asunción. In sum, a legacy of colonial militarization, high perceived levels of threat, and a low-intensity conflict during independence facilitated power centralization, the strength of the military, and an incorporation of the rural poor through the army.

The Paraguay-Argentina comparison illustrates this point. If one were to rank comparatively the effects of the wars of independence and subsequent conflicts during the first phase of state making on the economies and territories of Paraguay and Argentina, one would find that these two countries come closer to each other than to any of the other cases. In both, the wars did not disrupt the urban environment and caused little damage to the more densely populated areas. As in Paraguay, the Argentine struggle for independence was characterized by low-intensity combat around the city and its periphery, and more intense engagements on the frontiers. Still another aspect of the conflict that places Paraguay closer to Argentina relates to the reaction of Buenos Aires and Asunción to foreign invasions. The response of Buenos Aires to the 1807 British invasions and Asunción's response to the threat of foreign invasion after independence triggered similar effects; that is, both cities became the epicenter of army building and cemented an alliance of state makers and the officer corps. Also, both succeeded to a great degree in integrating the rural populations into the sphere of government influence without party mediation, and both quickly dominated the regional caudillos of their immediate hinterland.

The key Paraguayan and Argentine state makers in the first phase of state formation, Rosas and Francia, were offered "unlimited powers" by the ruling coalition.[41] Francia did something that Rosas perhaps wanted to do but could not fully accomplish; that is, El Dictador was able to destroy the old political elite by deporting foreigners, particularly Spaniards, and replacing them with his own appointees.[42] With the case of Colombia in mind, it is important to note as well that from the onset of state formation, the Paraguayan Church, as a possible institutional resource for party building, was weakened and eventually absorbed into the state.[43]

The Commercialization of Agriculture, Development, and State Building

The economics of the Francia era and the success of its policy of isolation testify to what, for most social science theory, may appear to be an anomalous correlation between the pace of power centralization and economic policy. Most literature on all the other cases, especially (and for good reasons) Argentina, claims a direct connection between economic development, greater "exposure to trade,"[44] and power centralization. Although economic growth and state expansion can definitely be correlated, the analysis in this book did not find a solid tie between greater levels of economic development and a faster pace of power centralization. Paraguay confirms these findings.

During the first phase of nation building, when the state was able to successfully centralize power, expand the bureaucracy, and even control a labor system based on slavery, growth was far from spectacular. Indeed, one can comfortably argue that recession, rather than growth, paralleled the thrust toward power centralization. White (1978:60) states that during the first decades of republican rule and under Francia's mild "popular dictatorship," trade contracted and led to a clear phase of recession. This encouraged the government to intervene in the economy and play a leading role in development. Others have echoed this opinion and shown that the Francia era presented clear features of economic decline.[45]

How much centralization did the state achieve in this context of quite modest economic performance? I would say that the state gained a considerable degree of centralization and pursued a rather aggressive policy of intervention in the economy. Pastore (1994a:593), who disagrees with the scholarship that emphasizes the power of the state under Francia, concludes that private property in land was "seriously circumscribed," and "in addition to owing much of the country's land, the state also became much more of a cattle rancher and a rent collecting landlord" and had a much bigger say in "whether or not people became landlords." Indeed, the state resembled a soft monarchy more than a republic.

Wars and Party Activity

What is left for us to assess is the impact of war and perceived level of threat on the parties that emerged in Paraguay. During the first phase of state formation, one cannot talk about parties. Rather, cliques of notables and family kinship networks acted as pressure groups in the cabildo and later in the *junta guvernativa* (which somewhat resembled parties but remained groups of notables). Some of these cliques did build networks that reached into the countryside, but civil society did not produce party organizations comparable to those examined in chapters 2 and 3.

To an extent, one can argue, these protoparties emerged as an outgrowth of the legislature, as in Argentina. This polity broke down with the Paraguayan War, which had "revolutionary consequences" for Paraguayan society.[46] Reminiscent of Uruguay (although later in the nineteenth century), the erosion of old institutions under foreign occupation encouraged the formation of cleavages, which divided the emerging civilian leadership. These cleavages and a weakened government provided a window of opportunity for party building during the period of occupation.[47] One cannot stress enough the influence of the Paraguayan War and foreign occupation on party formation. After all, as Harris Gaylord Warren (1985:4–5) and Paul H. Lewis (1993:19–26) have shown, Paraguayans in exile constituted the fundamental leadership of the new "clubs" that gave origin to the Colorado and Liberal parties. Although it is true that parties in Paraguay rank among the oldest in Latin America, only in the 1870 constitution did they become central for nation building.[48] In that decade, the country began its "Colorado era," which lasted from 1878 until the revolution of 1904.[49] The three decades of Liberal Party rule that followed can be taken as an intermediate, rather than final, phase in the construction of the Paraguayan polity.

Why did Paraguay, despite this period of party dominance, not follow the steps of Uruguay or Colombia? The answers can be found in variables that are already well known to the reader. First, there is the legacy of the first phase of nation building, which separated Paraguay from the other two. Second, given the traumatizing experience of the War of the Triple Alliance, and the remnants of a strong army under foreign occupation, the pattern of conflict that Paraguay inherited when it embarked on party politics differed from that in both Colombia and Uruguay. The Paraguayan Colorado era, despite its claims of being a competitive political system, still featured a much larger degree of centralization and nepotism than Colorado-dominated Uruguay or Conservative-dominated Colombia. The Paraguayan Colorado oligarchy, for instance, comprised a (small) Congress of twenty-six deputies and thirteen senators and maintained power by the simple expedient of "preventing Liberals from voting."[50] Although electoral fraud can be found in all the cases considered, the low competitive profile of the political system under the Colorado administration[51] reached levels reminiscent of the Francia era. One cannot help but think of Rosas and his long legacy, even after his defeat at the battle of Caseros. In Paraguay, no one could access office without approval from the ruling clique. The Liberals did not gain power until 1904, and they finally did so by the power of arms rather than elections. As expected, at least from the standpoint of the argument presented in this book, the resulting polity was characterized by a leading military establishment, scarce party competition, and a stronger state.

Conclusions

This book attempts to formulate an empirically grounded theory that, I hope, offers some counterintuitive propositions. My emphasis on war making and collective action is by no means an argument about the irrelevance of other factors; rather, it completes a picture that, I suggest, has not been fully drawn. Because all the cases in this book experienced intense war making at the time of nation building, however, one might accuse me of telling only part of the story. To be more persuasive, my comparisons should have included a case (or cases) in which the level of conflict approached much lower levels or, ideally, zero. Of course, nation building in general, and in the nineteenth century in particular, was rarely peaceful—so cases approaching a zero level of conflict are almost nonexistent.

In my defense, I would also point to the inclusion of Paraguay, a case in which the level of conflict was very low, at least during the early phases of state building. The lesson learned from comparing Paraguay with Argentina, which experienced a conflict of higher intensity during independence, is that the *type* of conflict was more critical to the formation of the polity than the intensity. These two countries ended up sharing important features of state making, which can be traced back to similarities in the war pattern during the initial stages of nation building. They both fought independence in their frontier, and their urban centers and economies suffered no serious damage as a result of war. In both, the major city militarized to respond to the threat of foreign invasion, whether fictitious or real, and in both the urban environment became the epicenter of army building. As a result, the Paraguayan and Argentine armies became state makers.

Conflicts did achieve a high level of intensity, which at times determined radical ruptures between different phases of polity formation (such as the War of the Triple Alliance that destroyed the Paraguayan army) and had consequences for institution building among all the participant countries (such as the Guerra Grande in Uruguay, or the Guerra de los Mil Dias in Colombia). One could perhaps construct an argument around the intensity of conflict to explain differences among countries. Yet the one presented in this book emphasizes the type (rather than the intensity) of conflict.

The analysis at the heart of this book suggests both the truth and the limits of structural theories of state making and regime consolidation. Variables such as the switch toward commercial agriculture, the structure of the economy, the use of labor, the land-labor ratio, class conflict over the means of production, and the exposure of a country to the world economy *have* been basic in shaping state building. Institutional theory has also provided a useful lens to better examine regimes and institutions. Nonetheless, in the final analysis, this book has given centrality to the characteristics of war, concomitant collective action, and the manner in which the rural lower classes reacted to the organizational imperatives of conflict.

The way in which the rural poor were incorporated into the polity stood as a centerpiece of the argument presented here. Conflicts, decisions made by state makers as to how to secure control of the political process, and, very importantly, the collective action of the rural poor themselves shaped institutions and regimes. Whether the rural poor were militarily incorporated by parties or armies made a difference. In their treatment of the "rural threat," Uruguay and Colombia came closer to each other. Argentina stood aloof but in many important ways resembled Paraguay. Venezuela opted for a different route of incorporation that resembled neither of the others, and least of all Paraguay's. The resemblance between Paraguay and Asia, the Middle East, or Eastern Europe may, I hope, open further interesting avenues of comparative research. The same goes for the suggested similarities between Venezuela (and at times Colombia) and the Ottoman case, in terms of the participation of the rural poor in mercenary armies and the widespread use of banditry.

The type of war, rather than the number of wars a country experienced during the process of nation building, shaped the polity—and states did not necessarily weaken when engaged in frequent conflict. All depended on who fought the wars and where. In the River Plate, for instance, despite having experienced a larger number of wars during state building, Argentina was perceived as more modern, pacific, and organized than Uruguay. A major difference between polity formation on the two shores of the River Plate was that in Argentina, a central army was a major contender in the struggle, and the capital city remained closer to the periphery of the conflict. On the other shore, in Uruguay, the opposite was true. In the 1870s, when the last challenge to power centralization rose from within the state bureaucracy in Buenos Aires, this war pattern changed somewhat. Yet the quick defeat of the insurrection expressed the predominance of urban politics over a hinterland that had been subdued during earlier phases of state building.

Confirming the findings of Eric A. Nordingler (1981, 1987), once in power, state officials and bureaucrats tried to shape institutions according to their own interests.[1] Not surprisingly, policy makers sought insulation and autonomy when designing institutions and regulating power distribution and resources. A more interesting and counterintuitive finding, however, was that state officials did not always find it convenient to strive for these objectives. And although the identity and personality of state officials and bureaucrats did shape outcomes, these factors remained, for the most part, a poor predictor of what state makers could do. The intended and unintended consequences of their choices depended on the characteristics of an extrastate conflict that, quite often, they did not control.

The way class actors acted collectively shaped the way economic elites related to the central power and political institutions. Uruguay and Colombia shared a similar pattern of conflict that created like polities, but they differed in the degree of state autonomy because in Colombia, powerful sectors of the economic elites participated more actively in wars and party politics. Uruguay and Venezuela were different in most aspects of state building, except in their pattern of conflict, in which economic elites depended heavily on military caudillos who retained a great degree of independence and did not directly identify with the business sectors. Consequently, Uruguay and Venezuela both developed a larger degree of state autonomy. During the first period of state building in Argentina, conflict facilitated the elites' penetration of the state in the province of Buenos Aires and their alliance with the military. Under these circumstances, the state evolved less autonomously, thus placing Argentina closer to Colombia than to Uruguay. In terms of state capacity, however, Argentina and Colombia differed. As in many European cases, the central Argentine government could use a more powerful central army to subdue the regions. Finally, in Paraguay, a high perceived level of threat contributed to the early development of a central army and a state that controlled resources, all of which favored state autonomy and capacity. Geographically, unlike Uruguay or Argentina, Asunción held no privileged position to claim centrality in state making, but war allowed the city to control the process of nation building.

Conflict shaped party organization as well. The parties that formed during the nineteenth century in Uruguay and Colombia developed as flexible organizations that, to an extent, resembled Duverger's (1954) classification of a "cadre" party, in which the leadership is grounded in its lower power base, ideology tends to be blurred, and the party bureaucracy is decentralized. Nonetheless, by the end of the century, one finds that finances, recruitment, and campaigns were handled by the top members, as in highly institutionalized parties. A main reason for this transformation was that party modernization mirrored state formation, which is to be expected under a system of unmediated party rule. Thus, as the process of power centralization gained momentum, party bureaucracies became more centralized. Improvements in organization and discipline fell short, however, of making these parties fit the model set by European socialist or communist parties, or even parties in Britain. One must remember as well that Venezuela teaches us a different lesson in terms of the correlation between parties and the state: that until the 1890s, contrary to most of the literature, both state and the parties were weak.

In Argentina, starting with the military expeditions that followed the May Revolution and the elimination of party activity under Rosas, the conflict over self-rule strengthened the state and the military rather than the parties. In addition to propitious opportunities for economic growth, particularly in Buenos Aires, Entre Ríos, and Santa Fe, the military supremacy of Buenos Aires and its more centralized polity marked a path of state formation in which cleavages separating Federales and Unitarios did not provide a strong enough basis for a party system. In Venezuela, the conflict among caudillos followed by militias from the armies of independence did not consolidate a party system, either. And from the start in Paraguay, the military and the state occupied the political space of party organizations, with parties remaining a shabby force in state making.

We can explain not only the emergence of parties but also differences between parties by looking at types of conflict. Dissimilarities between parties customarily considered alike, such as the Uruguayan Blancos and the Colombian Conservadores, for instance, owe much to the adoption of different war strategies and patterns of collective action. The Blancos fought insurrections that seldom found strong support in the capital city, and the party reacted to Colorado dominance with sporadic outbursts of guerrilla warfare. Therefore, the party evolved as an assembly of loose organizations that seldom responded to a central authority. The Conservadores, however, retained a strong base in Bogotá and other urban centers, developed a more recognizable central body, and were able to organize a much more cohesive counterrevolution. Ideological disparities also related to different ways of acting collectively. The Blancos' libertarian, nationalistic, and rural-inspired creed owed much to their experience during the Guerra Grande and the siege of Montevideo. Unlike the Conservatives, the party developed an anti-European and antiurban platform and flatly rejected centralized authority.

Contrasts in party systems also responded, to a great extent, to different types of conflict. In Uruguay, the Portuguese invasions, the Guerra Grande, and the wars of the 1870s shaped the party system into a one-party-dominant system. The Colorado party penetrated the central army and consolidated the state against Blanco party militias in a situation in which dissident caudillos sought control of Montevideo, a city considered by all as the "natural" geographic site for the central state. Conflict resolution materialized in quotas of participation between the parties, consolidating the party system. On its part, Colombia underwent no foreign invasions and evolved into a complex pattern of insurrection that aimed at the autonomy of the regions. The result was a loose federal system in which party hegemony was more short-lived than in Uruguay, and the estados remained more independent. Quasi-independent urban centers throughout the national territory provided important bases of military support for party armies; therefore, unlike their Uruguayan counterparts, Colombian caudillos did not regard Bogotá as the "natural" epicenter of nation building. Indeed, jefes politicos customarily threatened secession from the federation, and agreements between ruling coalitions and the party in opposition took on a more complex character as conflict unfolded between the regions and between the estados and the central power.

War contributed to divide countries into different geographic sections and to identify villages, towns, and regions with specific political subcultures. This emerged clearly in Uruguay and Colombia but also applies to regional identification with Federales and Unitarios in Argentina. One can argue likewise for Venezuelan militias that developed strong regional roots and military cultures. In all cases, shared collective action, as well as persecution, contributed to create a history full of symbols, heroes, slogans, and martyrs, very familiar to the Paraguayan survivors of the War of the Triple Alliance. All of these factors added to the perception that political organizations and armies were much more than simple tools to realize certain ends. Those in power often persecuted the opposition and did so in the name of culture, ideas, and values, thereby strengthening subcultures of resistance attached to the adversary party, army, or region. In Uruguay, Colorado presidents such as Fructuoso Rivera came to the point of arresting anyone in the streets of Montevideo who would not wear a Red Party pin in his or her lapel. Similarly, vociferous anticlerical rulers in Colombia, such as Cipriano de Mosquera, mocked the killing of clergy as a contribution to the augmentation of the number of angels inhabiting the "realm beyond." Examples abound. The point is that organizations that channeled collective action became valuable in and of themselves to those who sought refuge, protection, and social advancement through their development.

The cultural background and ideological preferences of institution makers did matter, but the capacity of state makers to impose their ideological preferences on institutional design remained dependent, more than anything else, on the type of collective action that they were able to muster in society and the strength of the opposition. Liberal constitutional reform regarding citizenship rights is a case in point. Some of the most inclusive bills for legislation on issues related to the rights of citizens and their incorporation into the political system emerged in nineteenth-century Argentina and Colombia, countries that nonetheless evolved into more exclusive polities. To an extent, this applies as well to militarized Venezuela and Paraguay. In the former, some presidential candidates even proposed the widening of the suffrage to include "eighteen year olds and women."[2] In the latter, similar examples of "progressive" and advanced legislation were also seriously considered and implemented. In contrast, Uruguay did not produce comparable pieces of "advanced" legislation during the state formation period but became a "model" of democracy during the first decades of the twentieth century. This unexpected outcome points to the importance of the strength of the opposition. By the time of reform, wars had worn down the conservative bloc, and democratic reform found more propitious grounds to materialize. Indeed, one can suggest that the Liberals, both in Argentina and Colombia, pushed for daring bills of democratic reform precisely because they were trying to preempt a powerful opposition. In contrast, Uruguayan liberals did not feel threatened enough by the Blancos—thus the absence of radical legislation.

Patterns of urbanization, an old favorite variable of modernization theory and Marxism, did affect state formation. However, the comparison of these cases shows the limits of the approach. Argentina, on one hand, and Colombia and Venezuela, on the other, seem to confirm that urbanization favored power centralization. The more urban Argentina centralized power faster than the less urban Colombia and Venezuela. Nevertheless, Uruguay, as urban as Argentina—with a capital city that contributed approximately 80 percent of state revenues, controlled overseas trade, and had a monopoly on customs duties—followed a slower pace of power centralization that placed it closer to Colombia and Venezuela. And rural and less modern Paraguay, in comparison with Colombia, Venezuela, and Uruguay, centralized power much faster. Moreover, Argentina showed that modernization alone does not necessarily favor power centralization; it did so in that country because of a prior institutional history that discouraged political competition.

Given the differences in political outcomes that characterized the five cases, mode-of-production explanations do not seem to suffice to explain these variations, either. Although by the early twentieth century an industrialized sector emerged in countries such as Argentina, industrialization remained rather modest, and we can argue that all the cases considered here shared the same mode of production. The relations of production and their evolution also turned out to be poor predictors of political outcomes. In our cases, no drastic change occurred in the relations of production within the framework of the same mode of production, as argued by Robert Brenner (1976) regarding medieval Europe. In addition, the timing and scope of the transformations experienced by the relations of production in the five cases did not correspond with the deep changes they endured in institutions and regimes.

Democracy was not negatively affected or favored by whether farmers, artisans, and peasants—or, for that matter, workers in manufacturing—shared an important or shabby part of the evolution of these nineteenth-century economies. Despite a rather blurred differentiation between farmers and peasants in the literature, some favored farmers over peasants as a positive democratizing influence. Yet in the cases analyzed here, farmers made an uncertain contribution to democracy. For example, Uruguay, which lacked a significant farm sector, ended up becoming more democratic than Colombia or Paraguay, which possessed farm economies. The peasants' contribution to democracy remained ambiguous as well. Marx's negative views of the peasantry in relation to democratic outcomes need not be repeated—but perhaps the most attractive claim of this sort for the cases examined here comes from Barrington Moore (1966).

In Moore's argument, democracy in countries with a large peasantry (such as France) could emerge only by an early revolution before the switch to commercial agriculture. Asia (specifically China and Russia) furnished cases in which peasant revolutions (especially China) took place after modernization, and therefore these societies adopted totalitarianism under communist rule. Uruguay, which underwent what can be called a rural revolution before the switch to commercial agriculture, and had no peasantry, evolved into a more democratic regime and therefore seemed to provide support for the theory. For the opposite reasons, Paraguay seems to add reassuring proof. The country did not experience a rural revolution before the switch, possessed a large peasantry, and evolved into an authoritarian state. A distinguishing feature of Paraguay that contributes to explain this outcome, however, was that despite the nation's mild form of rural populism, the central army's strong role in the incorporation of rural labor prevented the emergence of independent grassroots movements or peasant parties—unlike in Eastern Europe. Colombia, with an important peasant sector, also offers ambiguous evidence. It disproves Moore's theory, because the country kept its peasantry almost intact but developed a party system conducive to democracy. And yet it may provide evidence to support those who see peasants as a negative influence, because the polity that emerged in Colombia remained exclusive, and thus many scholars have perceived both Colombian peasants and farmers as obstacles.[3] Finally, Argentina, if anything, demonstrates that without a peasant sector, a country can still find many other impediments to building a democratic polity. Indeed, the country differed from more democratic Uruguay by having a thriving farm sector, yet these farmers appear not to have significantly helped the cause of democracy.

Further testing, within and without Latin America, is needed to reformulate this argument in more encompassing and persuasive ways. As must all arguments that study long processes and look at critical junctures to examine the "origins" and development of polities and regimes, so must this one confront the threat of historical determinism. I hope, however, that the cases speak of the complex array of intervening variables that can address the final outcome, the significance of other theories, and the fallibility of my own.

Notes

Introduction

1 Chile, however, achieved stability faster than Argentina. The different pace of state building was partially related to the military's degree of development. In the 1830s, Chile decisively defeated Peru and Bolivia, but Argentina could no longer dominate rebellious Uruguay and failed to control Paraguay and Upper Peru.

2 Collier and Collier (1991:789) have used the term "state" to designate the "bureaucratic and legal institutions of the public sector and the incumbent of these institutions." I adopt this usage, which encompasses the government in the sense of "the head of state and the immediate political leadership" surrounding the head of state, plus the public bureaucracy, the legislature, and the armed forces. Because the formation and evolution of the state and the armed forces were not necessarily identical, however, the chapters on the cases treat them separately.

3 See for example Evans 1987; Mann 1988b; Migdal 1988; Nordingler 1987. I assume here that the state can be an autonomous structure with a "logic and interest of its own not necessarily equivalent to, or fused with, the interests of the dominant classes in society or the full set of member groups in the polity" (Skocpol 1979:27).

4 See for example Levi 1990; North 1981, 1990; Shepsle 1989; Silberman 1993; Rogowski 1974.

5 For example, regimes are classified as monarchy, aristocracy, and democracy, as well as, in Aristotle's words, their "corrupted forms": tyranny, oligarchy, and demagogy.

6 Procedural versions of democracy facilitate comparisons and are widely used in long-term comparative analysis. Following Rueschemeyer, Stephens, and Stephens (1992:43–44), I define democracy as entailing three criteria: (1) regular, free, and fair elections of representatives with equal and universal suffrage; (2) responsibility of the state to the elected parliament or congress; and (3) freedom of association and expression, and protection of individual rights.

7 See Gillis 1989; Howard 1984; Kennedy 1987; Porter 1994.

8 Although state makers in Argentina were able to construct a stronger state in close collaboration with the army, civilians still played a stronger role in building the polity in Argentina.

9 One also hears of the "Brazilian riddle," the "Paraguayan riddle," the "Venezuelan riddle," and so forth. Almost all literature on the United States has characterized that country as exceptional as well.

10 See Katzenstein 1978; Krasner 1978; Nordingler 1981; Skocpol 1979.

11 Claiming that it ignored important considerations outside the formal governmental framework, the Comparative Politics Committee of the SSRC argued in 1955 that the state was too narrow a focus for research. See Almond, Cole, and Macridis 1955.

12 Civil society was understood in the widest possible context of extrastatal agencies and manifestations of collective action, including grassroots organizations, churches, mass media, and interest groups of all kinds.

13 Silberman (1993) discusses the formation of bureaucracies and their evolution.

14 For Huntington, political parties embody the largest degree of autonomy and are in effect the handicrafters of the state. Huntington also makes the political system, by which he means principally the party system, rather independent from the national and international economy. For an example of the literature on the United States, see Chambers 1969.

15 For details on the concept of "critical juncture," see the useful treatment by Collier and Collier (1991:27–39). Junctures may include elections, the incorporation of the labor movement, the extension of the franchise, the passing of a new bill, the impact of international events or economic crises, and war.

16 See Rippy 1943; W. Robertson 1918; Rojas Mery 1946.

17 Lynch's (1986) work on the Spanish American revolutions remains one of the best comparative narrative histories of these events. To that, one must add Bushnell and Macaulay 1988; Tulchin 1973; the edited volume by Humphreys and Lynch (1964); Moses 1926; and the classic work of Halperín Donghi (1993).

18 See for example Centeno 1997; Domínguez 1980; López-Alves 1993b. The insightful work of Domínguez focuses on the wars of independence and therefore includes only the initial stage of the larger developments examined in this book. Bergquist (1986) also adopted a comparative approach to examining institution building but focused on a later period.

19 Remmer (1984) discusses the political trajectory.

20 See Cardoso and Faletto 1979; Rueschemeyer, Stephens, and Stephens 1992; Schwartz 1989; Sunkel and Paz 1970.

21 See figure 8.1 in Collier and Collier 1991:747.

22 In my analysis of Argentina in chapter 4, I focus mainly on the province of Buenos Aires, which includes the capital city and its hinterland. Data from the other provinces proved more difficult to find; yet even if information was more readily available, my central comparative interest would still rest with Buenos Aires because of its geographic, structural, and cultural similarities to Uruguay.

23 Argentina possessed a larger indigenous population, which resisted both conqueror and creole; but native inhabitants were in retreat, and their land was taken over by ranchers or government officials by the third decade after independence. Therefore, not only in the province of Buenos Aires but also in the cities of the Littoral and the Interior, European cultural influences—as in Uruguay—became quite dominant.

24 The state apparatus really did not penetrate the countryside or more fully develop its bureaucracy until after the Blanco Aparicio Saravia insurrection in Uruguay in 1904, and the Thousand Day War in Colombia in 1903.

25 Rosas was governor of the province of Buenos Aires from 1829 to 1832 and from 1835 to 1852. Timing is, of course, a relative notion. Although Argentina centralized power earlier than either Uruguay or Colombia, one can cite Argentina as an example of slower state building in light of the experience of Mexico or Brazil.

26 The literature on the United States is apparently enormous, and I have used the work of only a limited number of authors.

1 The Argument: War, Polities, and the Rural Poor

1 In addition to the sources cited in the introduction, see the reviews in Mann 1993:44–91; Migdal, Kohli, and Shue 1994:7–37.

2 See for example Anderson 1974; Barkey 1995; Bartlett 1991; Goldstone 1991; Kasaba 1988; Kennedy 1987; Kuhn 1980; Mann 1986, 1993; Migdal 1988; North 1981, 1990; Spense 1990; Tilly 1978, 1990.

3 See Moore 1966 on the commercialization of agriculture; Marx 1959 and Moore 1966 on the rise of a bourgeoisie; Rueschemeyer, Stephens, and Stephens 1992 on the formation and integration of the working class; Marx 1959 and Kemp 1993 on the growth of the industrial sector; Downing 1992 on the preexistence of medieval forms of constitutionalism; Brenner 1976, Dobb 1947, Rueschemeyer, Stephens, and Stephens 1992 on labor relations and the character of labor in agriculture under feudalism; and P. Anderson 1974 on the pervasive influence of "Roman law."

4 See also Hartz 1964:26–33.

5 See Laclau 1971; and the controversy in the *American Historical Review* triggered by Stern (1988:841), who concluded that to call Latin America "feudal" or "seigniorial" and to equate it with earlier Old World slavery, obscures more than clarifies the issue. See also Veliz 1980:16–28.

6 There was no bank in the region before 1808, and producers were limited to traditional sources of financing: guilds, the Catholic Church, and brokers or merchants. See Bushnell and Macaulay 1988:50.

7 See for example Ansaldi 1988; Puiggrós 1948, 1974.

8 See North and Thomas 1973; North 1990:395. For North, Marxist and neoclassical economic theory cannot fully explain the cohesiveness of group political action or the behavior of bureaucrats; hence his inclusion of ideology as a key element of state maintenance.

9 Mann makes this case for both Europe and the United States (1986:vol. 1:28).

10 El Salvador seems to have been an extreme case. According to Lindo-Fuentes (1990), the state could not collect the most basic income.

11 See Naquin and Rawski 1987:4–21; Spense 1990:90–116.

12 See Naquin and Rawski 1987:5–6; Spense 1990:51–53. It would be somewhat inadequate to apply the term "nobility" to elites in Latin America. Nonetheless, for the purpose of comparison, one can argue that the landed elites who engaged in war activity played a similar role.

13 P. Anderson 1974; Moore 1966; Skocpol 1979; Rueschemeyer, Stephens, and Stephens 1992.

14 There were exceptions, which will be analyzed in some detail in the next chapters.

15 This is a major argument of Barkey (1991, 1995).

16 Barkey 1995:9.

17 See Chapman 1993; Bushnell and Macaulay 1988; Madariaga 1955; Halperín Donghi 1993; Hartz 1964; Mora 1973; Morse 1964; Parry 1966; Rojas Mery 1946; Rock 1987; Veliz 1980; Wiarda 1992; Worcester 1992.

18 No state in Latin America—including Paraguay, which at one point did own large extents of land and slaves, and Venezuela, which was the largest landholder by the second decade of the twentieth century—compare to this situation.

19 See Goldstone 1991:365–68, 379. Rulers faced a significant decline in revenues. By the seventeenth century, open revolts by provincial officials and magnates were a common occurrence in the empire.

20 See Kasaba 1994:226.

21 Taken from the commentary of a contemporary who attributed to society the functions that literature on the West usually assigns to the state. See Kasaba 1994:208.

22 For dissident views on accepted notions about the weakness of the American state, see Bensel 1990; Skocpol 1992; Skowronek 1982.

23 See McFarlane 1985, 1995. There is a sizable body of literature on late-eighteenth-century rebellions.

24 Barkey 1995:176.

25 Even under Caroline absolutism, Sweden differed from absolutist states everywhere in Europe, since its military was a citizen army loyal to the constitution. For details, see P. Anderson 1974; Downing 1992:chap. 8.

26 Barkey 1995:230.

27 See Naquin and Rawski 1987:4. During the decline of Ming China, the Manchus created so-called Banners, which performed functions similar to political parties in early Latin America. Banners became administrative units for registration, conscription, and mobilization.

28 Here I must thank Miguel Centeno and Jonathan Rosenberg, who pointed out that these suggestions could also apply to Porfirian and revolutionary Mexico.

29 See for example Chambers 1969; Degler 1959; Hartz 1955; Huntington 1981; Morone 1990; Lipset 1963, 1990; Wood 1972.

30 See Dinkin 1982; Shefter 1979.

31 Downing 1992:54.

32 Ibid.

33 The fuero was a body of privilege and rights, "jurisdictions, functions and obligations accorded to a town, corporation, association, classes, or individuals by charter or law granted by the Crown" (Gilmore 1964:23).

34 See, for instance, Andrews's analysis of these events (1985:127).

35 The term "political revolution" refers exclusively to changes in government institutions and ruling coalitions. It means that institutional change was significant enough to create a new polity, but it does not imply radical changes in the mode of production or the structure of class relations.

36 Lynch 1992:82.

37 See Veliz 1980.

38 See Blainey 1973:ix.

39 Tilly (1990:12) argues that Britain, France, and Brandenburg-Prussia, for instance, cannot be taken as general models of state making.

40 With the exceptions of Gourevitch 1986 and Katzenstein 1985, most literature on political economy has focused on cleavages and coalition type, rather than institution type. Rogowski's (1989) "exposure to trade" and Wallerstein's (1974) overall integration of national units into the "world system" contribute to understanding cleavages and type of coalition but remain insufficient to explain types of polities.

41 See Bollen 1979.

42 Rueschemeyer, Stephens, and Stephens 1992:165.

43 See Lindo-Fuentes 1990; Dunkerley 1988.

44 The same applies to table 1.4.

45 Waisman argues that in the 1940s, Juan Peron and state corporatism appealed to most of Argentina's economic elites because they perceived the "activated" labor movement as a serious threat from below.

46 See López-Alves 1989b:32–45; Rogowski 1989; Rueschemeyer, Stephens, and Stephens 1992:165–66; Stephens 1989.

2 Gauchos, Ranchers, and State Autonomy in Uruguay, 1811–1890

1 See Lanzaro 1986; Weinstein 1975.

2 See López-Alves 1993a.

3 See López-Alves 1995.

4 For details, see López-Alves 1993a.

5 Congress did not immediately pass this bill, but it was finally approved in 1932.

6 For a fuller discussion of batllismo and its importance in Uruguayan political history, see López-Alves 1993b:5–15. The other major party in this two-dominant-party system was the Blanco, or Nationalist, Party.

7 Batlle died in 1929, but his political legacy did not. As Finch (1981:2) wrote, "batllism refers to a national style or ideology of development within which Uruguayan public life was conducted from early this century to the end of the 1960s." For most Uruguayan scholars, the so-called "Batlle era" began in 1902 and ended with the Great Depression in 1929.

8 See Barrán and Nahum 1979–1986; Louis 1969; Panizza 1990; Vagner 1980a, 1980b.

9 See Barrán and Nahum 1979–1986.

10 By 1829, customs duties provided 582,234 pesos of a total state revenue of 751,040 pesos. By 1872, the state's income totaled 8,099,554 pesos, out of which 7,207,907 came from customs duties. In Barrán and Nahum 1967–1978:vol. 1:186.

11 *New York Times,* 15 October 1856, 3. On 4 November 1856, the *Times* reported on Uruguay's financial situation after the war.

12 For a complete description of the state's poor resources, see President Pedro Varela's *Presidential Report to the Cámaras, February 1875,* which shows the disastrous state of the bureaucracy and the inadequacy of state agency resources.

13 The military remained in power until 1983, when civilians gained state control.

14 The country's first constitution (1830) remained the same until 1917, and little change took place in the basic design of state institutions during state building.

15 Attempts to change the original document abounded (1838, 1842, 1851, 1853, 1878, and often during the 1880s). On the constitutional debate of the first half of the nineteenth century, see Sala de Touron and Alonso Eloy (1986–1991:126–27).

16 Tellingly, contemporaries used several names to refer to the territory today known as Uruguay, including *Banda del Norte, Banda Septentrional,* or *Banda de los Charruas.* In the north, no one was certain where the Banda began and Brazil ended. The first two designations expressed the location of Uruguay in relation to the capital of the viceroyalty, Buenos Aires. The latter referred to the presence of nomadic Charrua Indians who originally inhabited that territory.

17 As Real de Azúa (1984b:74) argued, initiatives to change the constitution, or to modify the state bureaucracy that it called for, came to be perceived as a move against the motherland.

18 See articles 153–58. The constitution called for a strong president and no permanent vice president. The annually elected president of the senate acted as vice president under extreme circumstances.

19 Pivel Devoto (1942:esp. vol. 1:236), for instance, argued forcefully that differences in ideas constituted the major cleavage in party building.

20 Reyes Abadie (1977), for instance, notes the "unusual" influence of liberal ideas in Montevideo. Some of the recent work on Batlle also acknowledges the dominant liberal (and even socialist) content of Batllista discourse and argues that it is a crucial building block in the development of this party and the nation at large. See Panizza 1990:esp. 37–55.

21 This view has been quite pervasive, and yet not articulated in a clear-cut hypothesis. For such arguments, see Stewart Vargas 1970; McDonald 1978; Pendle 1963; Weinstein 1975.

22 See Pivel Devoto 1956:vol. 2:138–39.

23 The first partidos de ideas were created in the 1850s (e.g., Andres Lamas and his *Unión Liberal* in 1855), but they peaked in the 1870s under principismo, or parties of principle, rather than those moved by loyalties to leaders or the spoils of war. This movement inspired the emergence of the *Partido Radical* (Radical Party) in 1872, and the *Partido Constitucional* (Constitutional Party) in 1880.

24 See Barrán and Nahum 1967–1978:201–9; Juan Oddone 1956:esp. 7–20; Reyes Abadie 1977:33–49; Pivel Devoto 1956:vol. 2:chap. 3; de Torres Wilson 1973:37–45.

25 These theories suggest that a more even land distribution created more

egalitarian political views, favored more inclusive political institutions, and encouraged entrepreneurial talents.

26 See Barrán and Nahum 1967–1978:vol. 1:part 5; Kleinpenning 1995:170.

27 Chapter 3 discusses the literature that saw a decisive step toward democracy in Colombia's 1850s "artisan revolt."

28 See, for instance, Marx 1959, 1967:vol. 3; and Moore 1966, especially on the contrasting experiences of England and China.

29 See Barrán and Nahum 1967–1978:vols. 1, 3; Denoon 1983; Finch 1981. Unlike their counterparts in Argentina, Uruguayan landowners played a modest role in the frozen-beef trade, which primarily engaged landowners in the South and Littoral but left most livestock producers in the large central and northern areas marginally integrated into the trade.

30 The British, Basque, Irish, French, and others played key roles, such as founders Benjamin Pourcel and Perfecto Giot.

31 See Barrán and Nahum 1967–1978:vol. 1:sec. 5.

32 See Barrán and Nahum 1979–1986:vol. 1:109.

33 Quoted in Reyes Abadie 1977:27.

34 Pivel Devoto 1942:58, 207, 209, 224; Zum Felde 1920; Reyes Abadie 1977, 1990. Charles Darwin (1933) described Uruguay as "virtually empty." Regarding a trip through the country, he wrote of "thick trees and green plains, with no visible sign of human proximity."

35 Real de Azúa (1961) uses the term "patricians."

36 See Barrán and Nahum 1979–1986:vols. 1–8; Barrán and Nahum 1967–1978:vols. 1–7; Reyes Abadie, Bruschera, and Melogno 1968; Reyes Abadie and Vázquez Romero 1981:vols. 1–4; Sala de Touron et al. 1970; Sala de Touron and Alonso Eloy 1986–1991:vols. 1–2.

37 Their contribution has no parallel in the literature on Uruguay or even in the general literature on nineteenth-century Latin America. Reyes Abadie and Vázquez Romero's (1981) encyclopedic volumes on Uruguay are the only possible comparison. Yet despite painstaking details and microscopic use of archives, there is a vacuum of themes and questions in the Reyes Abadie and Vázquez Romero collection.

38 See Barrán and Nahum 1967–1978:vol. 1:83 and passim; vol. 2:74–76.

39 This argument runs throughout Barrán and Nahum 1967–1978; 1979–1986. See especially their study on the 1890s economic crisis and the responses it triggered (1967–1978:vol. 3).

40 The inefficiency that characterized rural enterprises responded to a market structure lacking incentives for more entrepreneurial and risky behavior.

41 See Sala de Touron and Alonso Eloy 1986–1991:vol. 1:52–53. Most historiography indeed coincides with Sala de Touron and Alonso Eloy's account that the rivalry with Buenos Aires explains tariffs and the terms of trade.

42 See Sala de Touron and Alonso Eloy 1986–1991:esp. vol. 2:112, 152, 224–38.

43 Curiously, although Sala de Touron and Alonso Eloy (1986–1991:vol. 2:223 and passim) briefly compare Argentina under Rosas, they do not seem to perceive that the comparison challenges both mode-of-production and dependency approaches (see chapter 1).

44 Sala de Touron and Alonso Eloy (1986–1991:vol. 2:320) place an unwarranted (according to their own historical data) emphasis on the impact of foreign influence on economic development. See their poorly fitting comparison with Mexico.

45 Patriots included gauchos, Indians who abandoned the Jesuit missions after the order's expulsion, deserters from the Spanish and Portuguese armies, indigenous groups (of Charrua, Guaraní, or Chana origin), and creole elites who consolidated before the large waves of European immigrants. Sala de Touron and Alonso Eloy (1986–1991:vol. 2:58–107) describe these "precursor nationals."

46 See de Herrera (1984).

47 See López-Alves 1989b.

48 See Garcia 1956; de Herrera 1984. Emphasis on the personality of the gaucho and the struggles of rural populations and caudillos in the forging of this unique political culture is also found in Pivel Devoto 1956:esp. vol.2; Pivel Devoto and Ranieri de Pivel Devoto 1948a.

49 Nineteenth-century authors, such as Bauza (1876, 1887), had long subscribed to this view as well.

50 Despite frequent references to the characteristics Uruguay shared with other lands of recent settlement, few sources (see Denoon 1983) include Uruguay in comparisons of this nature.

51 A full list of references would be too lengthy, but good examples include the edited volumes by Real de Azúa (1968b, 1984a).

52 See Barrán and Nahum 1967–1978:vol. 3:76–77.

53 On the United States, see Hartz 1955, 1964; Huntington 1968; Morone 1990; Wood 1972, 1992.

54 Departments close to Montevideo (Colonia and Canelones) also hosted large numbers of Europeans.

55 From the (revised) census of 1877. Starting in 1839, Italian immigrants outnumbered all others, including Spaniards, French, Brazilians, and British ("Sulla Propieta Territoriale Degli'Italiani Nel Dipartamento di Montevideo," *Bolletino Consulare* 16 [March 1879], Roma, Biblioteca Ministero degli Affari Esteri). Italian migration peaked in the late 1860s and early 1870s.

56 Archivo de Ministerio de Asuntos Exteriores (MAS). Serie Politica, Legajo 2707, Folio no. 24 (March 1887), Madrid.

57 He argued that a comparison of geography and natural resources, rather than in terms of culture, is much more appropriate.

58 See Vanger 1980a, 1980b.

59 Most figures suggest that Uruguay's export industry peaked in the 1920s, or even the late 1930s and 1940s, after the initiation of political reform. See Finch 1981. I argue hereafter that the conservative bloc's weakness explains much of Batlle's success.

60 In the final analysis, Sala de Touron and Landinelli (1984) agreed with the latter position. Batlle's demagogic machinations fooled the working class into fighting for bourgeois interests, hampering the formation of a labor party.

61 See Sala de Touron and Landinelli 1984. For a detailed discussion of these issues, see López-Alves 1995.

62 See López-Alves 1993b:56–58.

63 Soon, imported goods brought to Uruguay via Argentina doubled those entering through the port of Montevideo. Additionally, goods reached northern Argentina and Peru through Buenos Aires.

64 General Console G. B. Raffo, "Commercio e Navigazione del Porto de Montevideo," in *Bolletino Consolare*, vol. 2 (Torino: Biblioteca Ministero degli Affari Esteri, 1863), 883.

65 Quoted in Barrán and Nahum 1967–1978:vol. 1:111.

66 For details, see table on public debt in Barrán and Nahum 1967–1978:vol. 1:187.

67 Public Record Office, Foreign Office 51, 160 (16 July 1870). From Munro to the earl of Clarendon (dispatch no. 20:90), "On the disastrous conditions of city and countryside." See also Foreign Office 51, 167, dispatch no. 11, Buenos Aires (13 September 1870).

68 The Spanish viceroyalty founded Montevideo in 1723 as a garrison to stop the advances of the Portuguese. In 1875 the British ministry of foreign affairs accurately described the emerging state as "originally [a] part of the Spanish Vice-royalty of Buenos Aires [which] became the object of a long and ruinous war between Brazil and the Argentine Confederation which only terminated in the year 1828 through the mediation of the British Government." Public Record Office, Foreign Office 51, 179:112, private. *Brief Sketch of the Political History of Uruguay* (printed in the Offices of the Ministry of Foreign Affairs, London, 1875).

69 Pivel Devoto 1942:vol. 1:96.

70 Common to Latin America, this represented a division between Ministeriales (inspired by the political and administrative life of the cabildos) and their republican challengers.

71 A consular report in 1863 noted that "in agreement with the historical record it can be guaranteed that without the impulse and cooperation

given by political groups of neighboring countries to the revolutionary element of the Banda Oriental . . . peace would have never been disturbed nor blood would have been shed or the industry of foreigners and Nationals obstructed from following its natural development." Attached to dispatch no. 2, confidential, Montevideo, 19 September 1863 (Pacco 357, classification of Rugero Moscati, Ministere Degli Affari Estere, Roma: Tipografia Reservata, 1963).

72 Following contemporaries and current literature on Uruguay, I use "revoluciónes de partido" to mean wars between the parties. Uprisings led by party factions, such as the conservatives and "fusionists" against Flores (1855), or the Revolución Tricolor insurrection against President Varela (1875), are not considered revoluciónes de partido; nor is the Blanco Aparicio Saravia revolt (1903) against President Batlle y Ordoñez a typical revolución de partido. In that instance, a government backed by its professional army fought a rural insurrection.

73 Table 2.5 does not include the Colorado government of Venancio Flores, who took office by armed insurrection in 1865.

74 President Giro integrated his cabinet with Blancos and Colorados who had fought the Guerra Grande, and he tried to form an alliance. Pereira aspired to create a third party, the Partido Nacional, which had no relation to the Blanco Party, an organization that adopted this name much later. Finally, under Berro, the use of party slogans was declared illegal and their use subject to penalties.

75 Public Record Office, Foreign Office 51, no. 160, decree 6, confidential, Montevideo (10 April 1870). From John Munro to the earl of Clarendon.

76 Quoted in Machado 1984:vol. 1:46.

77 See Barrán and Nahum 1989 for a similar argument in terms of the participation of the rural poor.

78 See Barrán and Nahum 1989:72.

79 From 15 November 1781. Quoted in Barrán and Nahum 1989:72.

80 On these issues, see Campal 1964; see also his articles in the weekly *Marcha* during 1964 and 1965, which give details of rural unemployment and the social consequences of the expansion of latifundia ranching in the late colonial period.

81 See Barrán and Nahum 1989:104–8; Machado 1984:vol. 1:47–52.

82 "Many times I heard him complain that few sons of distinguished families in the country wanted to fight under his command perhaps because of the deprivations and struggles that go along with military life. This made him rely on the gauchos, in whom he found more resignation, more perseverance and endurance." *Escritos históricos del Coronel Ramon de Caceres,* quoted in Barrán and Nahum 1989:102.

83 See Zum Felde 1972:48.

84 From a letter to L. Galvan, in Bruschera 1969:66.

85 "Reglamento Provisorio de la Provincia Oriental para el Fomento de su Campana y Seguridad de sus Hacendados," 10 September 1815 (Biblioteca Nacional, Sala Uruguay).

86 Most reliable sources agree. In addition to those already cited, see Sala de Touron et al. 1970.

87 See Machado 1984:vol. 1; Reyes Abadie, Bruschera, and Melogno 1968; Reyes Abadie and Vázquez Romero 1981:vol. 2:281–461.

88 See Zum Felde 1920:107, 110; de Herrera 1984.

89 See Pivel Devoto 1942:vol. 1:30.

90 This is the so-called "generals' pact" of 1830. Rivera retained the *comandancia general de la campaña* (the general captaincy of the countryside). This cleavage became even deeper during the Guerra Grande.

91 Zum Felde (1920:125), for instance, writes that state makers who designed the constitution could not figure out "what went on beyond the citadel."

92 The project never prospered. See Sala de Touron and Alonso Eloy 1986–1991:vol. 2:190 on efforts to create a class of farmers loyal to the government.

93 *El Universal,* no. 866, 10 June 1832.

94 See Barrán and Nahum 1967–1978:vol. 1:558–61.

95 Article 11 established that "wage paid peons, paid servants, rank-and-file soldiers, and vagrants" could not vote. A tiny minority consisting of small farmers on the outskirts of Montevideo, who depended on the city's economy, were not considered part of the "dangerous" rural masses.

96 Compare this with Argentina and Colombia. Following the lead of the Rivadavian reforms in Buenos Aires in the 1820s, Argentine state makers in 1857 extended the franchise without restrictions to all males. The 1850s reforms in Colombia also proposed a fuller incorporation of the lower classes.

97 Caudillos often represented small rural proprietors in litigation involving land invasions, property rights, or the plight of entire populations vis-à-vis rich hacendados. See de la Torre, Rodríguez, and Sala de Touron 1972:chaps. 4, 6.

98 Details in Pivel Devoto 1942:vol. 2:154.

99 From a letter to Pedro Bustamante, 2 May 1876 (Montevideo, Sala Uruguay, Biblioteca Nacional).

100 See Zum Felde 1920. Reyes Abadie (1977:51) described Congress as the most "exquisite" forum of philosophical and political debate, as "a Parliament which is not a Parliament, but an Academy, a government that is not a body of government, but an Ateneo." See also Barrán and Nahum 1967–1978:esp. vols. 1, 3.

101 See for example Barrán and Nahum 1967–1978:vol. 1; Pivel Devoto and Ranieri de Pivel Devoto 1948a; Sala de Touron and Alonso Eloy 1986–1991; Reyes Abadie and Vázquez Romero 1981:vol. 2; Zum Felde 1920.

102 See Machado 1984:vol. 3:33.

103 Some estimate that the casualties sometimes rose to more than a thousand. For a full account, see Acevedo 1933:vol. 2:esp. 148–50, 311–18, 383–93.

104 Rosas's program was called *Defensa Americana* (American Defense) and preached the formation of a Latin American bloc against European penetration in the River Plate.

105 Approximately 2,500 French soldiers, 500 Italians, and 500 Argentine Unitarios were under the command of General Paz, who became the "Supreme Chief of the Defensa." Fifty foreign vessels also were ready to defend the city.

106 Montevideo, 2 February 1854. Secretaria de Estado (Archivo Ministerio de Asuntos Exteriores, Madrid, Serie Politica Uruguay, Legajo 2706, 1854–1865).

107 Public Record Office, Foreign Office 51, 41, no. 5, confidential, Montevideo (19 July 1846).

108 For details, see López-Alves 1993b:55–58.

109 Madrid, AME, Uruguay, Serie Politica, Legajo 2705, 1845–1853. Informe no. 120, Montevideo (31 December 1853).

110 Abundant and thorough citations of newspaper reports on the Guerra Grande can be found in Acevedo 1933:esp. vols. 2–3 and Barrán and Nahum 1967–1978:esp. vol. 1:28–47.

111 Quoted in Barrán and Nahum 1967–1978:vol. 1:37. *Asado* can be translated as "barbecue."

112 *El Defensor de la Independencia Americana,* no. 5, 11 October 1848.

113 "Mensaje del poder Ejecutivo a la Octava Legislatura de la Republica Oriental del Uruguay en la apertura de sus sesiones ordinarias." 15 February 1858. Printed in Montevideo, Imprenta de la Republica, and signed by Gabriel Pereira, Antonio de las Carreras, Andres A. Gomez, and Federico Nin Reyes (Sala Uruguay, Biblioteca Nacional, Montevideo).

114 Public Record Office, Foreign Office 51, 130, dispatch no. 31 (29 March 1865), William Loadstone to the earl of Clarendon.

115 Ibid.

116 Flores excluded Blanco support and enlarged the bureaucracy by appointing Colorados and Brazilian advisers to the state bureaucracy.

117 Public Record Office, Foreign Office 51, 143, dispatch no. 1 (28 July 1867).

118 Regarding the foreign body, see López-Alves 1993b:52–53. The quotation is taken from *Journal de Commercio* (Rio de Janeiro), 28 October 1855, 2.

119 Aware of the instability of his government, on 15 February 1868, Flores left his office in the hands of Pedro Varela, president of the Senate. Four days later, Flores was assassinated. For a fuller account of the Flores regime and the circumstances of his death, see López-Alves 1993b:55–56.

120 MDAE, Pacco 1481, Serie Politica, no. 35, Montevideo (12 December 1870). From Raffo to Viscount Venosta.

121 Such efforts materialized in the newspaper *La Democracia* and a party manifesto elaborated by El Club de los Nacionalistas in June 1872, in which the party rejected violence and argued for elections as the best and safest mechanism to guarantee the rights of political minorities.

122 In 1881 the Principista Colorados launched another manifesto in which, like the Blancos, they argued for individual liberties, political rights, civilian rule, and peaceful transfers of power through elections.

123 Batlle was a general trained in France, a former Principista Colorado who had plotted against the first Flores administration in 1854. Like his predecessors, he appointed an overwhelming majority of his partisans to cámaras and ministries.

124 See Zum Felde 1972:24–26.

125 As Barrán and Nahum (1967–1978:vol. 1:195) put it, "The high command of the Timoteo Aparicio movement was a high command composed of estanciero-colonels and estanciero-captains."

126 One finds French, Basque, Italian, British, German, Spanish, and even some Dutch within this group of entrepreneurial estancieros. Large numbers of Brazilians and a sizable number of Argentines completed the picture. On foreign landowners, see Barrán and Nahum 1967–1978 and Sala de Touron and Alonso Eloy 1986–1991:vol. 2. On the composition of immigration in general, and percentages of immigrants settling on large and small property, a very good source is Kleinpenning 1995:235–90.

127 Conversations with José Pedro Barrán, Montevideo (July 1990). For details, see Barrán and Nahum's findings (1979–1986:vol. 1:226–27).

128 See the Latorre, Santos, and Tajes governments in table 2.5.

129 This practice started with the very party founders: Lavalleja, Rivera, and Oribe.

130 For example, in the 1870s, Colorado doctores established the *Club Liberal* (Liberal Club) and were able to recruit successfully among officers who became active members. See Pivel Devoto 1942:vol. 2:113.

131 It was at that time that *jefes militares* (military chiefs) loyal to the Blancos published a manifesto complaining about the increasing influence of urban politics in the countryside. See Pivel Devoto 1942:155.

132 Public Record Office, Foreign Office 51, 130, dispatch 39, Montevideo (18 April 1865). From J. Letteson to Earl Russell.

133 On 10 September 1870, the Italian chargé d'affaires reported, "The troops recruited by Blanco leaders were by and large mercenary troops . . . composed mainly by Italians" (Serie Politica no. 32, Pacco 1481, Moscati V, VI, Rome, MDAE).

134 On his administration, see Bengoa 1936; Fernandez Cabrelli 1975; Fernandez Saldana 1969; Reyes Abadie 1977. For an overview of Latorre and militarism as a whole, see as well Barrán and Nahum 1967–1978:vol. 1:479–585.

135 Italics mine. Communique delivered by hacendado Oscar Hordenana to the Foreign Diplomatic Body in Montevideo on 11 March 1876 (Biblioteca Nacional, Sala Uruguay).

136 Public Record Office, London, Foreign Office 51, 160, dispatch no. 20, Montevideo (16 July 1870). From John Munro to the earl of Clarendon.

137 Latorre had distinguished himself in suppressing the Revolución Tricolor (see table 2.4) against the Pedro Varela government and was known for his strong conviction that elected civilians, rather than the army, should finally rule.

138 See North 1981.

139 See Barrán and Nahum 1967–1978:vol. 1:486–522; Reyes Abadie 1977:34–57.

140 By 1877, the total amount of wire used in these enclosures amounted to 6,646 kilos, and by the end of the Latorre administration in 1880, the total kilos of wire had jumped to 14,127. See Mendez Vives 1975:12.

141 See Reyes Abadie 1977:44.

142 Quoted in Reyes Abadie 1977:72, from the original 1876 deposition.

143 The regime kept party politics alive by appointing an advisory committee composed of Blancos and (in larger numbers) Colorados.

144 In March 1876 the officer corps numbered 1,205 men, 3 brigade generals, 16 generals, 177 lieutenants, and 24 marines. By the end of his government, only 153 officers remained, and from a total of eight active battalions at the time of Latorre's ascension to power, there were only four when he stepped down from office. See Reyes Abadie 1977:71.

145 For details, see Sala de Touron and Alonso Eloy 1986–1991:vol. 1:part 1.

146 See Mendez Vives 1975:33.

147 Rome, MDAE, Serie Politica no. 125, Montevideo, Pacco 1483 (10 July 1887).

148 One was Gabriel Terra's (brief) military coup in the 1930s; the other and more consequential was the military takeover of 1973.

3 A Weak Army and Restrictive Democracy: Colombia, 1810–1886

1 La Regeneración has been one of the most studied periods of Colombian political history. For details on this movement, and Núñez's evolution and achievements in terms of power centralization, see, among others, Bergquist 1978; Florez 1987; Guillén Martínez 1986; Melo 1978, 1991a; Park 1985; Villalba Bustillo 1979.

2 In these elections, Liberals gained power after more than twelve years of electoral defeat. They began to use the denomination "Liberal Party" around 1841 or 1842. In 1848 Ezequiel Rojas published what constituted the platform of the party. As for the Conservatives, the label "Conservative Party" was used to define the opposition (J. M. Samper 1873:75). In 1849 Mariano Ospina Rodriguez and José E. Caro put together the first platform of the Conservative Party.

3 For a detailed account on the wars of independence and the events of the year 1810, see Ocampo López 1984:36–45. See also Bushnell and Macaulay 1988:chap. 5.

4 There are several sources on the Colombian Church as a social actor, as well as its connections with the conservative coalition. For a very good study on the social, political, and cultural influence of the church in the different regions, see Abel 1974; F. González 1987a, 1987b.

5 See for example Kalmanovitz 1984 and 1986; Ocampo López 1984; Villegas and Yunis 1978; Stoller 1992.

6 See Pérez 1989:13–16. Sixty percent of Colombian presidents came from small towns, 20 percent from provincial capitals, and only 20 percent from Bogotá.

7 See Jaramillo 1991 on the period preceding the Thousand Day War. Similar lessons can be learned from Bergquist 1978; Fals Borda 1969; Posada-Carbó 1994; Melo 1991a; Villegas and Yunis 1978.

8 See Arango 1981:vol. 1; Bergquist 1978; Palacios 1986.

9 For details, see Bushnell 1954, 1993; Galvis Madero 1970; and Ocampo López 1984, among others.

10 See Bushnell 1993:83.

11 See M. González 1984:398–409; Vázquez Carrizosa 1986:129–31.

12 See Molina 1987:99.

13 See his "Nuestro Sistema Tributario," 26–28.

14 Address to the Santander Congress, in M. Samper 1969:22, 50.

15 See Bergquist 1978:37.

16 See Chassen de López 1982:18; Vázquez Carrizosa 1986:204–5.

17 Tellingly, the country started this century with two events that show the weakness of both the state and the military: the Guerra de los Mil Dias and the separation of Panama (more hereafter).

18 See Melo 1991b:33.

19 The reduction of the state to a mere bystander is captured by Molina (1988–1989), and Vázquez Carrizosa (1986:esp. 94).

20 Tirado Mejía 1970:124.

21 Colombian women, for instance, had to wait until 1954 for the right to vote, casting ballots for the first time in the 1957 elections.

22 See Vázquez Carrizosa 1986:133–34.

23 In this era of "anarchy," Panama split as an autonomous state, followed by Antioquia, Bolívar, Cauca, Cundinamarca, Magdalena, and Santander. See Vázquez Carrizosa 1986:126–27.

24 Melo 1991c:18.

25 Italics mine. In Madrid, MAE, Colombia: Correspondencia Embajadas y Legaciones, 1881–1899, Legajo 1426, Serie Politica no. 67, Bogotá 17, November 1885.

26 See Melo 1991c:51–52.

27 See Bergquist 1978.

28 *Correo de la Ciudad de Bogotá,* open letter of Candido Justo Veritas, no. 146, 16 May 1822.

29 See for example L. González 1975; Caballero Calderon 1960.

30 See Wilde 1982:28–30.

31 See Fals Borda 1969:95–97.

32 See Kalmanovitz 1986:116–17, 185.

33 Ibid.; Melo 1991b:76.

34 See Colmenares 1968:71.

35 See Tirado Mejía 1970:114.

36 Taken from Medardo Rivas and cited in Colmenares 1968:69.

37 See Bushnell 1954:170–71.

38 Significantly, at that time the population of New Granada had reached two million, and the number of slaves had been reduced to twenty thousand; that is, their numbers had dwindled by half within a population that had more than doubled since the early years of the century. See Kalmanovitz 1986:94; Jaramillo Uribe 1985:22.

39 From Public Records Office 135, Foreign Office, no. 31, London, n.p.

40 Quoted in Arango 1981:63–64.

41 The artisan "revolution" has been mentioned at some length in most lit-

erature. On the artisans' influence in the regions, see Stoller 1992:chaps. 7, 9–11. On Bogotano artisans, see Sowell 1986.

42 See Kalmanovitz 1986:131.

43 For example, Vargas Martínez (1972) perceives them as democratic, and Molina (1987) as "socialist."

44 Gilmore 1964:11.

45 See Bushnell and Macaulay 1988:211.

46 Ibid., 212.

47 The term "Golgota" alludes to the martyr of Golgotha, Jesus Christ. See Bushnell and Macaulay 1988:210; Tirado Mejía 1970:118.

48 See Kalmanovitz 1986:173.

49 See Jiménez and Sideri 1985:17–169.

50 Bushnell 1993:75.

51 The formation of a hegemonic elite backed up by an industrializing economic project and enough military power was crucial in the United States. See Bensel 1990; Skowronek 1982; Rogowski 1989.

52 See Chassen de López 1982:24; Melo 1978:57; Tovar Zambrano 1991: 10–11.

53 The rate of expansion of the industry was phenomenal and had no precedent. See comparative figures in Melo 1978:76–78.

54 See Arango 1981:53–68.

55 See McGreevey 1971:35–41.

56 See Bergquist 1978:11; Melo 1991b:80.

57 See Park 1985:56.

58 See M. González 1984:404–8.

59 See Arango 1981:50–51.

60 Ibid., 54.

61 See Kalmanovitz 1986:97; Safford 1972a.

62 See Chassen de López 1982:14–16; Kalmanovitz 1984:288–93.

63 See Guillén Martínez 1986:36.

64 See Melo 1978:75.

65 For details, see Villalba Bustillo 1979:32–33. Also see, among others, Bushnell and Macaulay 1988:209–11; Pérez 1989:18.

66 See Lynch 1993:262–63. A very detailed account of Hilario López's reforms can be found in Molina 1988–1989:vol. 1:26. See also Nieto Arteta 1970:vol. 1:118.

67 See Melo 1978:66–67; Tirado Mejía 1970:132–33.

68 The classic work in this tradition is Nieto Arteta 1970.

69 See Chassen de López 1982:31.

70 See J. Samper 1873:85; Vázquez Carrizosa 1986:72–73.

71 For details, see Bushnell 1993:36–40.

72 Bushnell 1993:64–66. For a discussion of the well-known clashes between those who followed Bolívar and those who disagreed, see Bushnell and Macaulay 1988:83–104; Delpar 1981:1–5; Galvis Madero 1970.

73 See Bushnell and Macaulay 1988:88–112. On Bolívar's project and its decline, see also Galvis Madero 1970:321–71.

74 See Bushnell 1993:51–52.

75 On the constitution of 1821, see W. Gibson 1948:35–66.

76 According to the Liberal Samper (1873:85), the Conservative regime went back to a close marriage of state and church, established a much more centralized administration, attempted to impose a police state, and protected slavery.

77 See M. González 1984:188–90.

78 It would be redundant to re-create the events that led to this war and its development, as well as its effects on the party system. For details, see L. Caballero 1939; Jaramillo 1991; Villegas and Yunis 1978. A very good source on coalition formation is Bergquist 1978, who gives detailed analysis of the conflict. For wars in general, including this one, see Tirado Mejía 1970.

79 According to Pastrana Borrero 1984:12.

80 Congress initiated the amendments of 1830, 1843, 1853, and 1858, and the General Assembly promoted the rest. See Tobón Sanín 1979:117.

81 From 1832 to 1858, present-day Colombia was referred to as New Granada, and between 1853 and 1863 as the *Confederación Granadina* (Granadian Confederation). From 1863 to 1886, the name *Los Estados Unidos de Colombia* (the United States of Colombia) was adopted, and finally, in 1886, the country approved the name *República de Colombia* (Republic of Colombia).

82 According to George Welby, British chargé d'affaires. Roma, MAE, Serie Politica, Pacco 533, Colombia 1891–1902, Report no. 10, 2 February 1901.

83 See Villegas and Yunis 1978:49–50.

84 Letter from George Burghall Watts to the British General Consulate in Cartagena, 16 August 1841. Public Records Office, Foreign Office, no. 135, Dispatch 36, London.

85 Letter to His Excellency General Carmona Aleibia, signed by P. W. Kelly, Her Majesty's General Consul, Cartagena, 9 September 1841. Public Records Office, Foreign Office, no. 4.

86 Bergquist (1978:6) casts doubts, however, on the "quest-for-spoils thesis" because of its inability to explain long periods of peace and stability in the twentieth century. He highlights, instead, the impact of export agriculture on the political system. Yet economic incentives may

work both ways. Stagnation could lure people into politics, while increasing economic opportunities could make posts that are connected with the political representation of powerful economic groups desirable.

87 Quoted in Fals Borda 1969:75.

88 The president, however, did have some leeway and was not necessarily bound to make appointments from the lists submitted by the assemblies, according to Article 85.

89 During the 1820s, President Santander supported laissez-faire measures (Bushnell 1954:129), and when the country did adopt protectionism, it always did so quite mildly (Vázquez Carrizosa 1986:23).

90 See Ospina Vázquez 1979:167, 197.

91 See Bergquist 1978; Kalmanovitz 1986:esp. 93.

92 Bushnell 1993:81.

93 According to the British chargé d'affaires at Cartagena, 4 September 1841. Public Records Office, Foreign Office 33, no. 4, London.

94 See Tobón Sanín 1979:123.

95 See Torres Velasco 1978:49.

96 For more on this line of argument, see Colmenares 1968:53–55, 131.

97 Safford (1972b:352–53) has pointed to the political difficulties faced by landed sectors.

98 See Posada-Carbó 1994. The level of competitiveness among Colombian parties ranks as high as the most competitive systems in the world, including the United States.

99 Although the idea remains in embryo, Safford (1972b:345) himself refers to the Guerra de los Supremos as a crucial stage in the formation of party alignments.

100 Report of the Spanish consul to Madrid. Correspondence, Legajo 1425, Archivo Ministerio de Asuntos Exteriores, Madrid.

101 Posada-Carbó (1994) has stressed the impact of nineteenth-century wars on party alignments and elections.

102 This insurrection was both a tax resistance movement and a defense of local autonomy against the colonial state (Camacho Roldán 1946:vol. 1:24–25).

103 See McFarlane 1985; Ocampo López 1984:67–75.

104 In Nieto Arteta's (1970:vol. 2:237) argument, newer colonos, with a "dynamic" entrepreneurial outlook, settled in the Oriente provinces. They were opposed by those who benefited from the *encomienda* system and the crown monopolies based on forced labor—what Nieto Arteta calls the economy of the highlands.

105 See Torres Velasco 1978:44–45. Bushnell and Macaulay (1988) and Bushnell (1954, 1993) also make a similar argument.

106 On similar arguments about party formation, see also L. González 1975:34–37; Buenaventura 1984:48–49. For a discussion on the origins of the parties and references to other various sources, see Delpar 1981:1–14.

107 See quotations from Ospina in Tirado Mejía 1970:108–9.

108 On these parties of the middle, see Cuervo and Cuervo 1946:vol. 2:54.

109 See Torres Velasco 1978:62–65.

110 Cuervo and Cuervo 1946:vol. 2:50.

111 See Torres Velasco 1978:63. Twenty merchants supported the Liberals as opposed to three who supported the Ministeriales. Agricultural producers were more divided, but those who also engaged in commerce tended to support the Liberals.

112 Quoted in *El Granadino,* 16 September 1842.

113 For details on the Mosquera uprising, see Bushnell 1993:90–96; Osterling 1989:67–70.

114 Osterling 1989:66.

115 For the modernizing and intellectual aspects of the Mosquera and following Liberal administrations during the so-called Olimpo Radical era, see Jaramillo Uribe 1985:45–46.

116 See Vázquez Carrizosa 1986:155.

117 See Osterling 1989:69.

118 Vázquez Carrizosa 1986:187.

119 See Guillén Martínez 1986:76–78.

120 See Bushnell 1993:151. In the Battle of Palonegro in 1900, 4,000 men were killed in a confrontation involving 25,000.

121 See Tamayo 1975:69–79; Villegas and Yunis 1978:72.

122 Details in Bushnell 1993:150.

123 See Villegas and Yunis 1978:62.

124 See Tirado Mejía 1970:176–77.

125 See for example Bergquist 1978; Bushnell 1993:152; Delpar 1981:3–5; Tirado Mejía 1970:14–15; Buenaventura 1984:49; Tobón Sanín 1979: 121–23; Nieto Arteta 1970:esp. vol. 1:110–18.

126 On the complexity of these issues at the provincial and town level, see Escorcia 1983:esp. vol. 3; Park 1985; Stoller 1992.

127 In Deas 1979:291.

128 Sanchez and others have argued likewise in Bergquist, Penaranda, and Sanchez's (1992) edited volume on Colombia.

129 Tirado Mejía 1970:106.

130 See Tobón Sanín 1979:123–25. In Duverger's model, parties virtually emerge within the legislature and then reach for support in society. This model is discussed further in this volume in "Conclusions."

131 See Procultura 1984:vol. 2:36 on the importance of cabildos and regional political organizing.

132 Fals Borda 1969:73.

133 The convent of Buen Pastor was taken by assault, and prostitutes who
were held in prison in its inner chambers were liberated. Businesses and
private homes were ransacked, and "the upper class and foreigners of all
nationalities remained defenseless, prey of the bestial rabble" (MAE,
Roma, Serie Politica, no. 36/26, Inventario 533, Bogotá, 22 January
1893).

134 See Molina 1987:113.

135 Letter of Herran to the war secretary during the Guerra de los Supremos, quoted in Tirado Mejía 1970:341.

136 From Luis María Mora, *Documentos,* cited in Tirado Mejía 1970:32. On
party alignments in this war, see also Bergquist 1978.

137 These four regions were the Cordillera Oriental (Cundinamarca, Boyacá, Santander, and Tolima), the Cauca region, the Antioqueño region, and the areas of the Atlantic coast. See Ospina Vázquez 1979;
Melo 1991a:72.

138 Lipset and Rokkan 1967.

139 See Delpar 1981:19–41. To compare results by province, see her tables
on 19–20, 24–25, 31, 34–35, 39–40.

140 See Bushnell's (1970:221) table. The category "other" shows, of course,
that there existed political organizing outside these major groupings,
but his data also demonstrate a sharp perception on the part of the
electors of the bipolarity of the party system.

141 See Tirado Mejía 1981:106–7.

142 Imposed by colonial rule, the *patronato real* gave secular authorities the
right to approve clerical appointments and collect religious taxes. The
Law of Ecclesiastical Patronage, passed on 28 July 1824, reestablished
the union between church and state after independence and was enforced intermittently until 1886.

143 See F. González 1987b:1–3.

144 Details to be found in F. González 1985, 1987a, 1987b.

145 See F. González 1985:25.

146 See Procultura 1984:427.

147 See F. González 1985:26.

148 See for example Bushnell 1954, 1993; Bergquist 1978; Maingot 1969;
Payne 1968; Tirado Mejía 1970; Sanchez Gómez 1991.

149 Leal Buitrago and Saxe Fernandez (1978) have focused more systemat-
ically on the army, yet their work focuses on the twentieth century rather
than the nineteenth.

150 See Payne 1968:121.

151 For details, see Leal Buitrago 1984:62.

152 See Bushnell 1954:249–86.

153 Details in Maingot 1969; the author draws from important primary sources.

154 One can argue that racial tension in the Colombian army was more intense than, for instance, in Venezuela, where part of the core elite was also mestizo, and officers of black or mestizo origins gained leading positions in the political system shortly after independence.

155 The most notorious were Simón Bolívar, Francisco de Paula Santander, José Antonio Páez, José María Córdoba, Antonio José de Sucre, and Juan José Flores.

156 See Osterling 1989:55.

157 See the analysis of this constitution provided by W. Gibson (1948:42–44). See also Bushnell 1954:18.

158 The list included both New Granadians and Venezuelans. In addition to El Libertador, prominent political figures such as Francisco de Paula Santander, José Antonio Páez, Juan José Flores, José María Córdoba, José María Obando, and Antonio José de Sucre were partisan-civilians who, although also generals and soldiers, had a feeble commitment to the military as an institution.

159 See Tirado Mejía 1970:33.

160 See Maingot 1969:332.

161 Obando had been a patriot military officer and was elected vice president from 1831 to 1832. He rebelled against the Marquez government (1840–1841) and was forced into exile from 1841 to 1849 before he gained the presidency.

162 See Molina 1987:135.

163 See Tirado Mejía 1970:22–24.

164 See Vázquez Carrizosa 1986:150–51.

165 Other studies on the period of La Regeneración confirm this view. See, for instance, the essays in Torres Velasco 1978.

166 See Consular Report by Italian Consul to Rome. Bogotá, 8 February 1893. Roma, MAE, Serie Politica, no. 63/42, Inventario, p. 533.

4 A Stronger State and Urban Military:
Argentina, 1810–1890

1 See also Ternavasio 1996.

2 See also Rock 1987:118–62; Ansaldi 1988; Botana 1979; Chiaramonte 1971; Cortés Conde 1979; Cortés Conde and Gallo 1967; Martire 1965; Merkx 1968; Ortiz 1955; Remmer 1984; Rock 1987; Scobie 1964, 1971.

3 See for example Scobie 1964; Rock 1996a.

4 See for example Ansaldi 1988; Cantón 1966; Germani 1971; Ferrer 1967:esp. 75–126; Oszlak 1985; Rock 1987; Stephens 1989; Rueschemeyer, Stephens, and Stephens 1992.

5 Cantón 1966:180. See also Rock 1987:154–57. By the early 1870s, one-third of the province of Buenos Aires was still occupied by indigenous peoples, but the so-called wilderness campaign of 1878 to 1879 liquidated the "Indian frontier."

6 See Rock 1975 for details on the rise of the Radical Party, its evolution, and social consequences.

7 See Cantón 1968:3.

8 Ibid., 4–6.

9 See for example Busaniche 1967; Carretero 1971b; Ravignani 1970.

10 Quoted in Cantón 1968:4 from an article by A. Maligne, "Historia militar de la República Argentina de 1810 a 1910," in *La Nación*, special issue, 25 May 1910.

11 See among others Halperín Donghi 1989b; Luna 1966; Lynch 1981, 1992.

12 See Cortés Conde 1979; Cortés Conde and Gallo 1967; Germani 1955; Gori 1964; Rock 1987.

13 See Botana 1979; Halperín Donghi 1980; Shumway 1991.

14 Rivadavia abolished the so-called *Colegios Electorales*—which negotiated the different appointees to the bureaucracy and imposed a system of open electoral competition—established by the May Revolution.

15 See Carretero 1971a; Colegio Militar de la Nación 1942; Halperín Donghi 1975, 1982, 1989b; Johnson 1994.

16 See Colegio Militar de la Nación 1942:12–16.

17 Koebel (1907) provided a telling (although impressionistic) comparative account of Argentina, Uruguay, and Chile, in terms of their degree of "modernity." Argentina ranked first and was comparable only to other prosperous lands of recent settlement outside Latin America.

18 Germani 1971:240.

19 Quoted in Halperín Donghi 1980:110 from letter to Posse, Rosario, 24 January 1870.

20 See for example Cardoso and Faletto 1979; Schwartz 1989.

21 See Rock 1987.

22 See Halperín Donghi 1980; Irigoin 1995.

23 The value of paper money had reached a desired equilibrium, and the national bank acquired enough credibility to control money transactions and to open an office of exchange in 1867. See Irigoin 1995:35.

24 On the profitability of land investment, see Halperín Donghi 1991, 1993; Schwartz 1989; and especially J. Sábato 1988:59.

25 For details, see Ortiz 1955:103–4.
26 See Bagú 1966; Cortés Conde 1979:32; Sáenz Quesada 1985:84, 105–6.
    See also Gallo 1976; Lynch 1993; J. Oddone 1975; Halperín Donghi 1975
    for a similar notion about the influence of rural culture on political elites.
27 H. Sábato 1990:23.
28 See Cortés Conde 1979:57–63.
29 See Cortés Conde 1993:63.
30 Quoted in *Review of the River Plate*, 11 March 1899.
31 For an entertaining study and vivid testimonial of the expansion of wheat
    and its social consequences, see Zeballos 1883:vol. 2.
32 Taken from the *Harpers Weekly*, quoted in Scobie 1971:119.
33 See Cortés Conde 1973, 1979; Irigoin 1995; H. Sábato 1990; J. Sábato
    1988; Scobie 1971; Rock 1987.
34 See Schwartz 1989. Schwartz argues that the ability of Argentine land-
    owners to pass over to the state the debt resulting from foreign loans
    favored their short-term interests but in the long run hurt Argentina's
    chances of achieving self-sustained development.
35 Gori 1964:22.
36 See Sáenz Quesada 1985:83, 85–86, 101.
37 Burgin 1946:23.
38 Quoted in Rock 1996b:35.
39 See Botana 1979:75.
40 See also Ferns 1960; Schwartz 1989.
41 Cited in Cantón 1966:23.
42 See for example Denoon 1983; Fogarty, Gallo, and Dieguez 1979; Platt
    and Di Tella 1985; Schwartz 1989.
43 See Fogarty 1985:22.
44 Urquiza seems to have adopted this widespread view as well; for ex-
    ample, see Bosch's (1971) study on Urquiza. Belgrano's (1966) auto-
    biography provides a similar perspective on the influence of European
    immigration.
45 Reported in *New York Times*, 19 July 1869.
46 Interpretations of the effects of Law 817, however, have been controver-
    sial. Some argued that in reality, the law worked against the establishment
    of a farm sector. See Ortiz 1955:101–5.
47 See Scobie 1964:190. The annual arrival of immigrants over departures
    shows a steady increase in net immigration, which in 1889 reached its
    nineteenth-century peak with the colossal figure of 200,000.
48 See Germani 1971:269. See his table comparing immigration to both
    countries (ibid.), and his analysis of immigration trends to Argentina
    (ibid., 267 and passim).
49 In *New York Times*, 20 December 1868.

50 For details, see Germani 1971:259–63.

51 See Alen Lascano 1975. For a more sophisticated argument about Rosas, see Busaniche 1967; Lynch 1981; Ravignani 1970.

52 The debate between Mariano Moreno and Cornelio de Saavedra, the clashes among members of the Generation of 1837 (Alberdi, Esteban Echeverría, and Sarmiento), and the controversy between this group and the Rosas regime are good cases in point.

53 Quote from Halperín Donghi 1980:li.

54 The Congress, modeled after the Constituent Assembly of 1789 France, abolished Indian labor services and *majorazgos* (titles of nobility and landed states inherited through primogeniture), banned the slave trade, and freed the children of slaves.

55 See Bushnell 1983:9. He writes that the ideas of the May Revolution should be considered exceptionally advanced.

56 Indeed, Halperín Donghi notices the sharp contrast between Alberdi's celebrated polemic with Sarmiento about institutional design, and the actual institutions that emerged in the aftermath of the Rosas administration.

57 See Clementi 1983:10.

58 See for example Rock 1993.

59 See Halperín Donghi 1991; see also J. Sábato 1988:155.

60 Chiaramonte 1983; Chiaramonte and Ternavasio 1995.

61 Although Halperín Donghi (1975:332) notes that the central army at the time was about two thousand strong, the federalist troops won the battle, and the directory in Buenos Aires was forced to dissolve.

62 In 1862 Mitre took office as the first president of the newly united Argentine republic. Domingo Faustino Sarmiento (1868–1874) and Nicholás Avellaneda (1874–1880) followed Mitre.

63 Sources on Mitre range from basic anecdotal narration to more serious analytical studies. Among others, see Gandía 1970; Jeffrey 1952; Levene 1963; Vega 1960; Rock 1987:125–31.

64 See Scobie 1964; Rock 1996a.

65 On the formation of the PAN and its evolution, see Botana 1979:66; Cantón 1966:19–21; Rock 1987:130–31.

66 He defeated his opponent, the Unitarist Mitre, by 146 votes to 79 in the electoral college. See Rock 1987:130.

67 Escapelo, *El Senado de 1890,* quoted in Botana 1979:114.

68 Remmer (1984) has argued precisely along these lines for Argentina.

69 In a single-party-dominant system, one party wins no less than 60 percent of the legislature while the rest win less than 40 percent. Colombia from the mid–nineteenth century to the early twentieth, for instance,

could be placed in this category. In a multiparty system in which three or more parties compete but one is dominant, the dominant party receives no less than 40 percent but no more than 60 percent of the seats. In a multiparty loose system, no single party receives more than 40 percent of the seats.

70 See Cantón 1966:13. On Yrigoyen and his movement, see Rock 1975; Sommi 1947.

71 Indeed, intimidation seemed to have been so powerful that the opposition leader in Rosario requested asylum in the British Consulate. Cf. Rock 1996b:33.

72 See for example Germani 1971; H. Sábato 1991, 1992; Rock 1975.

73 Quoted in Rock 1975:27.

74 Among others, Halperín Donghi (1975, 1989a) and the recent research of Chiaramonte and Ternavasio (1995) clearly point in this direction, showing the overwhelming importance of urban politics in nineteenth-century elections.

75 See, for instance, Bóron and Pedogaro 1985.

76 The junta interpreted the decisions of the Triunvirato as a move toward the centralization of power in Buenos Aires. The Triunvirato, on its part, accused the junta of acting on a "divisive" notion of sovereignty. See Chiaramonte 1995:11.

77 Johns and Rocchi (1991), for instance, have shown that by the late part of the nineteenth century, divisions over the tariff were quite flexible and issue oriented. This adds to evidence from the other two cases, in which the tariff remained an insufficient explanation of coalition formation.

78 Burgin 1946:102. The system of *emphyteusis* introduced by the Unitarios, for example, found resistance among large landowners because— among other things—it was meant to prevent the accumulation of unproductive land in a few hands; this would "retard their settlement and cultivation." In the decree of 10 May 1828, quoted in Burgin 1946:99. For a full explanation of the law of emphyteusis, see pp. 96–100.

79 Commercial and financial interests led the consolidation of the ruling coalition, and perhaps somewhat similar to English landowners, those in Argentina acquired a "commercial mentality" (J. Sábato 1988:46). Unlike in England, however, landowners behaved more as merchants than as producers, and the economy grew dependent on European imports (52, 155–58).

80 Given that small provincial industries were an important part of the economy, the protectionist coalition in Argentina formed a stronger bloc than in our other cases; see Burgin 1946:235–37.

81 See Cantón 1967:1–2.

82 For details, see Ternavasio 1996:8–9.

83 See Chiaramonte and Ternavasio 1995:20.

84 See Lynch 1981; Ibarguren 1962; Ramos Mejía [1945?].

85 See table with names of representatives in Chiaramonte and Ternavasio 1995:21.

86 See Halperín Donghi 1975:362.

87 See Levene 1947.

88 Cited in Chiaramonte and Ternavasio 1995:17. They note the precinct's argument that twenty of the "best quality votes" were equal to about two hundred lower-quality votes; the result was that two candidates who did not obtain the majority vote got elected because "they represented the rational majority and the true plurality" of recorded votes.

89 See further discussion on this issue in Halperín Donghi 1975:360 and passim.

90 *La Tribuna*, 1 April 1864. Cited in Cantón 1966:22.

91 See Ternavasio 1996:3.

92 Ibid., 8. On the pact and the controversy it created, see also Ibarguren 1962; Ravignani 1970.

93 Death and retirement were, according to Ternavasio (1996:19–20), the main causes of elite renovation. In these cases, Rosas solicited four or five names from his advisers and directly decided which candidate would take the vacant post in the lista unica.

94 See Vega 1960.

95 San Juan and La Rioja, for instance, became the grounds for bitter rivalry between Liberals and Federales. The Liberals finally defeated the Federales with a brutality reminiscent of the worst confrontations between Blancos and Colorados in Uruguay. For details, see Rock 1996a:44–53.

96 For a good anecdotal and detailed account of the conditions of the provincial militias and the national army at different stages of their development before 1870, see Pomer 1985.

97 See Lynch 1992:82.

98 See Halperín Donghi 1975:129, 1982:79.

99 Carlos Roberts 1938. For an overall analysis of this period of British invasions of the River Plate, see the extensive work of Street (1956, 1967). In-depth analysis on British trade with Latin America and the emergence of the so-called British informal empire can be found in Platt 1972.

100 See Halperín Donghi 1982:118–22.

101 Johnson 1994:27. The first failed coup, in 1809, was led by Martín de Álzaga, a Spanish loyalist; in 1810, a successful coup removed the Spanish viceroy Balthasar de Cisneros.

102 Halperín Donghi 1982:78.

103 For a full discussion on this militia and army buildup in the early years of the republic, see the extensive work of Halperín Donghi (1975, 1982:esp. 78–93, 1989a:esp. chaps. 1–2).

104 Moreno, secretary of the junta and head of an influential faction tinted with Jacobin overtones, failed to seize control of the government because his faction could not gain the support of the militia. After a failed coup, Moreno had to resign; he departed for Europe and died shortly thereafter.

105 The creation of the powerful *cuerpo de granaderos a caballo* (cavalry battalion) under the command of General San Martín is a good example; the granaderos' officer corps was overwhelmingly from Buenos Aires, but its rank and file came from the hinterlands.

106 Quoted in Halperín Donghi 1975:191.

107 The expression *guerra permanente* (permanent war), as a definition of the Rosas period, is taken from Halperín Donghi 1982:chap. 4.

108 Rock (1987:120) also includes a third phase starting in the 1890s that led to "a collapse into depression and revolution."

109 For a detailed account of the life and policies of Rosas, see Galvez 1949; Ibarguren 1962; Ramos Mejía [1945?]. For particulars on the manipulation of public opinion and the dictatorial character of the regime, see Dellepiane 1955:esp. 72–111. For a characterization of the repressive features of rosismo, see Busaniche 1955:55–81. For an overall and analytical account of the entire period, see Ravignani 1970; Lynch 1981.

110 Indeed, Bushnell (1983:124) remarks that this government was more conservative and centralized than its predecessors.

111 Chiaramonte (1995:94–95) reminds us that in the minds of those in government, the term *provincia* still referred to the administrative divisions of the Spanish viceroyalty; thus the provinces could not by definition be autonomous.

112 Cady (1929:vol. 1) remains the best source on European intervention in the River Plate during the Rosas period. He amply documents the policies of France, Great Britain, and the United States regarding Rosas, and the characteristics of foreign intervention from 1838 to 1850. For a view from within the regime, see Busaniche 1955:85–105; Galvez 1949:266–88.

113 Most sources agree that these facultades had no limits other than the conservation of the Catholic Religion and the defense and support of the federation.

114 See Saldias 1977:204.

115 To understand subsequent popular support for the regime, one should

note that before accepting, Rosas submitted his newly acquired power to a plebiscite in the city. He won by 9,316 votes to 4. See Ternavasio 1996:18.

116 For details, see Lynch 1981:esp. chaps. 5, 8.

117 See Colegio Militar de la Nación 1942:8–52, 125–33.

118 The Argentine army remained small only in comparison to Brazil's. With large numbers of Portuguese officers, the Brazilian imperial forces numbered about 10,000 soldiers, among which there were some 2,000 professional German soldiers who had helped establish Pedro I on the throne. See Saldias 1977:vol. 1:153.

119 Quoted in Lynch 1981:36 from a letter of Manuel Moreno to Ponsonby.

120 See Astesano 1960:64–66; Galvez 1949:143, 149.

121 For details see Lynch 1981:chap. 3; Ternavasio 1996:24.

122 See Busaniche 1967; Carretero 1971b.

123 Sáenz Quesada (1985:145–51) provides an entertaining account of the uprisings led by landlords during this phase of state building and the negotiations that followed.

124 See Lynch 1981:115–17 for more on these laws and control of labor mobility.

125 See Halperín Donghi 1975:359.

126 See Botana 1979:71; Lynch 1993:15.

127 See Dellepiane 1955:73–75; Busaniche 1955:55–57.

128 Manuel José García, quoted in report of Lord Ponsonby to Canning, Public Records Office, 5 December 1826, Foreign Office 6/13.

129 See Busaniche 1955:82.

130 All professionals, members of corporations, and interest groups were asked to use a pin on the left side with the colors of the federation and the label "Federación." In the case of the armed forces, the logo said "Federación o Muerte." For details, see Saldias 1977:vol. 263.

131 For Rosas's own views on political leadership in the rural areas, see his 1968 "Intrucciones a los mayordomos de estancias."

132 On popular support for the Rosas regime, see also Lynch 1981.

133 See Alen Lascano 1975:12–14; Lynch 1981:27.

134 See Kelly 1994:220–22. See also Kelly's view on Rosas's coordinated and successful efforts to capture African Argentine support (221–24).

135 Quotation from Oszlak 1985:37.

136 Ibid., 59. On Urquiza's confederación, its development, and its defeat, see pp. 58–63; Rock 1987:120–31.

137 Sáenz Quesada 1985:258.

138 See Botana 1979:75; Rock 1987:155.

139 Botana 1979:78.

140 For details on Urquiza's campaign against Rosas, see Colegio Militar de la Nación 1942:187–92. For a broader view on Urquiza and his military actions, see Bosch 1971; Saldias 1977:vol. 3. In addition, most books on Argentine history devote lengthy discussions to Urquiza. On the fall of Rosas, see also Rosas's (1968) own account.

141 Pomer 1985:284.

142 On the importance of this campaign, see, among others, Cortés Conde and Gallo 1967; Gasío and San Román 1977; Walther 1948.

143 On the importance of these caudillos, see Halperín Donghi 1989a. See as well the excellent work of Lynch on caudillos (1992) and on Rosas (1981).

144 Rock 1996b:3. See Rock 1996a and 1996b for illuminating details of caudillo insurrections during the 1860s and 1870s, and the magnitude of the military resources employed by the state against the insurgents.

145 See Oszlak 1985:88.

146 Details in Rock 1996a:24.

147 Ibid., 36.

148 Mitre's letter to Santiago Arcos, quoted in Giménez Vega 1961:41–42.

149 See Oszlak 1985:66–67.

150 Quoted in Pomer 1985:163 from testimonies of Dr. Manuel A. Saez.

151 Ibid.

152 See Halperín Donghi 1975:193. Racial tension in the army diminished only when blacks, Indians, and mulattoes, used for the most precarious and dangerous missions or as front liners, severely decreased in numbers.

153 See Halperín Donghi 1982:152–53. At that time, 250 officers were pushed into retirement, and the wages for regular troops were reduced.

5 Two Alternative Paths of State Making: Venezuela and Paraguay

1 The expression is from Pastore (1994b:552), who has used the concept to characterize Paraguay under José Gaspar Rodríguez de Francia.

2 See Lott 1972:59.

3 See Bushnell and Macaulay 1988 on the dissolution of Gran Colombia and the characteristics of Venezuela. Carrera Damas (1983a, 1983b) offers a similar argument; see also Lombardi 1982:98–99.

4 Gilmore 1964:83.

5 See Quintero Montiel 1989:chap. 1, and 1990; Lott 1972:71.

6 See Fuenmayor 1984–1987:20–21.

7 Lombardi 1982:121.

8 See Domínguez 1980:102.

9 See Lombardi 1982:133–56. Also see Bushnell and Macaulay 1988 on the dissolution of Gran Colombia; and Carrera Damas 1983a; Gilmore 1964:71–74; and Quintero Montiel 1989, 1990 on caudillism.

10 Ewell 1984:7.

11 Ibid.; see also Lombardi 1982:166–68.

12 For details, see Ewell 1984:7–8; Lombardi 1982:271–79; Quintero Montiel 1990.

13 See Lott 1972:50–51.

14 See Castillo Blomquist 1987.

15 Fuenmayor 1984–1987:20.

16 See Carrera Damas 1983b.

17 See Hebrand 1995:6.

18 See Irwin 1990:16–17.

19 Ibid.

20 See Gilmore 1964:146.

21 See Quintero Montiel 1989:21.

22 For details, see Quintero Montiel 1989, 1990:42–51.

23 See Quintero Montiel 1989:49; Gilmore 1964:45.

24 Gilmore 1964:37.

25 Plumacher to Wilson, 10 September 1902, as quoted in Irwin 1990:15.

26 For an analysis of the Castro period and the qualitative transformation represented by his administration, see Quintero Montiel 1989:32–69.

27 Ibid., 91.

28 See Warren 1979.

29 See Lewis 1993:7.

30 See Pastore 1994b:550.

31 Ibid., 551.

32 A triumvirate was formed to substitute for the deposed Spanish governor, composed of representatives of the business community, two military officers, and the clergy. For details, see Pastore 1994b:552–53.

33 Ibid., 542.

34 See Williams 1979:17. Before independence, part of the filiado regiment served in the siege of Montevideo and participated in guerrilla wars against the Portuguese.

35 See White 1978:19.

36 Ibid., 36–37.

37 On Francia and his administration, see Pastore 1994b; Williams 1979:21–42; White 1978:61–125.

38 See Williams 1979:60–61.

39 See Cabanellas 1946.
40 Ibid., 171.
41 Williams 1979:48.
42 Ibid., 50–53.
43 In 1816 the government assumed financial "stewardship over the Church, collecting tithes and other church moneys and putting all clerics on a regular salary" (Williams 1979:57).
44 The expression is taken from Rogowski's 1989 argument about degrees of exposure to trade in relation to coalition formation.
45 See for example Pastore 1994a.
46 Lewis 1993:15.
47 See Warren 1979.
48 Lewis (1993:1–2), for instance, makes a case for the longevity of the Paraguayan parties.
49 For details, see Warren 1985.
50 Ibid., 28.
51 Ibid., 36–37.

Conclusions

1 For comparative work on less developed countries from this perspective, see Haggard 1990; for an interpretation of Brazilian politics using this approach, see Geddes 1994.
2 Ewell 1984:25.
3 For example, it has been argued that peasants prevented the hacienda from growing and adequately responding to markets. See Leal Buitrago 1984:18, 68–70. Also, farmers had been said to have contributed to perpetuating a system of "oppressive labor relations on a small scale" (Colmenares 1968:59).

References

Abel, Christopher. 1974. "Conservative Party in Colombia: 1930–1953." Ph.D. diss., Oxford University.

Acevedo, Eduardo. 1933. *Anales históricos del Uruguay.* 3 vols. Montevideo: Poder Ejecutivo.

Alem, Leandro. 1933. *Autonomismo y centralismo.* Buenos Aires: Raigal.

Alen Lascano, Luis C. 1975. *Rosas.* Buenos Aires: Capital, Troisi y Vaccaro.

Almond, Gabriel, Taylor Cole, and Roy C. Macridis. 1955. "A Suggested Research Strategy in Western European Government and Politics." *American Political Science Review* 49, no. 4 (December): 1042–49.

Anderson, Benedict R. 1983. *Imagined Communities: Reflections on the Origin and Spread of Nationalism.* London: Verso.

Anderson, Perry. 1974. *Lineages of the Absolutist State.* London: New Left Books.

Andrews, George Reid. 1985. "Spanish American Independence: A Structural Analysis." *Latin American Perspectives* 12, no. 1 (winter): 105–32.

Ansaldi, Waldo. 1988. *Estado y sociedad en la Argentina del siglo XIX.* Buenos Aires: Centro Editor de América Latina.

Arango, Mariano. 1981. *Café e industria 1850–1930.* Vol. 1. Bogotá: Carlos Valencia.

Ardao, Arturo. 1971. *Etapas de la inteligencia uruguaya.* Montevideo: Departamento de Publicaciones, Universidad de la República.

Ares Pons, Roberto. 1967. *Uruguay: Provincia o nación?* Montevideo: Nuevo Mundo.

Argentine Commission of the Panama-Pacific Exposition. 1915. *The Argentine Republic.* San Francisco: Panama Pacific Exposition.

Arrubla, Mario, et al. 1985. *Colombia hoy.* 9th ed. Bogotá: Siglo XXI.

Astesano, Eduardo B. 1960. *Rosas: Bases del nacionalismo popular.* Buenos Aires: A. Pena Lillo.

Bagú, Sergio. 1966. *El plan economico del grupo rivadaviano (1811–1827).* Rosario, Argentina: Instituto de Investigaciones Históricas, Facultad de Filosofía y Letras, Universidad Naciónal del Litoral.

Bannon, John Francis, and Peter Masten Dunne. 1958. *Latin American Historical Survey.* Rev. ed. Milwaukee, Wis.: Bruce Publishing.

Barba, Enrique. 1972. *Como llego Rosas al poder?* Buenos Aires: Pleamar.

Barba, Enrique, et al. 1974. *Unitarios y federales.* Selection and prologue by Julio Godio. Buenos Aires: Granica.

Barkey, Karen. 1991. "The State and Peasant Unrest in Early Seventeenth Century France and the Ottoman Empire." *American Sociological Review* 56, no. 6 (December): 699–715.

———. 1995. *Bandits and Bureaucrats: The Ottoman Route to State Centralization.* Ithaca, N.Y.: Cornell University Press.

Barrán, José Pedro, and Benjamín Nahum. 1967–1978. *Historia rural del Uruguay moderno.* 7 vols. Montevideo: Banda Oriental.

———. 1979–1986. *Batlle, los estancieros y el imperio británico.* 8 vols. Montevideo: Banda Oriental.

———. 1989. *Bases económicas de la revolución artiguista.* Montevideo: Banda Oriental.

Bartlett, Beatrice S. 1991. *Monarchs and Ministers: The Rise of the Grand Council in Mid-Ch'ing China, 1773–1820.* Berkeley: University of California Press.

Bauza, Francisco. 1876. *Colonización industrial: Ensayo sobre un sistema para la república oriental del Uruguay.* Montevideo: Impreta el Naciónal.

———. 1887. *Estudios constitucionales.* Montevideo: A. Barreiro and Ramos.

———. 1929. *Historia de la dominción española en el Uruguay.* 2 vols. 3d ed. Montevideo: Talleres Gráficos el Democrata.

———. 1965. *Historia de la dominación española en el Uruguay.* With an introduction by Juan E. Pivel Devoto. Montevideo.

Beard, Charles. 1913. *An Economic Interpretation of the Constitution of the United States.* New York: Macmillan.

Belgrano, Manuel. 1966. *Autobiografía y otras paginas.* Buenos Aires: Universitario de Buenos Aires.

Bengoa, Juan Leon. 1936. *El dictador Latorre: Retrato del hombre y crónica de la época.* Buenos Aires: Claridad.

Bensel, Richard F. 1990. *Yankee Leviathan: The Origins of Central State Authority in America, 1859–1877.* Cambridge: Cambridge University Press.

Bergquist, Charles W. 1978. *Coffee and Conflict in Colombia: 1886–1910.* Durham, N.C.: Duke University Press.

———. 1986. *Labor in Latin America: Comparative Essays on Chile, Argentina, Venezuela, and Colombia.* Stanford, Calif.: Stanford University Press.

Bergquist, Charles, Ricardo Penaranda, and Gonzalo Sanchez, eds. 1992. *Violence in Colombia: The Contemporary Crisis in Historical Perspective.* Wilmington, Del.: SR Books.

Bioy, Adolfo. 1958. *Antes del novecientos: Recuerdos.* Buenos Aires: Impresora Argentina.

Blainey, Geoffrey. 1973. *The Causes of War.* New York: Free Press.

Bliss, Horacio William. 1959. *Del virreinato a Rosas: Ensayo de la historia económica Argentina, 1776–1829.* Tucuman: Richardet.

Bollen, Kenneth. 1979. "Political Democracy and the Timing of Development." *American Sociological Review* 44, no. 4 (August): 572–87.

Bonilla Saus, Javier. 1981. "La restructura capitalista del Uruguay: 1958–1976." In *América Latina estudios y perspectivas,* ed. Dictadura y Realidad Naciónal. Mexico: ERESCU.

Bóron, Atilio, and Juan Pedogaro. 1985. "Las luchas sociales en el agro argentino." In *Historia política de los campesinos latinoamericanos* 4, ed. Pablo González Casanova. Mexico: Siglo XXI.

Bosch, Beatriz. 1971. *Urquiza y su tiempo.* Buenos Aires: Raigal.

Botana, Natalio R. 1979. *El orden conservador: La política Argentina entre 1880 y 1916.* 2d ed. Buenos Aires: Sudamericana.

Brackenridge, Henry Marie. 1971. *Voyage to South America, Performed by Order of the American Government in the Years 1817 and 1818, in the Frigate "Congress."* 2 vols. London: printed for John Miller, 1820. Reprint, New York: AMS Press.

Brenner, Robert. 1976. "Agrarian Class Structure and Economic Development in Pre-industrial Europe." *Past and Present,* no. 70 (February): 30–75.

Bruschera, Oscar. 1969. "Artigas." In *Biblioteca de marcha* 3. Montevideo.

Bryce, James. 1901. *The American Commonwealth.* 2 vols. London: Macmillan.

Buenaventura, Nicolas. 1984. *Clases y partidos en Colombia.* Bogotá: CEIS.

Bulnes, Gonzalo. 1927. *Nacimiento de las repúblicas Americanas.* 2 vols. Buenos Aires: Libreria la Facultad, Juan Roldán.

Bunkley, Alison Williams. 1952. *The Life of Sarmiento.* Princeton, N.J.: Princeton University Press.

Burgin, Miron. 1946. *The Economic Aspects of Argentine Federalism: 1820–1852.* Cambridge: Harvard University Press.

Burkholder, Mark A., and Lyman L. Johnson. 1990. *Colonial Latin America.* New York: Oxford University Press.

Busaniche, José Luis. 1955. *Rosas visto por sus contemporaneos.* Buenos Aires: Guillermo Kraft Limitada.

———. 1967. *Juan Manuel de Rosas.* Buenos Aires: Theoria.

Bushnell, David. 1954. *The Santander Regime in Gran Colombia.* Newark: University of Delaware Press.

———. 1970. "Elecciones presidenciales colombianas, 1825–1856." In *Compendio de estadisticas históricas de Colombia,* ed. Miguel Urrutia Montoya and Mario Arrubla. Bogotá: Universidad Nacional de Colombia.

———. 1983. *Reform and Reaction in the Platine Provinces, 1810–1852.* Gainesville: University Press of Florida.

———. 1993. *The Making of Modern Colombia: A Nation in Spite of Itself.* Berkeley: University of California Press.

Bushnell, David, and Neill Macaulay. 1988. *The Emergence of Latin America in the Nineteenth Century.* New York: Oxford University Press.

Caballero Calderon, Eduardo. 1960. *Historia privada de los colombianos.* Bogotá: Biblioteca de Cultura Colombiana.

Caballero, Lucas. 1939. *Memorias de la guerra de los mil dias.* Bogotá: "Aguila negra" editorial.

Cabanellas, Guillermo. 1946. *El dictador del Paraguay, Dr. Francia.* Buenos Aires: Claridad.

Cady, John F. 1929. *Foreign Intervention in the Río de la Plata, 1838–50: A Study of French, British, and American Policy in Relation to the Dictator Juan Manuel Rosas.* 2 vols. Philadelphia: University of Pennsylvania Press.

Camacho Roldán, Salvador. 1946. *Memorias.* 2 vols. Bogotá: Biblioteca Popular de Cultura Colombiana.

———. 1976. *Escritos sobre economia y política.* Bogotá: Instituto Colombiano de Cultura.

Campal, Esteban. 1964. *Hombres, tierras, y ganados.* Montevideo: Arca.

Campal, F. 1964. "Importancia económica y social del reglamento de 1815." *Marcha* (20 June).

Cantón, Darío. 1966. *El parlamento argentino en épocas de cambio: 1890, 1916, y 1946.* Buenos Aires: Editorial del Instituto.

———. 1967. *Los partidos políticos argentino entre 1912 y 1955.* Buenos Aires: Instituto Torcuato Di Tella.

———. 1968. "Military Intervention in Argentina: 1900–1966." Working Paper. Buenos Aires: Instituto Torcuato Di Tella.

———. 1973. *Elecciones y partidos políticos en la Argentina: Historia, interpretación y balance, 1910–1966.* Buenos Aires: Siglo XXI.

Cardoso, Fernando Henrique, and Enzo Faletto. 1979. *Dependency and Development in Latin America.* Berkeley: University of California Press.

Carrera Damas, Germán. 1983a. "Estructura de poder interna y proyecto nacional immediatamente despues de la independencia: El caso de Venezuela." Working Paper no. 128. Washington, D.C.: Wilson Center, Latin American Program.

———. 1983b. "Sobre la cuestion regional y el proyecto nacional venezolano en la segunda mitad del siglo 19." In *La unidad naciónal en América Latina,* ed. Marco Palacios. Mexico: El Colegio de Mexico.

———. 1984. *Una nación llamada Venezuela: Proceso sociohistórico de Venezuela (1810–1974).* Caracas: Monte Avila.

Carretero, Andres M. 1971a. *Anarquia y caudillismo: La crisis institucional en febrero de 1820*. Buenos Aires: Pannedille.

———. 1971b. *La llegada de Rosas al poder*. Buenos Aires: Pannedille.

———. 1972. *La propiedad de la tierra en la época de Rosas*. Buenos Aires: El Coloquio.

Carrillo, Jorge Hernandez. 1940. *Santander y la Gran Colombia*. Bogotá: ABC.

Castillo Blomquist, Rafael. 1987. *José Tadeo Monagas: Auge y consolidación de un caudillo*. Caracas: Monte Avila.

Castro, Antonio P. 1944. *Nueva historia de Urquiza: Industrial, comerciante, ganadero*. Buenos Aires: Imprenta de la Editorial Araujo Cepeda, José.

Centeno, Miguel. 1997. "War and Blood: State-Making in Latin America in the Nineteenth Century." Unpublished manuscript.

Cepeda, José. 1945. *Tres capitulos de la vida de Urquiza*. Entre Ríos: Concordia.

Chambers, William Nisbet. 1969. "Party Development and Party Action: The American Origins." In *American History: Recent Interpretations*, ed. Abraham S. Eisenstadt. 2 vols. New York: Thomas Y. Crowell.

Chapman, Charles Edward. 1933. *Colonial Hispanic America: A History*. New York: Macmillan.

Chassen de López, Francie R. 1982. *Café y capitalismo: El proceso de transición en Colombia, 1880–1930*. Mexico: Universidad Autonoma del Estado de Mexico.

Chiaramonte, José Carlos. 1971. *Nacionalismo y liberalismo económicos en Argentina, 1860–1880*. Buenos Aires: Solar Hachette.

———. 1983. "La cuestion regional en el proceso de gestacon del estado nacional argentino: Algunos problemas de interpretación." In *La unidad nacional en América Latina*, ed. Marco Palacio. Mexico: El Colegio de Mexico.

Chiaramonte, José Carlos, and Marcela Ternavasio. 1995. "Procesos electorales y cultura política." *Ciencia Hoy* (Buenos Aires) 5, no. 30.

Clementi, Hebe. 1983. *El radicalismo, trayectoria política*. Buenos Aires: Siglo XXI.

Codigo rural de la provincia de Buenos Aires. 1870. Expanded with the modifications introduced in the same work by the Argentine Rural Society. Buenos Aires: Imprenta Americana.

Colegio Militar de la Nación. 1942. *Cronología de las campañas militares en que actuo el ejercito argentino*. Buenos Aires: Ministerio de Guerra y Marina.

Collier, David, and James E. Mahon Jr. 1993. "Conceptual 'Stretching' Revisited: Adapting Categories in Comparative Analysis." *American Political Science Review* 87, no. 4 (December): 845–55.

Collier, Ruth Berins, and David Collier. 1991. *Shaping the Political Arena: Critical Junctures, the Labor Movement, and Regime Dynamics in Latin America*. Princeton, N.J.: Princeton University Press.

Colmenares, Germán. 1968. *Partidos políticos y clases sociales*. Bogotá: Universidad de los Andes.

Coppedge, Michael. 1991. "Institutions and Cleavages in the Evolution of Latin American Party Systems." Paper presented at the Annual Meeting of the American Political Science Association.

Cortés Conde, Roberto. 1973. "The Growth of the Export Economies: Latin America in the Second Half of the Nineteenth Century." In *Problems in Latin American History: The Modern Period*, ed. Joseph S. Tulchin. New York: Harper and Row.

——. 1979. *El progreso argentino: 1880–1914*. Buenos Aires: Sudamericana.

——. 1993. "The Growth of the Argentine Economy, c. 1870–1914." In *Argentina since Independence*, ed. Leslie Bethel. New York: Cambridge University Press.

Cortés Conde, Roberto, and Ezequiel Gallo Jr. 1967. *La formación de la Argentina moderna*. Buenos Aires: Paidós.

Crow, John A. 1992. *The Epic of Latin America*. 4th ed. Berkeley: University of California Press.

Cuervo, Angel, and Rufino José Cuervo. 1946. *Vida de Rufino Cuervo y noticias de su época*. 2d ed. Bogotá: Prensas de la Biblioteca Nacional.

Dahl, Robert. 1956. *A Preface to Democratic Theory*. Chicago: University of Chicago Press.

——. 1971. *Polyarchy: Participation and Opposition*. New Haven, Conn.: Yale University Press.

Darwin, Charles. 1933. *Viaje de un naturalista alrededor del mundo*. Vol. 2. Barcelona: Iberia.

Deas, Malcolm. 1973. "Algunas notas sobre la historia del caciquismo en Colombia." *Revista de Occidente*, no. 127 (October): 118–38.

——. 1979. "Poverty, Civil War, and Politics: Ricardo Gaitan Obeso and His Magdalena River Campaign in Colombia, 1885." *Nova Americana* (Torino), no. 2.

——. 1980. "Los problemas fiscales en Colombia durante el siglo XIX." In *Ensayos sobre historia económica colombiana*. Bogotá: Fedesarrollo.

——. 1983. "La presencia de la política nacional en la vida provinciana, pueblerina y rural de Colombia en el primer siglo de la república." In *La unidad nacional en América Latina: Del regionalismo a la nacionalidad*, ed. Marco Palacios. Mexico: El Colegio de Mexico.

Degler, Carl N. 1959. *Out of Our Past: The Forces That Shaped Modern America*. New York: Harper.

Dellepiane, Antonio. 1955. *Rosas*. Buenos Aires: Santiago Rueda.

———. 1957. *El testamento de Rosas, la hija del dictador: Algunos documentos significativos.* Buenos Aires: Editorial Oberon.

Delpar, Helen V. 1981. *Red against Blue: The Liberal Party in Colombian Politics, 1863–1899.* Tuscaloosa: University of Alabama Press.

Delpech, Emilio. 1944. *Una vida en la gran Argentina: Relatos desde 1869 hasta 1944.* Buenos Aires: Peuser.

Denoon, Donald. 1983. *Settler Capitalism: The Dynamics of Dependent Development in the Southern Hemisphere.* New York: Oxford University Press.

Diaz, Benito. 1967. "Organización de la justica de campaña en la provincia de Buenos Aires." In *Trabajos y Comunicaciones,* no. 16. La Plata: Universidad Nacional, Facultad de Humanidades.

Diaz Alejandro, Carlos F. 1985. "Argentina, Australia, and Brazil before 1929." In *Argentina, Australia, and Canada: Studies in Comparative Development, 1870–1965,* ed. D. C. M. Platt and Guido Di Tella. Oxford: Macmillan.

Díaz Díaz, Fernando. 1984. "Estado, iglesia, y desamortización." In *Manual de Historia de Colombia.* 2d ed. Bogotá: Procultura: Instituto Colombiano de Cultura.

Diaz Uribe, Eduardo. 1986. *El clientelismo en Colombia: Un estudio exploratorio.* Bogotá: Ancora.

Dinkin, Robert J. 1982. *Voting in Revolutionary America: A Study of Elections in the Original Thirteen States, 1776–1789.* Westport, Conn.: Greenwood Press.

Dobb, Maurice. 1947. *Studies in the Development of Capitalism.* New York: International Publishers.

Domínguez, Jorge I. 1980. *Insurrection or Loyalty: The Breakdown of the Spanish American Empire.* Cambridge: Harvard University Press.

Downing, Brian M. 1992. *The Military Revolution and Political Change: Origins of Democracy and Autocracy in Early Modern Europe.* Princeton, N.J.: Princeton University Press.

Dunkerley, James. 1988. *Power in the Isthmus: A Political History of Modern Central America.* London: Verso.

Dupuy, Daniel Hammerly. 1970. *San Martín y Artigas: Adversarios o colaboradores?* With a preface by Emilio Ravignani. Buenos Aires: Editorial Noel.

Duverger, Maurice. 1954. *Political Parties: Their Organization and Activity in the Modern State.* Trans. Barbara and Robert North. New York: Wiley.

Elster, Jon. 1982. "Marxism, Functionalism, and Game Theory: The Case for Methodological Individualism." *Theory and Society* 11, no. 4 (July): 453–82.

———. 1990. "When Rationality Fails." In *The Limits of Rationality,* ed. Karen Schwers Cook and Margaret Levi. Chicago: Chicago University Press.

Engels, Friedrich. 1978. "The Origins of the Family, Private Property, and the State." In *The Marx-Engels Reader,* ed. Robert Tucker. New York: W. W. Norton.

Escorcia, José. 1983. *Desarrollo político, social y económico, 1800–1854.* Bogotá: Fondo de Promoción de la Cultura del Banco Popular.

Escudé, Carlos. 1988. *Gran Bretãna, estados unidos, y la declinación Argentina, 1942–1949.* Buenos Aires: Editorial de Belgrano.

Evans, Peter B. 1987. "Foreign Capital and the Third World State." In *Understanding Political Development: An Analytic Study,* ed. Myron Weiner and Samuel P. Huntington. Boston, Mass.: Little, Brown.

Ewell, Judith. 1984. *Venezuela: A Century of Change.* Stanford, Calif.: Stanford University Press.

Fals Borda, Orlando. 1969. *Subversion and Social Change in Colombia.* Trans. Jacqueline D. Skiles. Rev. ed. New York: Columbia University Press.

Fernandez Cabrelli, Alfonso. 1962. *Masoneria y sociedades secretas en la luchas emancipadoras.* La Paz: Vanguardia.

———. 1975. *Coronel Latorre: Su gobierno, su obra, su final.* Montevideo: Grito de Asencio.

Fernandez Saldana, José. 1969. *Latorre y su tiempo.* Montevideo: Arca.

Ferns, Henry Stanley. 1960. *Britain and Argentina in the Nineteenth Century.* Oxford: Clarendon Press.

Ferrer, Aldo. 1967. *The Argentine Economy.* Trans. Marjory M. Urquidi. Berkeley: University of California Press.

Finch, Martin Henry John. 1981. *A Political Economy of Uruguay since 1870.* New York: St. Martin's Press.

Florez, G., Lenin, and Adolfo Atehortua C. 1987. *Estudios sobre la regeneración.* Bogotá: Valencia.

Floria, Carlos Alberto, and Cesar A. Garcia Belsunce. 1993. *Historia de los argentinos.* 2 vols. Buenos Aires: Larousse.

Fogarty, John. 1985. "Staples, Super Staples, and the Limits of Staple Theory: The Experiences of Argentina, Australia, and Canada Compared." In *Argentina, Australia, and Canada: Studies in Comparative Development, 1870–1965,* ed. D. C. M. Platt and Guido Di Tella. New York: St. Martin's Press.

Fogarty, John, Ezequiel Gallo, and Hector Dieguez. 1979. *Argentina y Australia.* Buenos Aires: Instituto Torcuato Di Tella.

Franco, Luis. 1945. *El otro Rosas.* Buenos Aires: Claridad.

Fuenmayor, Juan Bautista. 1984–1987. *Historia de la Venezuela política contemporanea, 1899–1969.* 3d ed. Caracas: Talleres Don Bosco.

Gallo, Ezequiel. 1970. "Agricultural Colonization and Society in Argentina: The Province of Santa Fe (1893)." Ph.D. diss., Oxford University.

———. 1976. *Farmers in Revolt: The Revolutions of 1893 in the Province of Santa*

Fe, Argentina. London: Institute of Latin American Studies, University of London.

Galvez, Manuel. 1934. *Este pueblo necesita.* Buenos Aires: A. Garcia Santos.

———. 1949. *Vida de don Juan Manuel de Rosas.* Buenos Aires: Editorial Tor.

Galvis Madero, Luis. 1970. *La Gran Colombia.* Vol. 7 of *Historia extensa de Colombia,* ed. Academia Colombiana de la Historia. Bogotá: Lerner.

Gandía, Enrique de. 1970. "Belgrano, Mitre, y Alberdi." *Investigaciones y ensayos,* no. 9 (July–December): 15–52.

Garavaglia, Juan Carlos, and Jorge Gelman. 1989. *El mundo rural rioplatense a fines de la época colonial: Estudios sobre producción y mano de obra.* Buenos Aires: Cuadernos Simon Rodríguez, Biblos.

Garcia, Flavio A. 1956. *Una historia de los orientales y de la revolución hispanoamericana.* 2 vols. Montevideo: Medina.

Gasío, Guillermo, and María C. San Román. 1977. *La conquista del progreso, 1874–1880.* Buenos Aires: La Bastilla.

Geddes, Barbara. 1994. *Politician's Dilemma: Building State Capacity in Latin America.* Berkeley: University of California Press.

Germani, Gino. 1955. *Estructura social de la Argentina: Analisis estadistico.* Buenos Aires: Raigal.

———. 1971. *Política y sociedad en una época de transición: De la sociedad tradicional a la sociedad de masas.* 4th ed. Buenos Aires: Paidós.

Giberti, Horacio C. E. 1970. *Historia económica de la ganaderia Argentina.* Buenos Aires: Solar Hachette.

Gibson, Herbert. 1893. *The History and Present State of the Sheep-Breeding Industry in the Argentine Republic.* Buenos Aires: Ravenscroft and Mills.

Gibson, William Marion. 1948. *The Constitutions of Colombia.* Durham, N.C.: Duke University Press.

Gillis, John R., ed. 1989. *The Militarization of the Western World.* New Brunswick, N.J.: Rutgers University Press.

Gilmore, Robert Louis. 1956. "Nueva Granada's Socialist Mirage." *Hispanic American Historical Review,* no. 2 (May): 190–210.

———. 1964. *Caudillism and Militarism in Venezuela, 1810–1910.* Athens: Ohio University Press.

Giménez Vega, Elias S. 1961. *Actores y testigos de la triple alianza.* Buenos Aires: A. Pena Lillo.

Goldstone, Jack A. 1991. *Revolution and Rebellion in the Early Modern World.* Berkeley: University of California Press.

González, Fernan E. 1985. "Iglesia y estado en Colombia durante el siglo XIX (1820–1860)." In *Documentos ocasionales,* no. 30. Bogotá: CINEP.

———. 1987a. "Problemas políticos y regionales durante los gobiernos del olimpo radical." Unpublished manuscript. Bogotá: CINEP.

———. 1987b. "Iglesia católica y sociedad colombiana: 1886–1986." Unpublished manuscript. Bogotá: CINEP.

González, Libardo. 1975. *El estado y los partidos políticos en Colombia.* 2d ed. Bogotá: Editorial Latina.

González, Margarita. 1984. "Las rentas del estado." In *Manual de historia de Colombia.* Vol. 2, Procultura. Bogotá: Instituto Colombiano de Cultura.

Goodwin, Paul B. 1977. "The Central Argentine Railway and the Economic Development of Argentina, 1854–1881." *Hispanic American Historical Review* 57, no. 4 (November): 613–32.

Gori, Gastón. 1964. *Immigración y colonización en la Argentina.* Buenos Aires: Editorial de la Universidad de Buenos Aires.

Gourevitch, Peter Alexis. 1986. *Politics in Hard Times: Comparative Responses to International Economic Crises.* Ithaca, N.Y.: Cornell University Press.

Griffin, Charles C. 1965. "The Enlightenment and Latin American Independence." In *The Origins of the Latin American Revolutions, 1808–1826,* ed. and with an introduction by Robert Arthur Humphreys and John Lynch. New York: Knopf.

———. 1973. "Were There Revolutions?" In *Problems in Latin American History: the Modern Period,* ed. Joseph S. Tulchin. New York: Harper and Row.

Grompone, Antonio Miguel. 1963. *Las clases medias en el Uruguay.* Montevideo: Río de la Plata.

Guerra, F. Xavier. 1994. "The Spanish American Tradition of Representation and Its European Roots." *Journal of Latin American Studies* 26, no. 1 (February): 1–35.

Guillén Martínez, Fernando. 1986. *La regeneración: Primer frente nacional.* Bogotá: Carlos Valencia.

Haddox, Benjamin E. 1965. *Sociedad y religion en Colombia: Estudio de las instituciones religiosas colombianas.* Trans. Jorge Zalamea. Bogotá: Tercer Mundo.

Haggard, Stephan. 1990. *Pathways from the Periphery: The Politics of Growth in the Newly Industrializing Countries.* Ithaca, N.Y.: Cornell University Press.

Halperín Donghi, Tulio. 1972. *Revolución y guerra: Formación de una elite dirigente en la Argentina criolla.* Buenos Aires: Siglo XXI.

———. 1975. *Politics, Economics, and Society in Argentina in the Revolutionary Period.* Trans. Richard Southern. New York: Cambridge University Press.

———. 1980. *Projecto y construcción de una nación: Argentina, 1846–1880.* Caracas: Biblioteca Ayacucho.

———. 1982. *Guerra y finanzas en los origenes del estado Argentina, 1791–1850.* Buenos Aires: Editorial de Belgrano.

———. 1987. *El espejo de la historia: Problemas argentinos y perspectivas hispanoamericanas.* Buenos Aires: Sudamericana.

———. 1989a. "El surgimiento de los caudillos en el marco de la sociedad rioplatense postrevolucionaria." *Estudios de historia social.* Universidad Autonoma de Mexico.

———. 1989b. *Historia Argentina: De la revolución a la confederación rosista.* Buenos Aires: Paidós.

———. 1991. "The Buenos Aires Landed Class and the Shape of Politics in Argentina, 1820–1930." Discussion Paper no. 85. Madison, Wis.: University of Wisconsin Center for Latin America.

———. 1993. *The Contemporary History of Latin America.* Ed. and trans. John Charles Chasteen. Durham, N.C.: Duke University Press.

Hardin, Russell. 1982. *Collective Action.* Baltimore: Johns Hopkins University Press for Resources for the Future.

———. 1990. "The Social Evolution of Cooperation." In *The Limits of Rationality,* ed. Karen Schweers Cook and Margaret Levi. Chicago: University of Chicago Press.

Hartlyn, Jonathan. 1983. "Colombia: Old Problems, New Opportunities." *Current History* 82, no. 481 (February): 62–65, 83–84.

———. 1988. *The Politics of Coalition Rule in Colombia.* New York: Cambridge University Press.

Hartz, Louis. 1955. *The Liberal Tradition in America: An Interpretation of American Political Thought since the Revolution.* New York: Harcourt, Brace.

———. 1964. *The Founding of New Societies: Studies in the History of the United States, Latin America, South Africa, Canada, and Australia.* New York: Harcourt, Brace and World.

Hebrand, Veronique. 1995. "Ciudadania y participación política: Venezuela, 1810–1830." Paper presented at the Institute for Latin American Studies, Conference on Nineteenth Century Latin America (May).

Hernandez Carrillo, Jorge. 1940. *Santander y la Gran Colombia.* Bogotá: ABC.

Herrera, Luis Alberto de. 1984. *La paz de 1828.* Montevideo: República Oriental del Uruguay, Cámara de Representantes, 1989. Montevideo: Tradinco.

Herrera Soto, Roberto. 1982. *Las ideas conservadoras en Colombia.* Bogotá: Universidad la Gran Colombia.

Hobsbawm, Eric J. 1981. *Bandits.* Rev. ed. New York: Pantheon Books.

Howard, Michael. 1984. *The Causes of War and Other Essays.* 2d ed. Cambridge: Harvard University Press.

Humphreys, Robert Arthur, and John Lynch, eds. 1964. *The Origins of the Latin American Revolutions, 1808–1826.* New York: Alfred Knopf.

Huntington, Samuel. 1968. *Political Order in Changing Societies*. New Haven, Conn.: Yale University Press.

———. 1981. *American Politics: The Promise of Disharmony*. Cambridge, Mass.: Belknap Press.

———. 1991. *The Third Wave: Democratization in the Late Twentieth Century*. Norman: University of Oklahoma Press.

Ibarguren, Carlos. 1962. *Juan Manuel de Rosas: Su vida, su drama, su tiempo*. Buenos Aires: Theoria.

Inglehart, Ronald. 1988. "Renaissance of Political Culture." *American Political Science Review* 82, no. 4 (December): 1203–30.

Innis, H. A. 1933. *Problems of Staple Production in Canada*. Toronto: Ryerson Press.

Irazabal, Carlos. 1980. *Venezuela: Esclava y feudal*. Caracas: Ateneo.

Irigoin, María Alejandra. 1995. *Las finanzas publicas en la formación del estado: Moneda e instituciones en el estado de Buenos Aires, 1852–1862*. Working Paper no. 18. Buenos Aires: Universidad Torcuato Di Tella.

Irwin, Domingo G. 1990. "Notas sobre los empresarios políticos de la violencia en la Venezuela de la segunda mitad del siglo XIX." *Tierra Firme* 8, no. 29.

Islamoglu-Inan, Huri, ed. 1987. *The Ottoman Empire and the World Economy*. Paris: Editions de la Maison des Sciences de l'homme.

Jaramillo, Carlos Eduardo. 1991. "Antecedentes generales de la guerra de los mil dias y golpe de estado de 31 de julio de 1900." In *Nueva historia de Colombia*, vol. 1, ed. Álvaro Tirado Mejía. Bogotá: Planeta.

Jaramillo Uribe, Jaime. 1985. "Etapas y sentido de la historia de Colombia." In *Colombia hoy*, 9th ed., ed. Mario Arrubla et al. Bogotá: Siglo XXI.

Jeffrey, William Hartley. 1952. *Mitre and Argentina*. New York: Library Publishers.

Jessop, Bob. 1990. *State Theory: Putting Capitalist State in Its Place*. University Park: Pennsylvania State University Press.

Jiménez, Margarita, and Sandro Sideri. 1985. *Historia del desarrollo regional en Colombia*. Bogotá: Fondo Editorial CEREC.

Johns, Michael, and Fernando Rocchi. 1991. "Industrial Capital and the City of Buenos Aires, 1880–1920." Paper presented at the American Historical Association Annual Meeting, Chicago.

Johnson, Lyman J. 1994. "The Military as Catalyst of Change in Late Colonial Buenos Aires." In *Revolution and Restoration: The Rearrangement of Power in Argentina, 1776–1860*, ed. Mark D. Szuchman and Jonathan C. Brown. Lincoln: University of Nebraska Press.

Kalmanovitz, Salomón. 1984. "El regimen agrario durante el siglo XIX en Colombia." In *Manual de historia de Colombia*. 2d ed. Bogotá: Procultura: Instituto Colombiano de Cultura.

——. 1986. *Economía y nación: Una breve historia de Colombia.* Bogotá: Siglo XXI.

Kasaba, Resat. 1988. *The Ottoman Empire and the World Economy: The Nineteenth Century.* Albany: State University of New York Press.

——. 1994. "A Time and Place for the Nonstate: Social Change in the Ottoman Empire during the 'Long Nineteenth Century.' " In *State Power and Social Forces: Domination and Transformation in the Third World,* ed. Joel Migdal, Atul Kohli, and Vivienne Shue. New York: Cambridge University Press.

Katzenstein, Peter J., ed. 1978. *Between Power and Plenty: Foreign Economic Policies of Advanced Industrial States.* Madison: University of Wisconsin Press.

——. 1985. *Small States in World Markets: Industrial Policy in Europe.* Ithaca, N.Y.: Cornell University Press.

Kay, Cristobal. 1989. *Latin American Theories of Development and Underdevelopment.* New York: Routledge.

Kelly, Kevin. 1994. "Rosas and the Restoration of Order through Populism." In *Revolution and Restoration: The Rearrangement of Power in Argentina, 1776–1860,* ed. Mark D. Szuchman and Jonathan C. Brown. Lincoln: University of Nebraska Press.

Kemp, Tom. 1993. *Historical Patterns of Industrialization.* 2d ed. New York: Longman House.

Kennedy, Paul M. 1987. *The Rise and Fall of the Great Powers: Economic Change and Military Conflict from 1500–2000.* New York: Random House.

Kinsbruner, Jay. 1994. *Independence in Spanish America: Civil Wars, Revolutions, and Underdevelopment.* Albuquerque: University of New Mexico Press.

Kleinpenning, Jan M. G. 1995. *Peopling the Purple Land: A Historical Geography of Rural Uruguay, 1500–1915.* Amsterdam: CEDLA.

Koebel, William Henry. 1907. *Modern Argentina: The Eldorado of Today, with Notes on Uruguay and Chile.* London: Francis Griffith.

Krasner, Stephen D. 1978. *Defending the National Interest: Raw Materials Investments and U.S. Foreign Policy.* Princeton, N.J.: Princeton University Press.

Kuethe, Allan J. 1994. "Military and Society." In *Latin American Revolutions, 1808–1826: Old and New World Origins,* ed. and with an introduction by John Lynch. Norman: University of Oklahoma Press.

Kuhn, Philip A. 1980. *Rebellion and Its Enemies in Late Imperial China: Militarization and Social Structure, 1796–1864.* Cambridge: Harvard University Press.

Laclau, Ernesto. 1971. "Feudalism and Capitalism in Latin America." *New Left Review,* no. 67 (May–June): 19–38.

Lamas, Andres. 1933. *La legislación agraria de Bernardino Rivadavia.* Prologue by Manuel Herrera y Reissig. Buenos Aires.

Lamas, Mario Daniel, and Diosma E. Piotti de Lamas. 1981. *Historia de la industria en el Uruguay: 1730–1980.* Montevideo: Cámara de la Industrias del Uruguay.

Lanzaro, Jorge L. 1986. *Sindicatos y sistema político: Relaciones corporativas en el Uruguay, 1940–1985.* Montevideo: Fundación de Cultura Universitaria.

Laski, Harold. 1938. *A Grammar of Politics.* New Haven, Conn.: Yale University Press.

Leal Buitrago, Francisco. 1984. *Estado y política en Colombia.* Bogotá: Siglo XXI.

Leal Buitrago, Francisco, and John Saxe Fernandez. 1978. *Política e intervención militar en Colombia.* Bogotá: Los Comuneros.

LeGrand, Catherine. 1984. "Labor Acquisition and Social Conflict on the Colombian Frontier, 1850–1936." *Journal of Latin American Studies* 16, no. 1 (May): 27–49.

Levene, Ricardo H. 1940. "Los sucesos de mayo." In *Historia de la nación Argentina* 5, part 2, ed. Ricardo H. Levene. Buenos Aires: Universidad de Buenos Aires.

———. 1947. "La anarquia de 1820 en Buenos Aires." In *Historia de la nación Argentina* 6, part 2, ed. Ricardo H. Levene. Buenos Aires: Universidad de Buenos Aires.

———. 1963. "Presidencia de Mitre." In *Historia argentina contemporanea* 1, Academia Naciónal de la Historia. Buenos Aires: Universidad de Buenos Aires.

Levi, Margaret. 1990. "A Logic of Institutional Change." In *The Limits of Rationality,* ed. Karen Schweers Cook and Margaret Levi. Chicago: Chicago University Press.

Lewis, Paul H. 1993. *Political Parties and Generations in Paraguay's Liberal Era, 1869–1940.* Chapel Hill: University of North Carolina Press.

Lijphart, Arend. 1975. "Comparative Politics and Comparative Method." *American Political Science Review* 65, no. 3 (September): 686–702.

Lindo-Fuentes, Hector. 1990. *Weak Foundations: The Economy of El Salvador in the Nineteenth Century, 1821–1898.* Berkeley: University of California Press.

Lipset, Seymour Martin. 1963. *The First New Nation: The United States in Historical and Comparative Perspective.* New York: Basic Books.

———. 1990. *Continental Divide: The Values and Institutions of the United States and Canada.* New York: Routledge.

Lipset, Seymour Martin, and Stein Rokkan, eds. 1967. *Party Systems and Voter Alignments: Cross-National Perspectives.* New York: Free Press.

Liu, Alan P. L. 1992. "The 'Wenzhou Model' of Development and China's Modernization." *Asian Survey* 32, no. 8 (August): 696–711.

Lleras Restrepo, Carlos. 1946. *La obra económica y fiscal del liberalismo.* 2 vols. Bogotá.

Lombardi, John V. 1982. *Venezuela: The Search for Order, the Dream of Progress.* New York: Oxford University Press.

López, José Hilario. 1942. *Memorias.* 2 vols. Bogotá: Biblioteca Popular de Cultura Colombiana.

López-Alves, Fernando. 1989a. "Why Do Unions Coalesce? Labor Solidarity in Colombia and Uruguay." Ph.D. diss., University of California–Los Angeles.

———. 1989b. "Crises and Liberation Fronts in Latin America: The Case of the Uruguayan Tupamaros." *Journal of Terrorism and Political Violence* 1, no. 2 (April): 202–41.

———. 1993a. "Why Not Corporatism? Uruguay in the 1940s." In *Latin America in the 1940s: War and Postwar Transitions,* ed. David Rock. Berkeley: University of California Press.

———. 1993b. *Between the Economy and the Polity in the River Plate: Uruguay, 1811–1890.* London: Institute of Latin American Studies, University of London.

———. 1995. "Pacts behind Institutions: Organized Labor and Democracy in Uruguay, 1900–1990." Paper presented at the Latin American Studies Association International Congress, Washington, D.C.

Lott, Leo B. 1972. *Venezuela and Paraguay: Political Modernity and Tradition in Conflict.* New York: Holt, Rinehart and Winston.

Louis, Julio A. 1969. *Batlle y Ordóñez: Apogeo y muerte de la democracia burguesa.* Montevideo: Nativa Libros.

Luna, Felix. 1956. *Yrigoyen.* Buenos Aires: Raigal.

———. 1966. *Los caudillos.* Buenos Aires: Jorge Álvarez.

Lynch, John. 1958. *Spanish Colonial Administration, 1782–1810: The Intendant System in the Viceroyalty of the Rio de la Plata.* London, University of London: Athlone Press.

———. 1981. *Argentine Dictator: Juan Manuel de Rosas, 1829–1852.* New York: Oxford University Press.

———. 1986. *The Spanish American Revolutions: 1808–1826.* 2d ed. New York: Norton.

———. 1992. *Caudillos in Spanish America: 1800–1850.* New York: Oxford University Press.

———. 1993. "From Independence to National Organization." In *Argentina since Independence,* ed. Leslie Bethell. New York: Cambridge University Press.

Mac Cann, William. 1939. *Viaje a caballo por las provincias argentinas, 1847*. Buenos Aires: Imprenta Ferrari.

Machado, Carlos. 1984. *Historia de los orientales*. 3 vols. Montevideo: Banda Oriental.

Madariaga, Salvador de. 1955. *El ocaso del imperio español en América*. Buenos Aires: Sudamericana.

Main, Jackson Turner. 1965. *The Social Structures of Revolutionary America*. Princeton, N.J.: Princeton University Press.

Maingot, Anthony P. 1969. "Social Structure, Social Status, and Civil-Military Conflict in Urban Colombia, 1810–1858." In *Nineteenth Century Cities: Essays in the New Urban History*, ed. Stephan Thernstrom and Richard Sennett. New Haven, Conn.: Yale University Press.

Mann, Michael. 1986. *The Sources of Political Power*. Vol. 1, *A History of Power from the Beginning to A.D. 1760*. New York: Cambridge University Press.

———. 1988a. "European Development: Approaching a Historical Explanation." In *Europe and the Rise of Capitalism*, ed. Jean Baechler, John Hall, and Michael Mann. New York: Basil Blackwell.

———. 1988b. *States, War, and Capitalism: Studies in Political Sociology*. New York: Basil Blackwell.

———. 1993. *The Sources of Social Power*. Vol. 2. New York: Cambridge University Press.

Manzetti, Luigi. 1992. "The Evolution of Agricultural Interest Groups in Argentina." *Journal of Latin American Studies* 24, no. 3 (October): 585–616.

March, James G., and Johan P. Olsen. 1984. "The New Institutionalism: Organizational Factors in Political Life." *American Political Science Review* 78, no. 3 (September): 734–49.

Marmier, Xavier. 1948. *Buenos Aires y Montevideo en 1850*. Translation, prologue, and notes by José Luis Busaniche. Buenos Aires: El Ateneo.

Martínez Lamas, Julio. 1946. *Riqueza y pobreza del Uruguay: Estudio de las causas que retardan el progreso nacional*. 2d ed. Montevideo: Atlantida.

Martire, Eduardo. 1965. *La crisis Argentina de 1873–1876*. Buenos Aires: Zupay.

Martorelli, Horacio. 1978. *Urbanization y desruralización en el Uruguay*. Montevideo: Fundación de Cultura Universitaria, and Centro Latinamericano de Economia Humana.

Marx, Karl. 1959. "Eighteenth Brumaire of Louis Bonaparte." In *Basic Writings on Politics and Philosophy [by] Karl Marx and Friedrich Engels*, ed. Lewis S. Feuer. Garden City, N.Y.: Doubleday.

———. 1967. *Capital: A Critique of Political Economy*. Vol. 3, ed. Frederick Engels. New York: International Publishers.

Mazo, Gabriel del. 1971. "Alem y el federalismo argentino." Introduction to *Autonomismo y centralismo,* by Leandro N. Alem. Buenos Aires: Raigal.

McDonald, Roland. 1978. "Party Factions and Modernization: A Comparative Analysis of Colombia and Uruguay." In *Faction Politics: Political Parties and Factionalism in Comparative Perspective,* ed. Frank P. Belloni and Dennis C. Beller. Santa Barbara, Calif.: ABC-Clio.

McFarlane, Anthony F. 1985. "Civil Disorder and Popular Protest in Late Colonial Nueva Granada." In *Readings in Latin American History,* ed. Peter J. Bakewell, John J. Johnson, and Meredith D. Dodge. Durham, N.C.: Duke University Press.

———. 1995. "Rebellions in Late Colonial Spanish America: A Comparative Perspective." *Bulletin of Latin American Research* 14, no. 3.

McGreevey, William Paul. 1971. *An Economic History of Colombia, 1845–1930.* Cambridge: Cambridge University Press.

McLynn, F. J. 1979. "The Argentine Presidential Election of 1868." *Journal of Latin American Studies* 11, no. 2 (November): 303–23.

Melo, Jorge Orlando. 1978. *Los origines de los partidos políticos en Colombia.* Bogotá: Instituto Colombiano de Cultura, Coacultura.

———. 1985. "La republica conservadora." In *Colombia hoy,* 9th ed., ed. Mario Arrubla. Bogotá: Siglo XXI.

———. 1991a. "Del federalismo a la constitución de 1886." In *Nueva historia de Colombia,* vol. 1, ed. Álvaro Tirado Mejía. Bogotá: Planeta.

———. 1991b. "La evolución económica de Colombia: 1830–1900." In *Nueva historia de Colombia,* vol. 2, ed. Álvaro Tirado Mejía. Bogotá: Planeta.

———. 1991c. "La constitución de 1886." In *Nueva historia de Colombia,* vol. 1, ed. Álvaro Tirado Mejía. Bogotá: Planeta.

Mendez Vives, Enrique. 1975. *El Uruguay de la modernización: 1876–1904.* Montevideo: Banda Oriental.

Merkx, Gilbert Wilson. 1968. "Political and Economic Change in Argentina from 1870 to 1966." Ph.D. diss., Yale University.

Michels, Robert. 1949. *Political Parties: A Sociological Study of the Oligarchical Tendencies of Modern Democracies.* Trans. Eden Paul and Cedar Paul. Glencoe, Ill.: Free Press.

Migdal, Joel S. 1988. *Strong Societies and Weak States: State-Society Relations and State Capabilities in the Third World.* Princeton, N.J.: Princeton University Press.

Migdal, Joel S., Atul Kohli, and Vivienne Shue, eds. 1994. *State Power and Social Forces: Domination and Transformation in the Third World.* New York: Cambridge University Press.

Mill, John Stuart. 1991. *Considerations on Representative Government.* Buffalo, N.Y.: Prometheus Books.

Millot, Julio, and Magdalena Bertino. 1991–1996. *Historia económica del Uruguay*. Vol. 1. Montevideo: Fundación de Cultura Universitaria.

Mitre, Bartolomé. 1947. *Historia del Belgrano y de la independencia Argentina.* 4 vols. With a preliminary study by Angel Acuna. Buenos Aires: Estrada.

Moe, Terry M. 1986. "Interests, Institutions, and Positive Theory: The Politics of the NLRB." In *Studies in American Political Development.* New Haven, Conn.: Yale University Press.

———. 1990. "Political Institutions: The Neglected Side of the Story." *Journal of Law, Economics, and Organization* 6:213–53.

Molina, Gerardo. 1987. *Las ideas socialistas en Colombia*. Bogotá: Tercer Mundo.

———. 1988–1989. *Las ideas liberales en Colombia*. 3 vols. Bogotá: Tercer Mundo.

Montoya, Alfredo J. 1956. *Historia de los saladeros argentinos*. Buenos Aires: Raigal.

Moore, Barrington. 1986. *Social Origins of Dictatorship and Democracy: Lords and Peasants in the Making of the Modern World*. Boston: Beacon Press.

Mora, José María Luis. 1973. "The Corporate Spirit." In *Problems in Latin American History: The Modern Period,* ed. Joseph S. Tulchin. New York: Harper and Row.

Morone, James A. 1990. *The Democratic Wish: Popular Participation and the Limits of American Government.* New York: Basic Books.

Morse, Richard M. 1964. "The Heritage of Latin America." In *The Founding of New Societies: Studies in the History of the United States, Latin America, South Africa, Canada, and Australia,* ed. Louis Hartz. New York: Harcourt, Brace and World.

Moses, Bernard. 1926. *The Intellectual Background of the Revolution in South America, 1810–1824.* New York: Hispanic Society of America.

Mosquera, Tomás Cipriano de, and Saturnino Vergara. 1874. *Los partidos en Colombia: Estudio histórico político.* Popayan: n.p.

Mulhall, M. G., and E. T. Mulhall. 1885. *Handbook of the River Plate, Comprising the Argentine Republic, Uruguay, and Paraguay.* 5th ed. Buenos Aires: Trubner.

Murillo, Gabriel, and Israel Rivera Ortiz. 1973. *Actividades y estructura de poder en los partidos colombianos.* With the collaboration of Patricia Pinzon. Bogotá: Facultad de Artes y Ciencias, Universidad de los Andes.

Murillo Toro, Manuel. 1984. "La reforma fiscal y el impuesto unico, Santander, 1857." In *Los radicales del siglo XIX: Escritos políticos,* with selection, prologue, and notes by Gonzalo España. Bogotá: El Ancora.

Naquin, Susan, and Evelyn Rawski. 1987. *Chinese Society in the Eighteenth Century.* New Haven, Conn.: Yale University Press.

Newton, Jorge. 1966. *Historia de la sociedad rural Argentina, en el centenario de su fundación.* With the collaboration of Lily Sosa de Newton. Buenos Aires: Goncourt.

Nieto Arteta, Luis Eduardo. 1970. *Economia y cultura en la historia de Colombia.* 3d ed. Medellín: La Oveja Negra.

Nordingler, Eric A. 1981. *On the Autonomy of the Democratic State.* Cambridge: Harvard University Press.

——. 1987. "Taking the State Seriously." In *Understanding Political Development: An Analytic Study,* ed. Myron Weiner and Samuel P. Huntington. Boston: Little, Brown.

North, Douglass C. 1981. *Structure and Change in Economic History.* New York: Norton.

——. 1990. *Institutions, Institutional Change, and Economic Performance.* New York: Cambridge University Press.

North, Douglass C., and Robert Paul Thomas. 1973. *The Rise of the Western World: A New Economic History.* Cambridge: Cambridge University Press.

Ocampo, José Antonio. 1990. "Las importaciones colombianas en el siglo XIX." In *Ensayos sobre historia económica colombiana.* Bogotá: Fedesarrollo.

Ocampo López, Javier. 1984. "El proceso político, militar, y social de la independencia." In *Manual de historia de Colombia.* 3d ed. Bogotá: Procultura, Instituto Colombiano de Cultura.

Oddone, Jacinto. 1975. *La burguesia terrateniente Argentina: Buenos Aires colonial, capital federal, provincia de Buenos Aires, provincia de Entre Ríos, territorios naciónales.* 2d ed. Buenos Aires: Libera.

Oddone, Juan Antonio. 1956. *El principismo del 70: Una experiencia liberal en el Uruguay.* Montevideo: Universidad de la República Oriental del Uruguay.

O'Donnell, Guillermo. 1979. "Tensions in the Bureaucratic-Authoritarian State and the Question of Democracy." In *The New Authoritarianism in Latin America,* ed. David Collier. Princeton, N.J.: Princeton University Press.

Olson, Mancur, Jr. 1965. *The Logic of Collective Action: Public Goods and the Theory of Groups.* Cambridge: Harvard University Press.

Ortiz, Ricardo M. 1955. *Historia económica de la Argentina, 1850–1930.* 2 vols. Buenos Aires: Raigal.

Ospina Vázquez, Luis. 1979. *Industria y protección en Colombia: 1810–1930.* Bogotá: Santa Fe.

Osterling, Jorge P. 1989. *Democracy in Colombia: Clientelist Politics and Guerrilla Warfare.* With a preface by Javier Sanin. New Brunswick, N.J.: Transaction.

Oszlak, Oscar. 1985. *La formación del estado argentino.* Buenos Aires: Editorial de Belgrano.

Otero, Miguel. 1948. *De guemes a Rosas.* With a preface by Dr. José Armando Seco Villalba and Miguel Sola. Buenos Aires: Sociedad Impresora Americana.

Palacios, Marco. 1980. *Coffee in Colombia, 1850–1970: An Economic, Social, and Political History.* New York: Cambridge University Press.

———. 1986. "El estado liberal colombiano y la crisis de la civilización en el siglo XIX." In *Boletin de historia y antiguedades,* no. 753: 401–18.

Palcos, Alberto. 1963. "La presidencia de Sarmiento." In *Historia Argentina contemporanea.* Vol. 1. Academia Naciónal de la Historia. Buenos Aires: El Alteneo.

Panizza, Francisco E. 1990. *Uruguay: Batllismo y despues: Pacheco, militares y tupamaros en la crisis del Uruguay batllista.* Montevideo: Banda Oriental.

Park, James William. 1985. *Rafael Núñez and the Politics of Colombian Regionalism, 1863–1886.* Baton Rouge: Louisiana State University Press.

Parry, John H. 1966. *The Spanish Seaborne Empire.* New York: Knopf.

Pastore, Mario. 1994a. "State-Led Industrialism: The Evidence of Paraguay, 1852–1870." *Journal of Latin American Studies* 26, no. 2 (May): 295–324.

———. 1994b. "Trade Contraction and Economic Decline: The Paraguayan Economy under Francia, 1810–1840." *Journal of Latin American Studies* 26, no. 3 (October): 539–95.

Pastrana Borrero, Misael. [1984?]. *Colombia, la vocación bipartidista en un siglo de historia.* Bogotá: Fundación Simón Bolívar, Academia Colombiana de Historia.

Pateman, Carole. 1980. "The Civic Culture: A Philosophical Critique." In *The Civic Culture Revisited: An Analytic Study,* ed. Gabriel A. Almond and Sidney Verba. Boston: Little, Brown.

Paula Pérez, Francisco de. 1939. *Política social: El partido conservador colombiano y los problemas sociales.* Bogotá: Lumen.

Payne, James L. 1968. *Patterns of Conflict in Colombia.* New Haven, Conn.: Yale University Press.

Pedraja Tolnan, Rene de la. 1978. *Los precios de los comestibles en la época del virreinato, 1740–1810.* Bogotá: Centro de Estudios Sobre Desarrollo Economica, Universidad de los Andes.

Peña, Milcíades. 1970. *Antes de mayo, formas sociales del trasplante español al nuevo mundo.* Buenos Aires: Fichas.

———. 1971. *Masas, caudillos y elites: La dependencia Argentina de Yrigoyen a Perón.* Buenos Aires: Fichas.

Pendle, George. 1963. *Uruguay.* 3d ed. New York: Oxford University Press.

Pérez Aguirre, Antonio. 1959. *25 años de historia colombiana, 1853 a 1878, del centralismo a la federación.* Bogotá: Academia Colombiana de Historia, Sucre.

Pérez, Hésper Eduardo. 1989. *Proceso del bipartidismo colombiano y frente nacional.* Bogotá: Centro, Universidad Nacional.

Perry, Elizabeth J. 1980. *Rebels and Revolutionaries in North China, 1845–1945*. Stanford, Calif.: Stanford University Press.

Phelan, John Leddy. 1978. *The People and the King: The Comunero Revolt in Colombia, 1781*. Madison: University of Wisconsin Press.

Picon-Salas, Mariano. 1991. *Los dias de Cipriano Castro*. Caracas: Monte Avila.

Pivel Devoto, Juan A. 1942. *Historia de los partidos políticos en el Uruguay*. 2 vols. Montevideo: Atlantida.

——. 1956. *Historia de los partidos y de las ideas políticas en el Uruguay*. Vol. 2, *La definición de los bandos: 1829–1838*. Montevideo: Medina.

Pivel Devoto, Juan, and Alcira Ranieri de Pivel Devoto. 1948a. *Historia de la república oriental del Uruguay (1830–1930)*. Montevideo: Raul Artagaveytia.

——. 1948b. *La amnistia en la tradición nacional*. Montevideo: Gaceta de Cultura.

Platt, D. C. M. 1972. *Latin America and British Trade, 1806–1914*. London: Adam and Charles Black.

Platt, D. C. M., and Guido Di Tella, eds. 1985. *Argentina, Australia, and Canada: Studies in Comparative Development, 1870–1965*. New York: St. Martin's Press.

Pomer, León. 1968. *La guerra del Paraguay ¡Gran negocio!* Buenos Aires: Caldén.

——. 1985. *Cinco años de guerra civil en la Argentina (1865–1870)*. Buenos Aires: Amorrortu.

Porter, Bruce D. 1994. *War and the Rise of the State: The Military Foundation of Modern Politics*. New York: Free Press.

Posada-Carbó, Eduardo. 1994. "Elections and Civil Wars in Nineteenth-Century Colombia: The 1875 Presidential Campaign." In *Journal of Latin American Studies 26:621–49*.

Poulantzas, Nicos Ar. 1968. *Political Power and Social Classes*. Trans. Timothy O'Hagan. London: New Left Books.

Procultura. 1984. *Manual de historia Colombia*. Vol. 2. Bogotá: Instituto Colombiano de Cultura.

Przeworski, Adam, and Henry Teune. 1970. *The Logic of Comparative Social Inquiry*. New York: Wiley Interscience.

Puiggrós, Ernesto. 1991. "El proceso inmigratorio en el Uruguay 1830–1940." In *La immigración española en el Uruguay, catalanes, gallegos, y vascos*, ed. Puiggrós et al. Washington, D.C.: OAS.

Puiggrós, Rodolfo. 1948. *Historia económica del Río de la Plata*. 2d ed. Buenos Aires: Siglo XXI.

——. 1974. "El feudalismo en América Latina." In *Cuadernos de pasado y presente*. Buenos Aires: Siglo XXI.

Quataert, Donald. 1983. *Social Disintegration and Popular Resistance in the Ottoman Empire, 1881–1908: Reactions to European Economic Penetration.* New York: New York University Press.

Quijano, Carlos. 1949. "La crisis del noventa." In *Revista de economía.* Montevideo: Facultad de Ciencias Económicas.

Quintero Montiel, Ines Mercedes. 1989. *El ocaso de una estirpe: La centralización restauradora y el fin de los caudillos históricos.* Caracas: Alfadil, Fondo Editorial Acte Científica Venezolana.

———. 1990. "La muerte del caudillismo en tres actos." In *Tierra Firme* 8, no. 29.

Rama, German W. 1969. "El ascenso de las clases medias." In *Enciclopedia Uruguaya* (Montevideo), no. 36.

Ramos Mejía, José María. [1945?]. *Rosas y su tiempo.* Buenos Aires: Orientación Cultural.

Ratto, Héctor R. 1944. "La campaña naval contra el poder realista de Montevideo." In *Historia de la Nación Argentina* 6, part 1, ed. Ricardo H. Levene. Buenos Aires: Universidad de Buenos Aires.

Ravignani, Emilio. 1970. *Rosas: Interpretación real y moderna.* Buenos Aires: Pleamar.

Real de Azúa, Carlos. 1961. *El patriciado uruguayo.* Montevideo: Asir.

———. 1968a. *Uruguay y sus problemas en el siglo XIX: Antologia.* Montevideo: Centro Editor de América Latina.

———. 1968b. *El Uruguay visto por los Uruguayos: Antologia.* 2 vols. Montevideo: Centro Editor de América Latina.

———. 1969. "Ejercito y política en el Uruguay." *Cuadernos de Marcha,* no. 23 (March).

———. 1984a. *Uruguay, una sociedad amortiguadora?* Montevideo: Banda Oriental, Centro de Informaciones y Estudios del Uruguay.

———. 1984b. *Ambiente espiritual del 900: Carlos Roxlo, un nacionalismo popular.* Montevideo: Arca.

Remmer, Karen L. 1984. *Party Competition in Argentina and Chile: Political Recruitment and Public Policy, 1890–1930.* Lincoln: University of Nebraska Press.

Restrepo, José Manuel. 1827. *Historia de la revolución de la república de Colombia.* 7 vols. Paris: Libreria Americana.

———. 1952–1963. *Historia de la Nueva Granada.* 2 vols. Bogotá: Cromos.

———. 1963. *Historia de la Nueva Granada.* Vol. 2, *1845–1854.* Bogotá: Editorial el Catolicismo.

Reyes Abadie, Washington. 1977. *Latorre: La forja del estado.* Montevideo: Banda Oriental.

———. 1989. *Historia del partido nacional.* Montevideo: Banda Oriental.

———. 1990. *Artigas y el federalismo en el Río de la Plata: 1811–1820.* Montevideo: Banda Oriental.

Reyes Abadie, Washington, and Andres Vázquez Romero. 1981. *Crónica general del Uruguay*. 4 vols. Montevideo: Banda Oriental.

Reyes Abadie, Washington, Oscar Bruschera, and Tabare Melogno. 1968. "Sentido actual del artiguismo: Reforma agraria e integración platense." In *Uruguay visto por los uruguayos: Antologia*, ed. Carlos Real de Azúa. Montevideo: Centro Editor de América Latina.

Rial Roade, Juan. 1980. *Estadisticas históricas del Uruguay, 1850–1930: Población, producción, agropecuaria, comercio, industria, urbanización, comunicaciones, calidad de vida*. Montevideo: Centro de Informaciones y Estucios del Uruguay.

———. 1983. *Población y desarrollo de un pequeño pais: Uruguay, 1830–1930*. Montevideo: Centro de Informaciones y Estudios del Uruguay, CIESU.

Rippy, James Fred. 1943. *Historical Evolution of Hispanic America*. New York: F. S. Crofts.

Roberts, Carlos. 1938. *Las invasiones inglesas del Río de la Plata (1806–1807) y la influencia inglesa en la independencia y organización de las provincias del Río de la Plata*. Buenos Aires: Jacobo Peuser.

Robertson, John Parish. 1920. *La Argentina en la época de la revolución. Cartas sobre el Paraguay: Comprendiendo la relación de una residencia de cuatro años en esa república, bajo el gobierno del dictador Francia*. Buenos Aires: Administración General Vaccaro.

Robertson, William Spense. 1918. *Rise of the Spanish-American Republics As Told in the Lives of Their Liberators*. New York: Appleton.

Rock, David. 1975. *Politics in Argentina, 1890–1930: The Rise and Fall of Radicalism*. Cambridge: Cambridge University Press.

———. 1987. *Argentina 1516–1987: From Spanish Colonization to Alfonsín*. Berkeley: University of California Press.

———. 1993. *Authoritarian Argentina: The Nationalist Movement, Its History and Its Impact*. Berkeley: University of California Press.

———. 1996a. "Factions, Rebellions, and State Making in Argentina in the 1860s." Unpublished manuscript.

———. 1996b. "Caudillos, Factions, and Outsiders: Politics in Argentina in the 1870s." Unpublished manuscript.

Rodríguez Molas, Ricardo E. 1968. *Historia social del gaucho*. Buenos Aires: Marú.

Rogowski, Ronald. 1974. *Rational Legitimacy: A Theory of Political Support*. Princeton, N.J.: Princeton University Press.

———. 1989. *Commerce and Coalitions: How Trade Affects Domestic Political Alignments*. Princeton, N.J.: Princeton University Press.

Rojas, Ricardo. 1922. *La argentinidad, ensayo histórico sobre nuestra conciencia nacional en la gesta de la emancipación, 1810–1816*. 2d ed. Buenos Aires: Libreria la Facultad.

Rojas Mery, Eulojio. 1946. *Independencia de Sudamérica hispana: Su grandeza y miserias. Estudio conjunto de los principales acontecimientos políticos y militares de la independencia, fundamentado en documentos de la época.* Montevideo: Caudio Garcia.

Rosa, José Maria. 1968. *La caida de Rosas.* 2d ed. Buenos Aires: Plus Ultra.

Rosas, Juan Manuel de. 1968. *Instrucciones a los mayordomos de estancias, con una biografía de Rosas por Pedro de Angelis, y notas y comentarios del ingeniero de Carlos Lemee.* Buenos Aires: Plus Ultra.

Rouquié, Alain. 1987. *The Military and the State in Latin America.* Trans. Paul E. Sigmund. Berkeley: University of California Press.

Rueschemeyer, Dietrich, Evelyne Huber Stephens, and John D. Stephens. 1992. *Capitalist Development and Democracy.* Chicago: University of Chicago Press.

Sábato, Hilda. 1990. *Agrarian Capitalism and the World Market: Buenos Aires in the Pastoral Age, 1840–1890.* Albuquerque: University of New Mexico Press.

———. 1991. "Political Participation in Buenos Aires." Paper presented at an informal conference at the University of California at Santa Barbara.

———. 1992. "Citizenship, Political Participation, and the Formation of the Public Sphere in Buenos Aires, 1850s–1880s." *Past and Present,* no. 136 (August): 139–63.

Sábato, Hilda, and Luis Alberto Romero. 1985. *Entre el ascenso y la caida: Trabajadores por cuenta propia en Buenos Aires, 1850–1880.* Buenos Aires: CISEA, Programa de Estudios de Historia Económica y Social Americana.

Sábato, Jorge F. 1988. *La clase dominante en la Argentina moderna: Formación y características.* Buenos Aires: CISEA, Grupo Editor Latinamericano.

Sáenz Quesada, María. 1985. *Los estancieros.* Buenos Aires: Editorial de Belgrano.

Safford, Frank. 1972a. "Commerce and Enterprise in Central Colombia, 1821–1870." Ph.D. diss., University of Michigan, Ann Arbor.

———. 1972b. "Social Aspects of Politics in Nineteenth Century Spanish America: New Granada, 1825–1850." *Journal of Social History* 5, no. 3 (spring): 344–70.

———. 1988. "The Emergence of Economic Liberalism in Colombia." In *Guiding the Invisible Hand,* ed. Joseph L. Love and Nils Jacobsen. New York: Prager.

———. 1992. "The Problem of Political Order in Early Republican Spanish America." *Journal of Latin American Studies* 24 (Quincentenary Supplement): 83–97.

Sala de Touron, Lucia, and J. E. Landinelli. 1984. "El movimiento obrero uruguayo." In *Historia del movimiento obrero en América Latina,* vol. 4, ed. Pablo González Casanova. Mexico: Siglo XXI.

Sala de Touron, Lucia, Julio C. Rodríguez, Nelson de la Torre, and Rosa Alonso Eloy. 1970. *La oligarquia oriental en la cisplatina.* Montevideo: Pueblos Unidos.

Sala de Touron, Lucia, and Rosa Alonso Eloy. 1986–1991. *El Uruguay comercial, pastoril y caudillesco.* Vols. 1–2. With collaboration of Julio C. Rodríguez. Montevideo: Banda Oriental.

Salazar, Oscar Rodríguez, ed. 1986. *Estado y economia en la constitución de 1886.* Bogotá: Contraloria General de la República.

Saldias, Adolfo. 1977. *Historia de la confederación Argentina.* 3 vols. Buenos Aires: EUDEBA.

Salinas, Reinaldo A., ed. 1985. *La cuestion agraria en la Argentina: Lo nuevo y lo viejo en los régimenes de propiedad, tenencia y renta de la tierra.* Buenos Aires: Anteo.

Salvatore, Ricardo D. 1992. "El mercado de trabajo en la campana bonaerense (1820–1860): Ocho inferencias a partir de narrativas militares." Paper presented at the Institute of Latin American Studies, University of London (November).

Sampay, Arturo Enrique. 1972. *Las ideas políticas de Juan Manuel de Rosas.* Buenos Aires: Juarez.

Samper, José María. 1873. *Los partidos en Colombia.* Bogotá: Imprenta de Echeverria Hermanos.

Samper, Miguel. 1969. *La miseria en Bogotá y otros escritos.* Bogotá: Universidad Nacional, Dirección de Divulgación Cultural.

Sanchez Gómez, Gonzalo. 1991. *Guerra y política en la sociedad colombiana.* Bogotá: El Ancora.

Schwartz, Herman M. 1989. *In the Dominions of Debt: Historical Perspectives on Dependent Development.* Ithaca, N.Y.: Cornell University Press.

Scobie, James R. 1964. *La lucha por la consolidación de la nacionalidad Argentina, 1852–1862.* Buenos Aires: Academia Naciónal de la Historia.

———. 1971. *Argentina: A City and a Nation.* 2d ed. New York: Oxford University Press.

———. 1974. *Buenos Aires: Plaza to Suburb, 1870–1910.* New York: Oxford University Press.

Scruggs, William L. 1900. *The Colombian and Venezuelan Republics.* Boston: Little, Brown.

Shefter, Martin. 1979. "Party, Bureaucracy, and Political Change in the United States." In *Electoral Studies Yearbook.* Vol. 5. Beverly Hills, Calif.: Sage Publications, 211–65.

Shepsle, Kenneth A. 1989. "Studying Institutions: Some Lessons from the Rational Choice Approach." *Journal of Theoretical Politics* 1, no. 2 (April): 131–47.

Shils, Edward. 1963. "On the Comparative Study of the New States." In *Old*

Societies and New States: The Quest for Modernity in Asia and Africa, ed. Clifford Geertz. New York: Free Press of Glencoe.

Shue, Vivienne. 1994. "State Power and Social Organizations in China." In *State Power and Social Forces,* ed. Joel Migdal, Atul Kohli, and Vivienne Shue. Cambridge: Harvard University Press.

Shumway, Nicolas. 1991. *The Invention of Argentina.* Berkeley: University of California Press.

Silberman, Bernard S. 1993. *Cages of Reason: The Rise of the Rational State in France, Japan, the United States, and Great Britain.* Chicago: University of Chicago Press.

Skocpol, Theda. 1979. *States and Social Revolutions: A Comparative Analysis of France, Russia, and China.* New York: Cambridge University Press.

———. 1992. "State Formation and Social Policy in the United States." *American Behavioral Scientist* 35, nos. 4–5 (March–June): 559–84.

Skowronek, Stephen. 1982. *Building a New American State: The Expansion of National Administrative Capacities, 1877–1920.* New York: Cambridge University Press.

Small, Melvin, and J. David Singer. 1982. *Resort to Arms: International and Civil Wars, 1816–1980.* With collaboration of Robert Bennett, Kari Gluski, and Susan Jones. Beverly Hills, Calif.: Sage Publications.

Smith, Peter H. 1969. *Politics and Beef in Argentina: Patterns of Conflict and Change.* New York: Columbia University Press.

Solberg, Carl E. 1970. *Immigration and Nationalism, Argentina and Chile, 1890–1914.* Austin: University of Texas Press.

Solberg, Winton U., ed. 1958. *The Federal Convention and the Formation of the American States.* New York: Liberal Arts Press.

Sommi, Luis V. 1947. *Hipólito Irigoyen, su época y su vida.* Buenos Aires: Monteagudo.

———. 1972. *La revolución del 90.* Buenos Aires: Gonzalo Pineda.

Sowell, David. 1986. "The Early Latin American Labor Movement: Artisans and Politics in Bogotá, Colombia, 1832–1919." Ph.D. diss., University of Florida.

Spense, Jonathan D. 1990. *The Search for Modern China.* New York: W. W. Norton.

Stein, Stanley J., and Barbara H. Stein. 1970. *The Colonial Heritage of Latin America: Essays on Economic Dependence in Perspective.* New York: Oxford University Press.

Stepan, Alfred. 1966. "Political Development Theory: The Latin American Experience." *Journal of International Affairs* 20, no. 2: 223–34.

Stephens, Evelyne Huber. 1989. "Capitalist Development and Democracy in South America." *Politics and Society* 17, no. 3 (September): 281–352.

Stern, J. Steven. 1988. "Feudalism, Capitalism, and the World System in the Perspective of Latin America and the Caribbean." *American Historical Review* 93, no. 4 (October): 829–72.

Stewart Vargas, Guillermo. 1970. *Oribe y su significación frente a Rosas y Rivera, 1958*. Buenos Aires: S. E.

Stinchcombe, Arthur S. 1968. *Constructing Social Theories*. New York: Harcourt, Brace and World.

——. 1978. *Theoretical Methods in Social History*. New York: Academic Press.

Stoller, Richard. 1992. "Liberalism and Conflict in Socorro, Colombia, 1830–1870." Ph.D. diss., University of Washington, Seattle.

Street, John. 1956. *La influencia britanica en la independencia de las provincias del Río de la Plata, con especial referencia al perido comprendido entre 1806 y 1816*. Montevideo.

——. 1967. *Gran Bretaña y la independencia del Río de la Plata*. Buenos Aires: Paidós.

Sunkel, Oswaldo, and Pedro Paz. 1970. *El subdesarrollo latinoamericano y la teoria del desarrollo*. Madrid: Siglo XXI de España.

Tamayo, Joaquin. 1975. *La revolución de 1899*. With prologue and indexes by José M. de Mier. Bogotá: Biblioteca Banco Popular.

Ternavasio, Marcela. 1996. *Hacia un regime de unanimidad: Política y elecciones en Buenos Aires, 1828–1850*. Buenos Aires: Instituto de Historia Americana y Argentina, Dr. Emilio Ravignani.

Tilly, Charles. 1978. *From Mobilization to Revolution*. Reading, Mass.: Addison-Wesley.

——. 1990. *Coercion, Capital, and European States, A.D. 990–1990*. Cambridge, Mass.: Blackwell.

——. 1993. *European Revolutions, 1492–1992*. Cambridge, Mass.: Blackwell.

Tirado Mejía, Álvaro. 1970. *Aspectos sociales de las guerras civiles en Colombia*. Bogotá: Instituto Colombiano de Cultura.

——. 1981. *El estado y la política en el siglo XIX*. 2d ed. Bogotá: El Ancora.

Tobón Sanín, Gilberto. 1979. *La lucha de clases y los partidos en Colombia*. Medellín: Aurora.

Torre, Nelson de la, Julio Rodríguez, and Lucia Sala de Touron. 1972. *Despues de Artigas (1820–1836)*. Montevideo: Pueblos Unidos.

Torres Velasco, Javier. 1978. *Los partidos políticos en Colombia*. 1st ed. Bogotá: ANIF.

Torres Wilson, José de. 1973. *Diez ensayos sobre historia uruguaya*. Montevideo: Banda Oriental.

Tovar Zambrano, Bernando. 1991. "La conomía colombiana, 1886–1922." In *Nueva historia de Colombia*, vol. 1, ed. Álvaro Tirado Mejía. Bogotá: Planeta.

Tulchin, Joseph S., ed. 1973. *Problems in Latin American History: The Modern Period.* New York: Harper and Row.

Turner, Frederick Jackson. 1920. *The Frontier in American History.* New York: Henry Holt.

Urrutia Montoya, Miguel, and Mario Arrubla, eds. 1970. *Compendio de estadísticas históricas de Colombia.* Bogotá: Dirección de Divulgación Cultural, Universidad Nacional de Colombia.

Vanger, Milton I. 1980a. *José Batlle y Ordoñez of Uruguay: The Creator of His Times, 1902–1907.* Waltham, Mass.: Brandeis University Press; Ann Arbor, MI: University Microfilms International.

———. 1980b. *The Model Country: José Batlle y Ordóñez of Uruguay, 1907–1915.* Waltham, Mass.: Brandeis University Press; Ann Arbor, Mich.: University Microfilms International.

Valcarcel, Carlos Daniel. 1982. *Rebeliónes coloniales sudamericanas.* Mexico: Fondo de Cultura Económica.

Van Loon, Hendrik Willem. 1943. *Fighters for Freedom: Jefferson and Bolívar.* New York: Dodd, Mead.

Varela, Pedro. 1875. *Mensaje del presidente de la república al abrirse el tercer periodo de la undecima legislatura.* Montevideo: Imprenta El Uruguay, Pasaje del Mercado Viejo.

Vargas Martínez, Gustavo. 1972. *Colombia 1854: Melo, los artesanos y el socialismo: La dictadura democratico—artesanal de 1854, expresión del socialismo utopico en Colombia.* [Bogotá?]: La Oveja Negra.

Vásquez-Presedo, Vicente. 1971–1988. *Estadisticas históricas Argentinas, 1875–1914.* 2 vols. Buenos Aires: Macchi.

Vázquez Carrizosa, Alfredo. 1986. *El poder presidencial en Colombia: La crisis permanente del derecho constitucional.* 3d ed. Bogotá: Suramericana Ltda.; Barranquilla: Libreria Norte.

Vega, Urbano de la. 1960. *El general Mitre: Historia, contribución al estudio de la organización nacional y a la historia militar del pais.* Buenos Aires.

Veliz, Claudio. 1980. *The Centralist Tradition of Latin America.* Princeton, N.J.: Princeton University Press.

Vicuna Mackenna, Benjamin. 1855. *La Argentina en el año 1855.* Buenos Aires: La Revista Americana.

Vieytes, Juan H. 1956. *Antecedentes económicos de la revolución de mayo: Escritos publicados en el semenario de agricultura, industria y comercio, 1802–1806.* With preface by Felix Weinberg. Buenos Aires: Raigal.

Villalba Bustillo, Carlos. 1979. *Entre Núñez y Uribe.* Bogotá: Tercer Mundo.

Villegas, Jorge, and José Yunis. 1978. *La guerra de los mil dias.* Bogotá: Carlos Valencia.

Waisman, Carlos H. 1987. *Reversal of Development in Argentina: Postwar*

Counterrevolutionary Policies and Their Structural Consequences. Princeton, N.J.: Princeton University Press.

Wallerstein, Immanuel. 1974. *Capitalist Agriculture and the Origins of the European World Economy in the Sixteenth Century.* 2 vols. New York: Academic Press.

Walther, Juan Carlos. 1948. *La conquista del desierto: Sintesis histórica de los principales sucesos ocurridos y operaciones militares realizados en la Pampa y Patagonia, contra los indios (años 1527–1885).* Vol. 2. Buenos Aires: Bibliotecha del Oficial.

Warren, Harris Gaylord. 1979. *Paraguay and the Triple Alliance: The Postwar Decade, 1869–1904.* With the assistance of Katharine F. Warren. Pittsburgh, PA: University of Pittsburgh Press.

———. 1985. *Rebirth of the Paraguayan Republic: The First Colorado Era, 1878–1904.* With the assistance of Katharine F. Warren. Pittsburgh, Pa.: University of Pittsburgh Press.

Weber, Max. 1941. *The Theory of Social and Economic Organization.* London: William Hodge.

Weinstein, Martin. 1975. *Uruguay: The Politics of Failure.* Westport, Conn.: Greenwood Press.

Werlin, Herbert. 1990. "Political Culture and Political Change." *American Political Science Review* 84, no. 1 (March): 249–59.

White, Richard Alan. 1978. *Paraguay's Autonomous Revolution, 1810–1840.* Albuquerque: University of New Mexico Press.

Wiarda, Howard J., ed. 1992. *Politics and Social Change in Latin America: Still a Distinct Tradition?* 3d ed. Boulder, Colo.: Westview Press.

Wilde, Alexander. 1982. *Conversaciones de caballeros: La quiebra de la democracia en Colombia.* Bogotá: Tercer Mundo.

Williams, John Hoyt. 1979. *The Rise and Fall of the Paraguayan Republic, 1800–1870.* Austin: University of Texas Press.

Williams Alzaga, Enrique. 1966. "La ganaderia argentina, 1862–1930." In *Historia Argentina contemporanea,* ed. Academia Naciónal de la Historia. Vol. 3. Buenos Aires: El Ateneo.

Winn, Peter. 1973. "British Informal Empire in Uruguay in the Nineteenth Century." *Past and Present,* no. 73 (November): 100–126.

Wood, Gordon S. 1972. *The Creation of the American Republic, 1776–1787.* New York: Norton.

———. 1992. *The Radicalism of the American Revolution.* New York: Alfred Knopf.

Worcester, Donald E. 1992. "The Spanish American Past: Enemy of Change." In *Politics and Social Change in Latin America: Still a Distinct Tradition?,* ed. Howard J. Wiarda. Boulder, Colo.: Westview Press.

Zeballos, Estanislao S. 1883. *Descripción amena de la república Argentina.* Buenos Aires: Peuser.

Zorroaquin Becu, Ricardo. 1958. *El federalismo argentino.* 3d ed. Buenos Aires: Perrot.

———. 1961. "Los grupos sociales en la revolución de mayo." In *Academia nacional de la historia.* Tercer Congreso Internacional de Historia de América. Buenos Aires.

Zorrilla, Ruben H. 1972. *Extracción social de los caudillos, 1810–1870.* Buenos Aires: La Pleyade.

Zum Felde, Alberto. 1920. *Evolución histórica del Uruguay: esquema de su sociologia, comprende la evolución social y política del pais desde los origenes hasta el presente.* Montevideo: Maximo Garcia.

———. 1972. *Proceso histórico del Uruguay.* Montevideo: Arca.

Index

Agriculture: 3, 42–43, 213, 219. *See also* Argentina: agriculture in; Colombia: agriculture in; Paraguay: agriculture in; Uruguay: agriculture in; Venezuela: agriculture in

Aguirre, Anastasio (Uruguay), 71, 84

Alberdi, Juan Bautista (Argentina), 152, 156, 190

Alonso Eloy, Rosa, 62, 69, 83

Anderson, Benedict R., 1, 11

Andueza Palacio, Raimundo (Venezuela), 198

Aparacio, Timoteo (Uruguay), 85–86, 90

Argentina: agriculture in, 142, 144, 146, 151–55, 169–70, 185, 188; alliance between capital and state in, 20, 39; antimilitarism in, 190; autonomism in, 168, 175; bureaucracy in, 144, 188; caudillos in, 142, 144, 158, 161–62, 172, 175, 179, 183, 186–89; centralism in, 168–69, 179–80; civil-military relations in, 145, 176–84, 191–92; civil society in, 28–29; class differences in, 169, 184; coalition formation in, 20, 39–43, 141–42, 155, 162, 164, 175, 186–88, 190, 192; Colombia compared to, 9–14, 139, 141–45, 151, 154, 156, 162, 164, 176–77, 182, 184–85; conservatism in, 43, 141–44, 159, 165, 179, 186; constitutions of, 140, 142, 144, 154, 179; coups d'etat in, 143, 172; cultural features of, 3, 11–13, 26, 66, 152, 156–67; development of democracy in, 41–43, 59, 66, 142, 144–45, 154–59, 166, 180, 218, 220; economic development in, 68, 92, 140–42, 144, 146, 151–57, 185; elections in, 171–75; exceptionalism of, 66, 146, 158; exports in, 43, 146, 152–54, 177–78, 186; federalism in, 137, 139, 142, 144, 164, 167, 183, 189, 217; "feudal" characteristics of, 16–17; foreign intervention in, 143, 159–66, 177–78, 208–9; foreign investment in, 144, 146, 152, 155, 185–86; founding fathers of, 158–59; ideology in, 144, 159, 168–69, 186; industry in, 156, 186; justices of the peace in, 162, 167, 181, 187, 189; labor in, 11, 44, 152, 154, 156, 182, 186, 190–91; liberalism in, 56, 142–44, 157–59, 180, 186, 217; military intervention in Uruguay of, 49, 69–70, 73–77, 81, 91; militia and military in, 29, 32, 34, 37–39, 43, 45, 71, 137, 141–44, 154–55, 157, 159, 162, 164, 166–68, 171–92, 195, 201, 206, 215; Paraguay compared to, 193, 204–11; political features of, 2, 11–13, 41–42, 140, 154–55, 157–58, 164, 167, 187; political parties in, 7, 29, 34, 37, 39, 40, 66, 141, 143–45, 155, 164–76, 182,

Colombia (*cont.*)
175; "feudal" characteristics of, 16–17; foreign intervention in, 128; frontier in, 108; guerrilla war in, 130; labor in, 13, 44, 107–9, 113, 116, 120, 125; liberalism in, 56, 105, 107, 110, 117, 123–24, 217; militia and military in, 12, 34, 37–39, 71–72, 97–99, 101, 103, 105, 107, 109–10, 117–18, 122, 125, 128–32, 134–39, 143, 166, 184, 210; peasantry in, 59, 108, 111, 220; political features of, 2, 12–13, 104, 114–15, 131–32; political parties in, 7, 12, 34, 37, 40, 42, 66, 97–99, 103, 105, 107–11, 114, 118–19, 125–28, 130–35, 139, 143, 164, 166–67, 173, 175–76, 197–98, 211, 215–17, 220; populism in, 110–12, 139; power centralization in, 13, 23, 34, 93, 96–97, 101–2, 112, 114, 117–18, 122–25, 128, 164, 185, 217–18; racial tension in, 136, 243 n.154; "riddle" of, 5; role of war in, 23, 37–39, 98, 103, 113, 117–22, 124–32, 137, 144–45, 216–17; rural mobilization in, 45–48, 103–5, 107, 118, 120, 125, 132, 134, 143, 181, 191, 207, 212; state formation in, 5, 21, 34, 37–45, 96–139, 181, 184–85, 214–15; taxation and tariffs in, 19, 101–2, 105, 113, 120, 123–24; urbanization in, 12, 96, 112, 218; Uruguay compared to, 9–14, 49–50, 61–63, 66, 68, 71–72, 74, 87, 96–99, 101, 104–5, 107, 126, 130–31, 133; wars for independence in, 74, 96, 104, 113, 117–21, 125, 127, 135–36, 145. *See also* Argentina: Colombia compared to; *Gran Colombia;* New Granada; Venezuela: military intervention in Colombia of

Colonial period: influences of, 1–2, 27–28, 36, 63, 65, 118, 151, 159, 208; militia and military in, 33, 35, 205, 208; rule during, 13, 16, 26, 75, 117–18, 133, 177. *See also* Argentina: wars for independence in; Colombia: wars for independence in; Cuba: wars for independence in; Mexico: wars for independence in; Peru: wars for independence in; United States: wars for independence in; Uruguay: wars for independence in; Venezuela: wars for independence in

Colorado Party: Paraguay and, 211; Uruguay and, 34, 50, 55–57, 61, 66, 69, 71, 77, 79–81, 83–88, 90–91, 93–95, 98, 130, 190, 204, 211, 216–17

Conservative Party (*Partido Conservadore*): Colombia and, 97–99, 105, 107, 110–12, 116, 118–19, 124–31, 133–34, 136–37, 139, 191, 197, 211, 216; Paraguay and, 206; Venezuela and, 198, 201–3

Constitutionalist Party (*Partido Constitucional*) (Uruguay), 55, 227 n.23

Corporatism, 4, 25–26, 29, 49, 143

Cortés Conde, Roberto, 146, 152–53

Costa Rica: development of democracy in, 57; state formation in, 21

Crespo, Joaquín (Venezuela), 198

Critical junctures, 7–8, 141, 220, 222 n.15

Crusade of the Thirty-three Orientals (Uruguay), 77–79

Cuba: economy of, 60; wars for independence in, 35

Deas, Malcolm, 101–2

Delpar, Helen V., 133

Democracy: definition of, 4, 221 n.6; feudalism as obstacle to, 16; origins

Fernando López-Alves is Associate Professor

in the Department of Political Science at the University of

California at Santa Barbara.

Library of Congress Cataloging-in-Publication Data
López-Alves, Fernando.
State formation and democracy in Latin America, 1810–
1900 / Fernando López-Alves.
p. cm.
Includes bibliographical references and index.
ISBN 0-8223-2450-4 (cl. : alk. paper) —
ISBN 0-8223-2474-1 (pa. : alk. paper)
1. South America—Politics and government—19th
century. 2. Democracy—South America—History—
19th century. I. Title.
JL1860.L66 2000
321'.0098'09034—dc21   99-045624